"In a world that is forever changing, we need futurists and pioneers to help us dream and get us to our desired destination. I believe David (Futurist) and Jonathan (Pioneer) have given us the map with this book to begin solving our health care crisis in America!"

—*H. William Montoya, Principal Owner & Founder,*
Montoya and Associates

"Futurist David Houle's latest publishing success, *The New Health Age*, is a reflective, well-researched work that examines the future of health care in America from a historical perspective. David and his co-author Jonathan Fleece are persuasively hopeful, charting a clear path to success. After reading this influential book, send it to your congressman!"

—*Richard Noyes, former Associate Director of the Center for Advanced*
Engineering Study, Massachusetts Institute of Technology

"*The New Health Age* leads the reader out of the muddle of tumultuous, emotional arguments that have characterized the debate about health care changes in the United States into a reasoned, clear discussion of the critical issues that will inform rational health care in the twenty-first century. This book will transform the public dialogue and restore our confidence that we will have an affordable, universal, healthy health care system in the near future. It is a must-read for everyone who cares about their own health and the health of the nation!"

—*Judith A. Sedgeman, EdD, Director, Institute for Public Policy and*
Leadership, University of South Florida–Sarasota-Manatee

"End-of-life health care is an increasingly important part of health care reform. *The New Health Age* is a must-read for health care providers, institutions, and families who want to understand this critical issue as well as the positive changes that are ahead."

—*Gerry Radford, Chief Executive Officer, Tidewell Hospice*

"Dealing effectively with the revolutionary change occurring in health care requires some sense of what may be on the horizon. *The New Health Age* is a bold attempt to envision the future of health care treatments, delivery, and financing that should be of great value to lawyers, administrators, policymakers, and the public."

—*Thomas (Tim) Greaney, Chester A. Myers Professor,*
Director, Center for Health Law Studies,
Saint Louis University School of Law

THE NEW HEALTH AGE℠

THE FUTURE OF HEALTH CARE IN AMERICA

DAVID HOULE
JONATHAN FLEECE

sourcebooks

Printed in the United States of America.
VP 10 9 8 7 6 5 4

Table of Contents

PART I
HISTORY AND CONTEXT

PART II
THE DYNAMICS OF THE NEW HEALTH AGE

PART III
THE LANDSCAPE OF THE NEW HEALTH AGE

Acknowledgments

A great number of people helped and contributed to numerous aspects of this book. We would like to thank and acknowledge each one.

We are so grateful to and appreciative of Professor Thomas L. Greaney, Director of the Center for Health Law Studies, Saint Louis University (SLU) School of Law, for recognizing the importance of our book and connecting us with a fabulous team of SLU student researchers who provided us with tremendous supporting data and sources for the book. The Center for Health Law Studies consistently ranks as the top health law program in the nation by *U.S. News & World Report*. Combine that praise with the fact that Jonathan received his JD and Certificate in Health Law Studies from SLU and this relationship created a wonderful collaboration. We recognize Eric J. Knickrehm and Ann Schunicht, both School of Law students, and Jessica Claire Burt and Lauren Groebe, School of Law and School of Public Health students. You each have bright futures ahead of you, and we thank you for a job well done.

Next, throughout the book, we have included Vision Statements—perspectives, views, comments, and opinions written by national thought leaders within the health care sector. We praise and thank our Vision Statement contributors. Your Vision Statements provide readers with real applications and examples of how medicine and health care will exist in The New Health Age.

Special thanks go to Glen Tullman, CEO of Allscripts, and Lee Shapiro, President of Allscripts, because you both introduced and connected us—which Allscripts does so well as an electronic health records technology company—with so many of our Vision Statement contributors. Thank you to Paul Duck, CEO of Coastal Orthopedics, for your insights and perspectives about the importance of healthy corporate cultures and efficiency. Thanks to Robert Epstein, MD, MS, Chief Medical Officer and President of Medco Research Institute Medco Health Solutions, Inc., for your Vision Statement about medical advancements and the incredible breakthroughs around the corner. Thank you to Dr. Stuart Levine, Corporate Medical Director for HealthCare Partners Medical Group. Your leadership and work at HealthCare Partners, as evidenced in your Vision Statement, serves as a prized model for how integrated health care delivery can improve the quality of health care while controlling costs. We thank Andy Slavitt, Chief Executive Officer of OptumInsight, for his views about the need for productive innovation in health care. Thank you David Steinman, a Director with Navigant Consulting, for contributing your "Market of One" Change Vision, which enlightens readers about the future concept of value in health care.

Thank you goes to Mike Shatzkin, Founder and CEO of The Idea Logical Company. As a widely acknowledged advisor about digital change in the book publishing industry, your advice and wisdom have been essential to this book being published. Thank you Claire Holloway for all of your assistance and interest during the editing process. We also thank Dominique Raccah and Peter Lynch with Sourcebooks, who took charge of this project and transformed our words into a spectacularly laid out book.

We want to thank Jonathan's law firm, Blalock Walters, P.A., in Bradenton and Sarasota, Florida, for supporting him throughout the long research and writing process, particularly Jonathan's valued assistant Sarah Orendorff, who helped Jonathan stay organized, scheduled, and smiling every day.

Dedications

We dedicate this book to all those physicians, health care professionals, administrators, advisors, scientists, researchers, leaders, educators, and elected officials who have already begun the early state of transformation of health care and medicine in America. We dedicate this book to them and to the tens of thousands, and soon hundreds of thousands, of individuals who will join them to embrace and set the pace as we enter The New Health Age.

—David and Jonathan

For Victoria, again! Your support and understanding during the writing of this book is deeply appreciated.

—David

I dedicate this book to my wife, Amy, who for 20 glorious and heart-felt years of marriage has filled my life with everything necessary for good health—love, laughter, friendship, support, and intelligence. I dedicate this book to my three beautiful children, Nathan, Anna, and Colin, who will thankfully grow up to enjoy and benefit from The New Health Age. I also dedicate this book to my parents, David and Madge Fleece, and to my father-in-law, Peter Mattina, MD, who each spent their careers in health care. Your guidance and contributions to society and me continue to be inspirational to all.

—Jonathan

Authors' Notes

DAVID HOULE

As a futurist, I define what I do as being a catalyst to get people to think about the future and to then facilitate a conversation about that future. To do so, I ask audiences and readers to let me lift them up out of their day-to-day context with all the thoughts that they have about the present, all the opinions that they have about issues, and all of what they have been told to believe. Only by setting aside all of this mental noise can we really get a glimpse of what will be and what the future might look like. If one has a point of view, that viewpoint acts as a filter through which one looks at the world. If one is a technologist, for example, he will think that technology will solve everything. If someone identifies with a political party, then she will think that when that party has control, everything will improve. Almost everyone looks at life through these types of filters.

As a futurist, I try not to hold any such points of view as they inhibit my ability to see, sense, or envision the future. Holding a specific point of view will keep me from seeing the future clearly. I ask you to read this book without any preconceived filters, as they may well limit your ability to see all the possibilities, potential, change, and benefits of The New Health Age.

My first book, *The Shift Age*, was published in early 2008. In it, I set forth the idea that humanity had entered a new age, the Shift Age, and was leaving the Information Age. When *The Shift Age* was first published, many people questioned why I used the word "shift." Well, in the years since, the use of that word has exploded. It shows up every day in the media. The number of new books that have the word *shift* in the title has grown exponentially. Everyone now senses dramatic shifts in his or her lives and in the world. Almost every aspect of humanity and of how we live is in a relative rate of shift. We have entered a time of shift and transformation unparalleled in human history.

The three previous ages of humanity, the Agricultural Age, the Industrial Age, and the Information Age, were each named around how things were produced and how wealth was created and society changed. Each of these ages initiated profound transformations in the world. The Shift Age that we are now experiencing is shaped by three fundamental forces that have, are, and will reshape humanity for the next 10 to 15 years. These three forces are The Flow to Global, The Flow to the Individual, and Accelerating Electronic Connectedness. We will explore each of these forces of *The Shift Age* in Chapter 6. It is in the context of these three forces that we must also view The New Health Age.

The New Health Age is beginning exactly because of these forces and has begun as part of the Shift Age. I mention this as there are numerous references to the Shift Age and these forces in this book.

I thank the thousands of people who have let me know that *The Shift Age*, and my speeches related to the book, has profoundly changed the way that they look at the world around them. I thank the hundreds of CEOs and business owners who have told me that this view of the future has helped them reshape their visions of how they need to run their companies. To all of you, I say that I will publish an updated volume of *The Shift Age* by the end of 2011.

In 2010, Jonathan Fleece, my co-author of this book, and I were speaking about my sense that medicine and health care delivery were about to enter a new age that is historically inevitable and closely tied to the forces of the Shift Age. Jonathan is one of the most knowledgeable and accomplished health care attorneys and thinkers in America. He told me of how profoundly his health care law practice had changed in 2009 and 2010. It was these conversations that led us to define the period that we have now entered as "The New Health Age" and which inspired us to write the book that you now hold in your hands.

Jonathan Fleece

Almost overnight, everything changed. I have practiced health care law since 1997, representing health care professionals and institutions of all sorts—including many physicians. In 2009, my law practice transformed itself. Barack Obama had been sworn in as the 44th President of the United States; and soon thereafter, he declared that reforming America's health care system was one of his top agenda items. The president had enough Congressional support to see this goal through to the end, and the nation and many of my clients knew it.

Questions and uncertainty swirled through nearly every aspect of my professional life. What would health care reform look like? Who would be in control of health care after it was all said and done? Was the country headed toward a socialist-based health care model? How fast and to what degree would things change?

Not surprisingly, the most common questions surrounded everyone's own self-interest, including mine. How was health care reform going to change *my* world? What will reform mean for my family and me? Will my profession and my business be able to adapt to the new ways? Will the quality of health care be better or worse in America? Will I make more or less money? How will this nation and taxpayers pay for it all in the midst of great local and global economic turmoil?

By late 2009, even before Congress and the president had passed any health care reform laws, purely in response to the *anticipation* of a new health care system that few knew anything about, many of my clients began to react in unprecedented and unpredictable ways. Hospitals and physicians who had stood in opposition previously began to partner and align in rapid-fire fashion. I represented one group of doctors who had been functioning independently for decades, yet the impending threat of health care reform drove these physicians to sell their practices to a hospital system for next to nothing monetarily; and they each became salaried employees. The transaction took less than 60 days to complete, which was nearly unheard of in the commercial transactional world. (It typically takes longer than 60 days to sell or purchase a residential home, which is a far less complex transaction.)

Other groups of health care clients that had previously viewed themselves as competitors merged to become larger—based on the "safety in numbers" logic. Several health care technology clients feared that massive capital would be required to compete following health care reform, so they sold or aligned with other companies to increase their combined financial strength and market power. Examples of this sort were becoming the norm amidst the stir of health care reform.

Client after client demonstrated symptoms of fear, uncertainty, stress, and dissatisfaction, to levels and degrees that I have not previously witnessed. Since 2009 to date, I have represented more clients making substantial business decisions triggered by these emotions than in all prior years of my practice combined. Indeed, the business and profession of health care had changed, and in a substantial way.

During this dynamic period, it became clear to me that my clients lacked a resource to explain and justify their emotions and behaviors. I too was unable to locate a single source of information that could explain succinctly and effectively the market forces that were driving such new, but starkly different, activity.

So David, as an internationally acclaimed futurist, and I, as a national health care attorney, set out to coauthor a book that would fill the informational void that existed. Simply stated, this book shares knowledge about the transformational changes occurring in health care and organizes it clearly, to instill hope for a better tomorrow through a gained awareness.

The pursuit of knowledge and the eventual acquisition of it, whether we obtain it through education, life lessons, or otherwise, is what separates great citizens from all others, because without knowledge, humankind has no basis upon which to see a better tomorrow. Without knowledge, we simply exist versus contribute. The knowledge that readers can gain from *The New Health Age: The Future of Health Care in America* will help to foster contributions from all of us—contributions that we cannot even begin to comprehend, yet.

Introduction

This book is about the future of health care and medicine in America. We have entered a new time, a period that we call The New Health Age. This new age will usher our country into a historically inevitable, transformative process, where the entire landscape of health care delivery and the practice of medicine will change significantly. It will be a time of struggle and exhilaration, as our country will again be called upon to rise up to greatness. The challenge is huge, but the results and probable outcomes are worth the commitment and effort. The returns on this investment and commitment will be staggeringly large and positive for our nation.

As we wrote this book, the debate regarding the future of America's health care delivery system was politicized and largely driven by fear, uncertainty, and misinformation. No intelligent outcome can result if these limiting dynamics dominate and shape the debate surrounding health care. This book is not about advocating for or against any political platform or about taking a political side. Our greatest hope is that the book that you hold in your hands can provide an understanding of what lies ahead in The New Health Age and why this new age will occur, regardless of which political party may control federal, state, and local governments. The New Health Age will dawn irrespective of the swaying tides in Washington, D.C., and in every state capital city. We believe that the literal health of Americans and our very country are at stake and that it is essential to find a way to not only face but also embrace the inevitable changes rushing toward us.

We have tried to provide a large context for understanding so that all of us can begin with this challenge and opportunity better equipped to succeed as a country. In Part I, we first introduce you to The New Health Age. We then take a quick look back on the histories of medicine and health care delivery from the beginning of recorded history to the present day. Next, we look deeply into American health care as it exists today and look at what works, what doesn't work, and why the continued success of our very country is at risk if certain systems and practices do not change.

The rest of the book is a look into the future. In Chapter 6, we examine the large contexts of the twenty-first century and the Shift Age,[1] a new age that David introduced to us in his Author's Note for the present book. We describe the forces and dynamics that have reshaped and are reshaping our professional and personal lives as result of the Shift Age. We look at the medical breakthroughs just around the corner, as they are profound in their potential to alter how we view medicine, health care, and even life itself. Then, in Chapter 8, we point out that nearly 20 percent of America's economy is connected to health care and that many of the dynamics and changes that Americans have already embraced and accepted in the other 80 percent of our economy will now simply be occurring within health care.

Part II of the book deals with nine dynamic flows—changes and transformational movements—that are historic and forceful and that are driving the major shifts that are occurring, or about to occur, within health care. We believe strongly that the dynamic flows enumerated in Chapters 9 through 12 are the forces that, once explained, can provide the conceptual context for deeper understanding of what will occur in The New Health Age. Many readers, particularly those who work in health care, will already be familiar with some of these dynamic flows, but by gaining a greater understanding of each of the nine flows, we as individuals and we as a nation will be better equipped for the changing landscape of The New Health Age. These dynamic flows became clear to us as we immersed ourselves in research, history, and an analysis of global, national, technological, and economic trends. Understand these flows and you will embrace and feel less threatened by what has begun. It is these flows that, if fully understood, will allow physicians and others in health care to see the pathways to continued, if not greater, economic and personal satisfaction through your daily work.

In Part III, we look forward. The transition that we are entering will be hard and must be considered a short-term investment in a bright, longer term outcome. We provide a detailed analysis of what the future health care delivery landscape will look like. We identify the new structures and institutions that will begin to dominate health care delivery in the years ahead. The understanding of these new shapes and processes will provide those who embrace them with a sense of personal, economic, and social opportunity and growth. We understand that policy, legislation, and education are all critical points to moving the country forward, so we include a chapter suggesting what legislators and educators need to think about and do to help create the opportunity for dramatic success and triumph over out-of-control, ever-escalating costs and a downward spiral of the health of Americans. We point out that it is time for all American citizens to accept greater responsibility for their own health. Not only must we become more knowledgeable about health, but we must also use this knowledge to all become healthier as that will be one of the key ways to lower our health care costs and improve our quality of life. There is even a larger case to be made that the Race to a Healthy America, as we call for in this book, is the national challenge and opportunity of our times. Finally, we look ahead to suggest what the future landscape of health care and medicine in America will look like in 2015, 2020, and 2025.

The road ahead will be difficult. It will be contentious. Yet, don't despair; it will ultimately be truly transformative and inspirational. The necessary short-term investment of time, money, vision, and willpower can produce a long-term return for America that for many is currently incredibly difficult to see. We fervently hope that reading this book will provide the reader with the tools, thoughts, and understanding to see this future more clearly.

Let us all begin. Welcome to The New Health Age!

Part I

History and Context

The New Health Age

"We live in a moment of history where change is so speeded up that we begin to see the present only when it is already disappearing."

—R. D. Laing

We live in a transformational time in the history of medicine and health care. The twenty-first century will be a time of dramatic change, incredible breakthroughs, and totally altered thinking about health, medicine, and health care delivery. The years to 2020 will be filled with changes in how Americans think about health, how medicine is practiced, and how health care is delivered. These years will set the stage for a 50-year period that will be viewed as The New Health Age. Future generations will look back and thank those of us alive today for what we accomplished and initiated in this brilliant new age.

Ages are defined by historians because true clarity of human process and social change that can only be documented and seen in hindsight. When looked at through the lens of history, major historical events become clear demarcations of human change.

Biographies are not written about the unborn. Gutenberg was just preoccupied with inventing the moveable type press; he was a printer. Only later was it clear that this invention disintermediated knowledge and launched the Age of Science. In the future, historians will look back upon the simultaneous forces—the new global technological and economic realities and dynamic flows discussed in this book—occurring today as the clear beginning of The New Health Age. We write this book to provide a clear view of this new age that we have entered.

What we now face is an altering of course that will be very difficult, but historically necessary and significant. Centuries of thinking, practices, and morality will be called into question. Legacy thinking and old habits will hold us back. Vested interests, acting out of fear and ignorance, if not greed, will resist change. The unknown can be scary. The different can be resisted simply because it is. Emotion can easily cloud clear thinking.

As this book is being written, the words *health care* provoke fear and are deeply colored by politics. The conversations around health care are filled with uncertainty, misinformation, and anxiety. In such a climate, it is hard to have intelligent, rational discussions. It is even harder to see the future because all the baggage of legacy thinking from the past and the heated emotions of the present completely cloud any clear view of the future. The purpose of this book is to provide an understanding of the directional flows of the practice of medicine and health care delivery and to present a vision of the probable future of health care and the transformative landscape of medicine that is just around the corner.

In this book, we attempt to explain the larger overarching dynamics and forces that are driving this transformation. We present the nine dynamic flows that are the fundamental underpinnings of all change in health care. Only through a high-level, macro perspective can the direction be seen. The view of the future of medicine and health care is beautiful and breathtaking in its possibilities and potential. Will we achieve perfection in health care? Of course not, but humanity has reached a new time after millennia of trial and error, discovery, death, disease, and the evolution of beliefs that have continually been trumped by subsequent better substantiated beliefs.

Only now can we truly enter into The New Health Age, the age that ancient myths have prepared us for. Living forever? No, but certainly the reality of life expectancy moving to 100 to 125 years old. A life free of disease? Well, closer than we have ever been before. A time when the medical profession gets paid based on the health and wellness it provides? Absolutely! A time when health care providers* embrace technology and innovation to deliver care better? Yes! A time when we can genetically engineer our species to improve health, intelligence, longevity, and performance? Yes! A time when the failure of body parts triggers replacement by superior parts? Yes! A time when all Americans can, will, and must live healthier lives? Yes! Yes! A time when health care providers can continue to thrive economically? Absolutely!

We hope to provide you with an understanding as to the direction we are going, what the benefits will be, why the health costs to society and taxpayers will go down, and how we can all benefit—economically, socially, institutionally, emotionally, physically, and psychologically. We will place the coming transformation of health care delivery within the larger context of the trends and forces that have, are, and will transform human society, economics, and life. It is only through this larger context that the transformation that is now beginning can be understood.

To those who are fearful, we hope to allay your fears. To those who have succeeded economically in the past, we hope to con-

---

*When we use the phrase "health care provider(s)" in the book, it is meant to be all inclusive because most of the book is written about the health care delivery system as a whole versus singling out any one group of professionals or organizations. A "health care provider" for purposes of this book is any individual or institution involved in the delivery of health care services, including physicians, physician assistants, nurses, physical therapists, counselors, hospitals, surgery centers, long-term care providers, hospices, pharmacists, device companies, and others.

vince you that you can continue with this success. Indeed, a new game with new rules is upon us, but the opportunity to continue to succeed economically will still be a part of this new reality for people and organizations who choose to embrace it. To those who, in moments of private honesty, can admit general ignorance about health care reform, we hope to obliterate that ignorance with information, advice from experts, and explanations that will make you informed and ready to embrace The New Health Age.

In this book, our primary focus is on the United States. It is the richest country with the largest economy, yet many Americans continue to debate and question how the U.S. health care system should be organized and function. The time for unresolved discussion about the topic of health care in America is nearing an end. The time for resolution is now. The future of American health care is becoming clearer. As futurists, it is time for us to bring understanding and perspective to this process that has just begun. America must create a vision of the future that we can attain if we have the fortitude to move toward it.

Even though The New Health Age will be a new age for all humanity, this book addresses America's health care system and the state of health in the United States. Despite our book's national focus, make no mistake; the medical breakthroughs ahead have the potential to benefit everyone on the planet. The massive improvements ahead in health care delivery systems and in personal health will, we hope, be utilized by all countries. That said, inventions and breakthroughs take time to migrate across all strata of human society and they move through countries at different speeds. Some move slowly. Electricity was invented more than 100 years ago, but there are millions who live without it in their homes today. Some inventions and breakthroughs move quickly. Cell phones first became widely used in the 1980s. In 1985, there were only 700,000 cell phone subscribers. As this book was being written in 2011, there were an estimated 5 billion subscribers. We hope that all global citizens will be able to take advantage of The

New Health Age quickly; however, history shows us that this may not be the case.

We will write to the future. We will write about the trends and forces that even now are moving us into the Shift Age, into the twenty-first century, and into The New Health Age.

First, we need to take a quick look back at the history of medicine and health care, because such knowledge is essential to understanding why we are where we are today and where we are going tomorrow. An understanding of the past is essential to grasp the dynamics of the present and to get a glimpse of the future.

KEY POINTS

1. We live in a transformational time in the history of medicine and health care.

2. The conversations around health care are filled with fear, uncertainty, misinformation, and anxiety. In such a climate, it is hard to have intelligent, rational discussions.

3. In this book, we will explain the larger overarching dynamics and forces that are driving this transformation.

4. Although perfection can rarely be obtained, the view of the future of medicine and health care is beautiful and breathtaking in its possibilities and potential.

2

A Quick Look Back at the History of Medicine

"Medicine is not only a science; it is also an art. It does not consist of compounding pills and plasters; it deals with the very processes of life, which must be understood before they may be guided."

—Philipus A. Paracelsus

When placed within the hundreds of millennia of human existence on planet Earth, the history of medicine is incredibly brief. Learning about medicine from a historical perspective in a "big picture way" is extremely informative and offers valuable insights into modern health care as it exists now and as it continues to transform. This chapter walks us down the rapid path of medicine's progression over the ages. As we examine medicine's advancement, it becomes apparent that many aspects of medicine and health care today are deeply rooted in the events and traditions of the past.

Those of us alive today manifest the latest iteration of humanity, what anthropologists call Modern Man. Modern Man has been on this planet for approximately 150,000 years. Yet, it has only been in the last 4,500 years, or 3 percent of our time here, that there has been any real history of medicine. The scientific foundations of modern medicine have occurred in even less time, only in the last 150 years.

Much of what we know and experience as medicine and health care has come into being in the last one-tenth of 1 percent (0.1%) of our time on Earth in our current anthropological iteration. Health, wellness, and an ever-extending natural lifespan are very recent developments.

1. The ancient practices of medicine are rich with tradition, some of which continue to influence medicine today.

In ancient cultures, medicine and religion were significantly intertwined.[1] Illness was frequently attributed to demons, witches, astral influences, or the will of the gods.[2] Although some of these views continue to retain some influence (consider faith-based healing centers), the rise of scientific medicine over the past millennium has altered or replaced most of the historical mystical notions surrounding health care.[3]

The earliest documented medical care existed in Egyptian religious temples, where leaders provided basic treatments and cures to the sick.[4] In ancient Greece, temples dedicated to the healer-god Asclepius also opened their sacred doors to the ill.[5] The ancient Greeks slept and waited patiently in their temples for dreams to reveal diagnoses and treatments.[6] Dreams were perceived as vehicles for deities to communicate with their followers on earth.[7]

Dating from approximately 1000 BC, the Atharvaveda, a sacred text of Hinduism, is one of the first Indian manuscripts to discuss medicine. Rooted in ancient Eastern cultures, the Atharvaveda contains herbal prescriptions for various ailments.[8] In the first millennium BC, the literate and scholarly Indian system of medicine known as Ayurveda emerged.[9] The foundations of Ayurveda are a synthesis of traditional herbal practices, combined with a vast array of theoretical conceptualizations, dating from about 400 BC onward. The Ayurveda was birthed out of communities of Indian thinkers, with heavy influences from Buddhism.[10]

Ancient Chinese medical knowledge and practices also contributed heavily to medicine's evolution.[11] Much of Chinese medicine originated from empirical observations of disease and illness by Taoist physicians and reflects the classical Chinese belief that human experiences are an expression of causative principles originating from one's surrounding environment, at various levels. These causative principles, whether mystical, essential, or material, correlate as the expression of the natural order of the universe.

According to ancient Chinese philosophy, the human body is governed by Chi, or Qi, which can be translated to mean breath, air, energy, spirit or fluid, or life force.[12] The Chi is made up of the Yin and the Yang, two counterbalanced energy forces.[13] When Yin and Yang are in perfect balance, peace, well-being, and health are the result.[14] An imbalance of the Chi causes disease and poor health.[15]

As early as approximately 2700 BC, the intricate and admired practice of Chinese acupuncture had identified pressure points in the human body considered crucial for the healing process.[16] Chinese physicians of the day believed that manipulation of the body's pressure points could treat most diseases.[17]

2. A quick snapshot of the history of medicine demonstrates how far humanity has progressed over the centuries.

The following abbreviated snapshot outlining the history of medicine is by no means exhaustive, but it nonetheless shows how far we have come. Thousands of breakthroughs, inventions, and new practices have occurred just in the last few centuries. The following timeline demonstrates that medicine, as a part of the fabric of human society, is a mostly recent phenomenon.

2900 BC	The Egyptian Imhotep created rational theories of disease.[18]
460 BC	Birth of Hippocrates, the Greek father of medicine, who later began the scientific study of medicine.[19]
130 AD	Birth of Galen, one of the first known Greek physicians, who served the gladiators and important Roman emperors.[20]
1489	Leonardo da Vinci dissected corpses.[21]
1735	Claudius Amyand performed the first successful appendectomy.[22]
1865	Louis Pasteur identified germs as a significant cause of disease.[23]
1875	German physicist Wilhelm Röntgen discovered X-rays.[24]
1899	Felix Hoffman developed a process to manufacture aspirin.[25]
1913	Dr. Paul Dudley White pioneered the use of the electrocardiograph (ECG).[26]
1920	Earle Dickson invented the Band-Aid.[27]
1922	The first use of insulin to treat diabetes.[28]
1927	A tetanus vaccine was developed.[29]
1928	Sir Alexander Fleming discovered penicillin.[30]
1943	Selman A. Waksman discovered the antibiotic streptomycin.[31]
1945	The first commercial vaccine was developed for influenza.[32]
1950	Dr. John Hopps invented the first cardiac pacemaker.[33]
1953	Jonas Salk developed a polio vaccine.[34]
	James Watson and Francis Crick discovered the structure of the DNA molecule.[35]

1967	Dr. Christiaan Barnard performed the first human heart transplant.[36]
1971	Measles, mumps, and rubella vaccines were licensed.[37]
1974	First vaccine developed for chicken pox.[38]
1975	General Electric, Siemens, Toshiba, Elscint, and Shimadzu began to offer CAT scans.[39]
1978	First test-tube baby was born.[40]
1980	Smallpox was virtually eradicated.[41]
1983	HIV was identified.[42]
1996	Dolly the sheep became the first cloned mammal.[43]
2003	The Human Genome Project was completed.[44]

The most striking aspect of this timeline is the rapid acceleration of medical advancements during the twentieth century and into the twenty-first century. Modern medicine has essentially come into being over the last 150 years. Although each medical advance has been remarkable in its own right, several developments were true "game changers" for humanity.

The discovery of germs and bacteria radically changed how health care providers treated infections. Nurses would no longer move from soldier to soldier using the same sponges and water to clean patients' wounds in battlefield hospital tents. The invention of the X-ray gave physicians the ability to diagnose problems within the skeletal system and soft tissues. Vaccines eradicated horrific diseases that had previously killed or handicapped millions. With the invention of antibiotics, bacterial infection, as a cause of death, plummeted. Between 1944 and 1972, human life expectancy increased by eight years.[45] Such a large increase in life expectancy is largely credited to the introduction of antibiotics.[46] Humanity is just beginning to grasp the magnitude of the recently concluded Human Genome Project, which resulted in the identification of all human genes. Genes carry the instructions for the production of fundamental proteins that determine, among other things, how we look, how well our bodies metabolize food and fight infections, and sometimes even how we behave. Now that we have identified all human genes, the possible applications of this knowledge are virtually endless.

As we continue into the first part of the twenty-first century, new and exciting medical discoveries are continuously being integrated into our daily lives. It is a fabulous time to be alive as expanded medical knowledge, improved diagnostic capabilities, and enhanced disease treatments bring about a new era of health in the world.

3. Advancements in medical technology accompanied humanity's rapid growth in medical knowledge.

During the eighteenth century, physicians primarily used manual techniques to diagnose patients and study cadavers. It wasn't until the nineteenth century that the use of technology expanded and grew within health care and became an integral aspect of practicing medicine.

In the first half of the nineteenth century, certain inventions in medical technology, including the stethoscope, ophthalmoscope, and laryngoscope, transformed health care.[47] After the development of these devices, physicians were better able to see and hear critical parts of their patients' bodies, such as the eyes, lungs, and heart. Herisson's sphygmomanometer, developed in 1835, measured blood pressure.[48] In 1846, doctors put Hutchinson's device for measuring the vital capacity of the lungs into use.[49]

Today, the U.S. medical device and equipment market is incredibly innovative and the largest in the world.[50] The market is highly advanced and very competitive and was estimated at $94.4 billion in 2010.[51] Critical medical devices, implants, and equipment in use today include cardiac defibrillators (external and internal), pacemakers, stents, numerous orthopedic items, ventilators, diagnostic imaging, surgical drills, electronic thermometers, and ultrasonic nebulizers, just to name a few.

Prosthetics and orthotics have also transformed health care over the ages. Prosthetics have been mentioned since circa 440 BC when the Greek historian Herodotus wrote an account of Hegistratus, a Persian soldier, who was reported to have severed his own foot to escape his captors and then replaced it later with a wooden limb.[52] In recent years, significant advancements have occurred with artificial limbs and prosthetic implants.[53] New plastics and other materials, such as carbon steel, have made artificial limbs stronger and lighter, decreasing the amount of extra energy required to operate the limb.[54] The use of modern materials also means that artificial limbs look much more realistic.[55] Following major surgeries, such as hip replacements, patients can literally walk out of the hospital and go home, while continuing with some outpatient physical therapy.

4. Over the centuries, the practice of medicine and treatment of health care conditions have become increasingly interconnected and dependent upon pharmaceuticals.

The pharmaceutical industry was born because of the growth in the number of drugs and their increasing importance in the practice of medicine. The earliest pharmacy, or drugstore, dates back to the Middle Ages. Pharmacists in Baghdad opened the first known drugstore in 754 AD.[56] By the nineteenth century, drugstores had expanded and progressed into the traditional notion of a pharmaceutical company. In fact, many of the major pharmaceutical companies that still exist today, such as Pfizer[57] and Eli Lilly,[58] were founded in the late nineteenth century.

By the 1940s, following the discoveries of penicillin and insulin, drug companies manufactured pharmaceuticals in massive quantities and distributed them throughout the world. During the 1950s and 1960s, more drugs were developed, including the first oral contraceptive, known as "the Pill," as well as blood-pressure drugs, cortisone, and various psychiatric medications. Valium (diazepam), discovered and marketed in the 1960s, became one of the most prescribed drugs in history.

The pharmaceutical industry experienced explosive growth in the second half of the twentieth century due to the increased understanding of human biology and sophisticated manufacturing techniques. As the concept of managed care spread rapidly during the 1980s, efforts were focused at containing rising medical costs through the development of more medications targeted at disease prevention and maintenance, such as Procardia for angina and hypertension[59] and Humulin, a form of biosynthetic insulin used to treat diabetes.[60] Advanced and efficient distribution and supply chains were developed that further promoted the industry's rapid growth.

The 1990s continued to bring change to the pharma industry, with new marketing outlets such as the Internet and television. The Internet enabled consumers to purchase drugs more easily. "Direct-to-consumer advertising" proliferated on radio and television. In 1990, pharmaceutical companies spent an estimated $47 million on "direct-to-consumer" advertising. In 2001, such spending climbed to $2.7 billion,[61] a more than 50-fold increase in a little over 10 years.

In 2011, projected global pharmaceutical sales will likely top $880 billion.[62] United States' sales will be in the range of $310 billion, which will represent more than one-third of the total.[63] At these sales amounts, America will continue to retain its position as the largest pharma market in the world.[64] At $310 billion, drugs comprise a major component of America's spending on health care.[65]

Looking back, pharmaceuticals have cured or treated countless diseases and health conditions and have changed the face of health care across the globe. New drugs are being developed constantly in an effort to chase and discover the next miracle. Today, drugs are an integral component of modern society, which has enabled the pharmaceutical industry to amass great power and influence economically, politically, and socially in America.

Significant medical advancement applicable to the human race is a relatively recent development in humanity's time on Earth. Modern medicine is less than two centuries old. By looking back at the history of medicine, we see how far we have come and can better appreciate how the pace of inventions, discoveries, and breakthroughs is accelerating.

Next, let's examine how the health care profession and delivery systems have evolved.

KEY POINTS

1. The human history of medicine is a recent one.

2. The world of modern medicine that we live in today started in the Industrial Age some 150 years ago.

3. Advancements in medical technology accompanied the breakthroughs of modern medicine.

4. Although pharmaceuticals had humble beginnings, today drugs are an integral component of modern society, which has enabled the pharmaceutical industry to amass great power and influence economically, politically, and socially in America.

5. The speed of invention, discoveries, and breakthroughs is accelerating.

A Quick History
of Health Care
Delivery and
Payment Systems

*"He's the best physician that knows the worthlessness
of the most medicines."*

—Benjamin Franklin

Health care delivery has its own unique history and humble beginnings. Knowledge of the roots of health care delivery is critical to setting the framework for understanding where health care is today and where it is going tomorrow.

Over the centuries, health care professions, delivery systems, and institutions developed and grew as advancements in medicine emerged. To understand how isolated scientific discoveries in various laboratories turned into life-changing and lifesaving procedures, we now examine the history of health care delivery. Although America's health care system is the primary focus of this chapter, we will compare the U.S. model to other countries' in a few sections.

The following timeline highlights some of the most significant events in the history of health care delivery:

4th century BC	The Sinhalese (Sri Lankans) built organized homes where the sick and injured could receive care.[1]
1st century AD	The Romans opened medical homes, especially during times of war, to care for sick and injured soldiers.[2]
5th to 15th centuries AD	European monasteries and convents provided hospital-type destinations where monks and nuns served as caregivers.[3]
754 AD	Arabian pharmacists opened the first known drugstore in Baghdad.[4]
10th century AD	The cradle of Western medical education, the medical school, was established in Salerno, Italy.[5]
1524	The first hospital in the Americas, the Hospital of Immaculate Conception (Hospital de Nuestra Senora O Limpia Concepcion), was established in Mexico City.[6]
1663	The first hospital in the British colonies was established by the East India Company on a small military infirmary on Manhattan Island.[7]
18th century AD	Public hospitals began to appear in towns and cities throughout Europe.[8]
1847	The American Medical Association was founded.[9]

1861	The first U.S. private health insurance plan was developed.[10]
1883	One of the first forms of government-funded health care was created in Germany by the German Health Insurance Bill.[11]
1889	The American Hospital Association was founded.[12]
1906	The American Association for Labor Legislation (AALL) was founded in an attempt to mandate American health insurance coverage through government regulation.[13]
1911	The National Insurance Act of 1911 was passed as a first step toward establishing a national health care system in Great Britain.[14]
1929	Blue Cross was formed as a nonprofit insurance corporation in the United States.[15]
1935	The Social Security Act was signed into law by Franklin Delano Roosevelt.[16]
1943	The Wagner-Murray-Dingell Bill was the first legislation introduced to enact compulsory insurance in the United States; however, without official support from President Roosevelt, the bill died in committee.[17]
1948	Following the end of World War II, 48 United Nations General Assembly countries, including the United States, signed the Universal Declaration of Human Rights, which includes Article 25, which gives all people the right to a standard of living adequate for health and well-being.[18]
1954	A change in federal law provided grants for the construction of U.S. nursing homes in an attempt to raise the quality of care for the elderly.[19]

1965	President Lyndon B. Johnson signed legislation for the federal Medicaid and Medicare programs.[20]
1966	Follow-up visits by nurses after hospital discharge became reimbursable by the Medicare Act of 1966, sparking rapid growth in the home health industry.[21]
1974	The first hospice in the United States was established in New Haven, Connecticut.[22]
1983	The Reagan administration created Diagnostic Related Groups (DRGs) to limit the length of hospitals stays covered byMedicare.[23]
1994	President Clinton's health care reform bill was defeated.[24]
2006	President George W. Bush signed Medicare Part-D into law, providing subsidized prescription drugs to Medicare beneficiaries.[25]
2010	President Barack Obama signed the Patient Protection and Affordable Care Act (PPACA).[26]

Health care delivery has clearly progressed over the centuries alongside advancements in medicine. The timeline provides just a snapshot of the development of health care delivery. Now let's examine some of the more significant events in more detail.

1. When most Americans think of health care delivery, they think of hospitals. What is the history of the hospital?

Some of the world's first organized homes for treating the sick and injured were established by the Sinhalese (Sri Lankans) during the period from 543 BC to the fourth century AD.[27] Another early example of medical homes, later termed hospitals, was the infirmaries the ancient Romans set up to care for injured soldiers during times of war.[28]

As Christianity grew, the Roman Catholic Church assumed a major role in caring for the sick, injured, and dying in society.[29] During the Middle Ages, many monasteries and convents became hospital-like destinations, with monks and nuns serving as the primary caregivers.[30]

In the Americas, records show that the first hospital, the Hospital of Immaculate Conception (Hospital de Nuestra Senora O Limpia Concepcion), was built in Mexico City in 1524.[31] In the British colonies, the first hospital was established by the East India Company as a small military infirmary on Manhattan Island in 1663.[32]

By the mid-nineteenth century, a variety of private and public hospitals had been established in most European countries and in the United States. In continental Europe, the new hospitals were typically built and run from public funds. Alternatively, the traditional hospital model in the United States was a private nonprofit institution, usually sponsored by a religious denomination. These early hospitals were largely tax exempt due to their charitable purpose, but they provided only a limited amount of charitable medical care. Private nonprofit hospitals were supplemented by bigger public hospitals in major U.S. cities, many of which would affiliate with medical schools for teaching and research purposes. By the second part of the twentieth century, for-profit hospital chains arose in the United States.

Today, nearly 5,800 hospitals with an estimated 944,277 staffed beds exist in the United States.[33] Hospitals are a critical pillar within the American health care system.

2. After societies established hospitals, other health care delivery institutions emerged, including home health, nursing homes, and hospice.

As the delivery of health care advanced, new institutions and organizations formed alongside hospital institutions. Although the home health care industry established its initial roots toward the beginning of the nineteenth century, home health really took off in the early part of the twentieth century when insurance companies began to write policies that covered this service.[34]

On August 14, 1935, President Franklin Delano Roosevelt signed the Social Security Act into law. Social Security provided matching grants to states for "Old Age Assistance Payments" to retired workers; however, under the program, people living in public institutions were not eligible to receive these payments, thus private old-age homes—nursing homes—emerged.[35]

Nursing homes and home health continued to expand in the 1960s when the Medicare program became law and covered nursing visits for patients who had been discharged from the hospital.[36] In the early 1980s, both sectors received another boost when President Reagan made sweeping Medicare reform by establishing the DRG (Diagnostic Related Group) reimbursement system. In an attempt to reduce hospitalization costs, DRGs limited patients' hospital stays based on their diagnosis. After a DRG-established hospital length-of-stay period expired, Medicare stopped paying a hospital, regardless of a patient's true medical condition. Home health and nursing home care provided a "safety net of care" for these patients. Reagan's DRG system was arguably the federal government's first significant step toward reforming health care payment models.[37]

Dame Cecily Saunders, who is considered the mother of the modern hospice, created the hospice care concept in the 1960s.[38] She believed in the need for and benefits to providing unique and specialized care for the dying and shared those views with the health care community. Organizers established the first hospice in the United States in New Haven, Connecticut, in 1974.[39] Today, hospice adopts a holistic philosophy and type of care that focuses on the palliation of terminally ill patients' symptoms, whether physical, spiritual, social, or emotional in nature. Thanks to Dame Saunders' early efforts, hospices serve a vital role by helping patients and their families during the end of life.

3. The history of the professionalization of physicians.

Health care delivery would not be what it is today without doctors. Although effective health care delivery requires physical structures and organized institutions, without doctors to coordinate and deliver the care, health care facilities would be nothing more than building shells. The origin of the medical profession may have had humble beginnings, but it has since evolved into one of the most highly regarded professions in America, if not the world.

During the tenth century, universities and the first medical schools emerged in Italy. The "practice of medicine" began to develop, as physicians began to depend less on the "gospel" of medical texts and started to rely more on applying knowledge based on their individual experiences and expertise. As described in Chapter 2 in the discussion of the ancient Greeks' use of dreams to determine diagnoses and treatments, early healers based many of their treatments on religious beliefs and traditions. Medicine's movement away from its ties with religion was a critical step toward transforming medical education and the discipline itself into a formalized and recognized profession.[40]

In the early American colonies, the role of the physician was more informal than it was in England.[41] Many viewed colonial doctors as alternative healers, in part, because there was no distinction between the medical profession and other trades. The barber was no different from the colonial doctor.

Over time, doctors came to benefit from the use of developing sciences, such as chemistry. By the nineteenth century, American doctors applied their knowledge of evolution, psychiatry, and the beginnings of genetics and immunology to the practice of medicine. Even with this impressive growth in knowledge, doctors still lacked educational standards and formal training and were a fragmented group.[42] Without educational standards, certification, or professionalization, a physician could only gain a good reputation through the opinions held in his or her local community.

During the nineteenth century, U.S. society became increasingly stratified based on socioeconomic class. This increased stratification propelled the creation of standards required to practice medicine. The concentration of wealth drove wealthier Americans to seek the best of everything—the best clothing, homes, and doctors. In order to separate the "best" doctors from the others, advanced educational degrees and certifications developed.

The American Medical Association (AMA) was founded in 1847 with the goal of representing the interests of both physicians and patients. In the same year, the AMA established standards for medical education and the MD degree.[43]

During the very early years of the twentieth century, competition among those who provided health care increased. Clinics without physicians, known as dispensaries, became popular as the number of American immigrants increased. The number of dispensaries in New York City increased from an estimated 100 in 1900 to 574 by 1910, with the goal of providing lower-cost care.[44]

The "cure-all" medications of the time also threatened the early medical profession. "Cure-all" medicines promised the ability to heal nearly every ailment and were not prescribed by doctors. This practice began to undermine doctors' medical expertise. Sales of non-doctor-prescribed medication grew from $74.5 million in 1904 to $141.9 million by 1909.[45]

Contract medicine, where companies would contract directly with doctors for reduced, fixed fees, also began to transform the medical profession during the early 1900s. The railroad, mining, and lumber industries were among the first to develop these contract models because their employees needed access to care in remote locations while engaging in high-risk activities.[46] As corporations grew during the Industrial Age, many adopted similar health care models for their employees; however, many doctors perceived contract medicine as a threat to their profession.

The combined effects of an increasingly stratified society, dispensaries, cure-all medicines, and the rise of contract medicine all led to the advancement of American medical education in an effort to separate "real doctors" from other less learned providers of health care services. In 1910, the AMA and the Carnegie Foundation completed a joint study, which ultimately led to the recommendation for 4-year medical schools that would combine teaching, research, and clinical internships.[47] This American model of physician education, birthed nearly 100 years ago, continues today.[48]

Most physicians in the early nineteenth century practiced general medicine, but with advancements in medical education and medicine the number of specialty physicians began to grow at a rapid rate during the twentieth century. During the 1930s, one in every four doctors was a medical specialist.[49] By 1980, four out of five doctors were specialists due to the expanding knowledge required for diagnosis and treatment.[50] In addition, the increasing number of sophisticated medical devices and equipment required specialized skills to operate. Today, the U.S. Census Bureau recognizes 26 physician specialties.[51]

Approximately 822,000 physicians are licensed to practice medicine in the United States.[52] Numerous "mid-level" professionals, such as nurses, nurse practitioners, and physician assistants aid physicians in their practices. The modern doctor also relies on advanced equipment and technology to practice medicine, including surgical lasers, robots, and high-powered magnetic imagers.

Society regards being a physician as a very prestigious and lucrative career. Doctors play a critical role in the health care delivery system and possess one of the most powerful instruments within the system—"the pen," which will soon be replaced by the keypad, as more and more physicians migrate toward electronic medical records. Physicians make the initial medical evaluations, order diagnostic tests, admit patients to hospitals, write prescriptions, order physical therapy, refer patients to home health agencies and other long-term care facilities, and determine hospice eligibility, referring patients for services across the vastly complex health care continuum. America's Health Insurance Plans, one of the country's largest health insurance associations, reported in 2010 that a typical physician can direct up to $30,000 of health care spending a day.[53] Without physicians, the health care system would come to a complete and utter stop. Doctors remain at the core of American medicine.

4. As medicine, diagnostic tools, treatments, and cures advanced over the ages, the costs for health care began to rise, leading to the formation of insurance and other payment systems.

The cost to deliver medical care increased with advances in medicine, diagnostic tools, treatments, and cures. At the same time, moral and public policy debates ensued surrounding the need to provide affordable and accessible health care to larger population groups.

Despite the tremendous growth of medical knowledge, the beginnings of a formal structure for health care delivery, and the birth of the medical profession, many of the early medical advancements noted in the timelines within these chapters primarily benefited royalty, the aristocracy, and the wealthy. Political leaders and those with wealth typically had relationships with religious institutions that provided health care and had medical knowledge. Thus, the elites had greater access to health care. Those without means were fortunate to receive whatever form of charity care was available.[54]

In response, health care access and payment systems advanced alongside the growth of medicine. In Europe, government-sponsored programs were developed to increase access and to cover increasing health care costs. One of the world's first forms of government-funded health care dates back to Germany with the passage of the German Health Insurance Bill of 1883,[55] the Accident Insurance Bill of 1884,[56] and the Old Age and Disability Insurance Bill of 1889.[57] In Great Britain, the National Insurance Act of 1911 created a universal and national form of health care that covered most employed persons and their dependents.[58]

The first private insurance plans in the United States originated in the 1860s, primarily to cover health care for illnesses and injuries during the Civil War. After the Civil War, developing corporations in the United States began to implement early forms of employee health insurance, either by contracting directly with physicians to provide care, as discussed earlier, or under new premium-based plans.[59] By the 1920s and 1930s, American businesses began to form the first employer group health plans.[60]

Blue Cross and Blue Shield (BCBS) was formed as a nonprofit corporation and entered the health care insurance scene in the 1930s.[61] BCBS's success is attributed to its ability to offer physicians and hospitals discounted fees for services in return for delivering them large numbers of patients.[62] The development of labor unions in the 1940s and 1950s increased employees' ability to bargain for enhanced employee benefit packages, such as employer-sponsored health insurance.[63] During World War II, the federal government imposed wage freezes, which limited companies' ability to attract workers by paying higher wages, so employers offered expanded health benefits to attract a better workforce, further solidifying America's employer-based health insurance model.[64]

The private health insurance system in the United States did not develop without debate. Dating back to 1906, organizers founded the American Association for Labor Legislation (AALL) to consolidate the newly created health insurance industry and to mandate coverage through government regulation.[65] The AALL's ultimate goal was to create compulsory health insurance for all Americans. Many insurance companies fought against any plan for consolidation of the industry and compulsory insurance.[66]

In the presidential campaign of 1912, Theodore Roosevelt stated, "No country can be strong if its people are sick and poor." In fact, he changed his party affiliations and joined the Progressive Party, which had adopted a plan to provide universal health insurance to every American.[67,68] Woodrow Wilson defeated Roosevelt in that election, and the national political debate over how to provide the best health care for Americans had begun.[69]

During World War I, AALL continued to push for universal health care coverage because a surprising number of soldier recruits showed poor health and disabilities.[70] The AALL viewed increased access to health care as a necessity to protecting the fighting young men and their families left at home.[71]

The AALL's efforts were again defeated. California's League for the Conservation of Public Health labeled AALL's proposal as "compulsory social health insurance" and proclaimed that "it was a dangerous device, invented in Germany, announced by the German Emperor from the throne in the same year he started plotting and preparing to conquer the world."[72] The League proclaimed that compulsory health coverage was "un-American" and a move toward socialism, in part due to its similarities to the German health system.[73]

By 1933, less than 6 percent of Americans had any form of health care coverage, and the United States was headed straight for the depths of the Great Depression.[74] In an effort to bring the nation out of the Depression's grip, Theodore Roosevelt's distant cousin, President Franklin D. Roosevelt, constructed the New Deal. Part of the New Deal included the creation of Social Security, which the President and Congress enacted to provide a safety net for the nation's elderly, sick, and disabled.[75]

Social Security firmly placed the U.S. government in the role of funding some degree of public welfare. The President's Committee on Economic Security, which set the agenda for the New Deal, debated heavily whether to include mandated health insurance into Social Security, but to ensure its enactment the Committee excluded any form of universal or national health care coverage from the legislation.[76]

The federal government's decision to exclude national health insurance from the New Deal prompted private insurance companies to expand their offerings quickly. Blue Cross expanded its network of hospital prepayment plans. Henry J. Kaiser developed worksite group medical practices (similar to HMOs) to provide comprehensive health coverage for his workers and others. Community-based physician medical societies developed their own insurance plans, which they would later name Blue Shield plans.[77]

After Roosevelt's reelection in 1936, debate surrounding the nation's obligation to ensure comprehensive health care ignited once again. In July of 1938, a National Health Conference on the future of the U.S. health care system took place. It featured intense debates and disagreements as to the correct path for health care in the United States, and any notion of compulsory or universal health care insurance was attacked.[78] The editor of the *Journal of the American Medical Association* at the time, Morris Fishbein, blasted compulsory health care insurance as "another step toward the breakdown of American democracy and a trend toward a system fascistic or communistic in character directly opposed to the democratic principle."[79]

In 1943, Senators Wagner, Murray, and Dingell proposed a series of bills that would expand Social Security into a tax-supported federal insurance plan for Americans.[80] The AMA and its supporters remained in opposition to the creation of any nationalized health care system, stating that it "would result in a deterioration of the health of the people…. The enactment of this bill will destroy the private practice of medicine; it will create a political system of medicine dictated by a federal bureaucracy."[81]

Legislation for universal health care coverage never made it to President Roosevelt's desk. Following Roosevelt's death in office, President Truman pushed for national health insurance, but his efforts were also defeated.[82]

After these early twentieth-century attempts to enact universal health care died, health insurance in the United States became predominantly a privately purchased good. Policy makers established that the government should only intervene when supplemental health coverage was needed. For instance, Social Security added disability coverage in 1954.

Despite debate and strong criticism, in 1965 President Lyndon B. Johnson had enough Congressional support to enact America's largest government-funded health care benefit program at the time, the Medicare and Medicaid programs, but their roles and functions were limited. Medicare focused on the elderly and disabled; Medicaid targeted those in poverty, especially children and mothers.[83]

By the early 1970s, surveys reported that three-quarters of American families perceived that "there [was] a crisis in health care in the United States."[84] Health care prices were skyrocketing, and many American had limited access to affordable health care. Following President Richard Nixon's election, the debate over improving health care access and controlling costs raged. Nixon became stalwart in his belief that a national health insurance plan was vital to the nation's success. In his 1974 State of the Union Address, Nixon proclaimed that "[t]he time is at hand this year to bring comprehensive, high quality health care within the reach of every American."[85] In the end, Nixon's call for universal health care coverage took a back seat to Watergate, and it did not advance.[86]

When Gerald Ford succeeded Nixon to the presidency, the United States was entering a deeper economic crisis. In the mid-1970s, energy costs were soaring and a recession loomed. President Ford reintroduced reforming health care legislation,[87] but he soon abandoned these efforts because Congress was not supportive.[88] President Jimmy Carter did not move toward providing universal health care either, and instead focused on containing health care costs.[89]

In step with President Reagan's campaign promises of smaller government, his administration gave states more power in health funding. President Reagan also reformed Medicare and Medicaid to create a more managed and competitive system. He established the transformative DRG system, as discussed in Chapter 3. The Reagan administration also made large funding cuts, including reducing health planning funding from $167 million in 1980 to $58 million by 1983.[90]

Bill Clinton defeated President George H. W. Bush for the presidency in 1992, and health care was a significant component of his campaign. Candidate Clinton promised to have a health care reform bill to Congress within his first 100 days in office. Clinton focused on the individual rights of the American citizen by promising no tax increases and marketing himself as a New Democrat who opposed big government. He also appealed to Americans' value of equality by promoting his plan for universal coverage to ensure access to quality and affordable health care for all Americans.[91]

When President Clinton took office in 1993, 66 percent of Americans favored national health insurance financed by taxes,[92] yet Clinton's proposal for universal coverage never became law. Opponents to the President's reform plans claimed that Clinton's ideas could lead to socialized medicine.[93] By June 1994, public support for the bill dropped to 44 percent,[94] and the Clinton health reform bill was defeated.

After the Clinton administration, President George W. Bush relied heavily on the self-regulation of the market to lower health care prices through provider competition.[95] President Bush's most significant health care policy decision came with the enactment of the Medicare Prescription Drug, Improvement, and Modernization Act of 2003[96] (known as Medicare Part D), which created a major federal government entitlement program to cover certain prescription drugs for the elderly.[97] President Bush also signed the Deficit Reduction Act of 2005 into law, which contained some of America's most significant cuts to Medicare and Medicaid spending.[98]

By the dawn of the twenty-first century, Americans had been debating health care reform for nearly one hundred years. Like many candidates for U.S. president before him, Barack Obama proclaimed an urgent need to reform the nation's health care system during his 2008 race for the presidency. Candidate Obama made health care a central component to his campaign.

After winning the 2008 election, in a September 9, 2009, address to Congress, President Barack Obama remarked that "I am not the first president to take up this cause, but I am determined to be the last."[99] In March 2010, President Obama signed the Patient Protection and Affordable Care Act (PPACA) into law, making it perhaps the most comprehensive health care reform law passed in American history. We set forth a brief overview of PPACA[100] in Chapter 4.

Although it seems that universal health insurance in America was often part of a populist platform, attempts to implement it have always been fraught with controversy. Today is no different. Whether Americans view PPACA as dangerously socialist or as just being too darned expensive, this chapter demonstrates how this country has fiercely opposed any sweeping health care reform efforts.

Although President Obama intends to be the last president to champion this cause, history shows that the politics of health care reform have indeed become a cyclical process of gradually expanding coverage that is then countered by the steady weight of the reluctance for rapid change.

Many Americans refer to the Patient Protection and Affordable Care Act (PPACA) of 2010 as "Obama Care" because President Obama was so closely tied to the passage of this current legislation. Although PPACA has certainly triggered debate and become the focus for discussions about the need for U.S. health care reform today, what is surprising is how many U.S. presidents have spoken about, addressed, and advocated for health care reform, long before the current president signed PPACA into law.

Ponder the following presidential statements, many of which partially resemble components of Obama Care:

Whether we come to [national health insurance] soon or later on, I am confident that we can devise a system which will enhance and not hinder the remarkable progress which has been made and is being made in practice of the professions of medicine and surgery in the United States.

—Franklin D. Roosevelt, November 14, 1934[101]

We should resolve now that the health of this nation is a national concern; that financial barriers in the way of attaining health shall be removed; that the health of all its citizens deserves the help of all the nation.

—Harry S. Truman, November 19, 1945[102]

We are behind every country pretty nearly in Europe in this matter of medical care for our citizens.

—John F. Kennedy, May 20, 1962[103]

*Many men can make many proposals. Many men can draft
many laws. But few have the piercing and humane eye which
can see beyond the words to the people that they touch. Few
can see past the speeches and the political battles to the doctor
over there that is tending the infirm, and to the hospital that is
receiving those in anguish, or feel in their heart painful wrath
at the injustice which denies the miracle of healing to the old
and to the poor. And fewer still have the courage to stake
reputation, and position, and the effort of a lifetime upon such
a cause when there are so few that share it.*

—Lyndon B. Johnson, July 30, 1965[104]

*I shall propose a sweeping new program that will assure
comprehensive health-insurance protection to millions of
Americans who cannot now obtain it or afford it, with vastly
improved protection against catastrophic illnesses.*

—Richard Nixon, February 6, 1974[105]

*We have the finest medical facilities and highly skilled,
dedicated health professionals. Yet many of our people still
lack adequate medical care, and the cost of care is rising so
rapidly it jeopardizes our health goals and our other important
social objectives.*

—Jimmy Carter, April 25, 1977[106]

*It's high time that we put health care costs under the knife and
cut away the waste and inefficiency. The growth in medical
costs is malignant and must be removed for the continued
health of the American people.*

—Ronald Reagan, June 23, 1983[107]

*Despite the dedication of literally millions of talented health
care professionals, our health care is too uncertain and too
expensive, too bureaucratic and too wasteful. It has too much*

fraud and too much greed. At long last, after decades of false starts, we must make this our most urgent priority, giving every American health security—health care that can never be taken away, health care that is always there.

—Bill Clinton, September 22, 1993[108]

I believe every American should have access to quality, affordable health care by giving consumers better information about health care plans, providing more choices such as medical savings accounts and changing tax laws to help more people, such as the uninsured and the self-employed, afford health insurance.

—George W. Bush, October 11, 2000[109]
(during his campaign for the presidency)

The question isn't how we can afford to focus on healthcare. The question is how we can afford not to. Because in order to fix our economic crisis and rebuild our middle class, we need to fix our health care system, too.

—Barack Obama, October 4, 2008[110]
(during his campaign for the presidency)

After a century of striving, after a year of debate, after a historic vote, health care reform is no longer an unmet promise. It is the law of the land.

—Barack Obama, March 23, 2010[111]

Indeed, recent health care reform laws, including PPACA, have stirred great controversy. Many in America outright oppose it. To be clear, we are not writing this book to take a position in the PPACA debate. In fact, this book is about stepping out of the political and public fight surrounding PPACA, while offering valuable perspectives to everyone who feels compelled to take sides (Republicans, Democrats, Libertarians, Tea Party Patriots,

Independents—everyone). Perhaps if we step back and examine PPACA against the backdrop of nearly 100 years of debating how the American health care system should function, "Obama Care" will be perceived more as "evolutionary" rather than as "revolutionary."

We end this chapter by concluding that the rates of development of modern medicine, the medical profession, and medical delivery systems have increased at a marvelous pace. The United States is currently poised to choose the direction of future innovations.

As we stand at this point, poised to shape The New Health Age, we must decide who should be granted access to the latest medical advancements and how they are to obtain these treatments. Who gets to decide who receives advanced medicine and who is to be left behind? Governments? The free market? Citizens? In order to begin to answer these questions, we must take stock of the current landscape of medicine and health care in America.

KEY POINTS

1. It is apparent that the early medical profession and related health care delivery systems have evolved into a market made up of advanced and complex systems and institutions.

2. As medicine, diagnostic tools, treatments, and cures advanced over the ages, the costs for health care began to rise, leading to the formation of insurance and other payment systems.

3. Health reform has been a presidential goal for nearly a century, ending with the historical passage of the Patient Protection and Affordable Care Act in March 2010.

4

The Present Landscape

"In the revelation of any truth, there are three stages. In the first it is ridiculed, in the second it is resisted, and in the third it is considered self-evident."

—Arthur Schopenhauer

We now look at the challenges and opportunities in health care today that are leading this nation into an era of transformation in medicine and health care delivery. Change is coming. The speed of this change is accelerating. The problem that many participants within the health care system have with this change is simply that there is change from the ways that things have been done. The recent past and the present context are places where most people and almost all institutions contain their thinking and points of view. When the known is comfortable, the unknown is often resisted.

We believe that the forces and the nine dynamic transformational flows that we discuss later in this book will provide you with a way to see that the change that has begun in America is an inevitable, natural, and historical next step in the evolution of both how medicine is practiced and how health care is delivered. Those who have deeply entrenched interests or who cannot think outside of their history are always resistant to change. As futurists, we know that where there is resistance there is also a view to what lies ahead, because when resistance is at its most intense it is usually a last stand against inevitable change.

One of the reasons for this book is to help everyone who participates in the American health care system to see that the changing landscape of medicine and health care that we are living in today is inevitable and completely understandable. Too much of the recent national discussion around health care has been based upon fear, uncertainty, and misinformation. Such negative states rarely coexist with creative innovation. We are hopeful that this book will lead America away from such pessimistic and counterproductive thinking.

Ask yourself the following questions. Have the profound advancements and achievements that have occurred in medicine and health care, as noted in Chapters 2 and 3, resulted in a health care system that all Americans understand and praise today? Is it possible that the current U.S. health care delivery system is "stuck in its ways of the past" despite its astonishing progression over the prior centuries?

Compare health care to the information technology sector. Computers continue to get more powerful for less cost. In 1990, a personal computer cost approximately $2,000, processed at 16 MHz, and had 2 MB of RAM and 80 MB of disk space.[1] In 2010, you can purchase a small laptop computer, which fits in your briefcase, for $500, processing at 2.0 GHz, with 4 GB of RAM and 500 GB of disk space.[2] You get a much better computer for less cost than 20 years ago. Unlike many other business sectors in the United States, have our gains in medical knowledge and technology over the years resulted in an efficient, integrated, and cost-effective health care system today?

Great progress is often followed by great challenges. Medicine has advanced rapidly in recent centuries; we've moved from understanding the very basics of human anatomy to today being able to map the human genome. Health care delivery systems have evolved from operating in simple surroundings to massive and complex institutions with infrastructures and equipment valued in the billions of dollars. But do modern and often disconnected and behemoth institutions, which possess tremendous capital and resources, provide "best in class" health care? We will share data and facts throughout this chapter that address this question.

The present landscape of health care in the United States and the focus of this chapter are summed up as follows:

> America's state of health, the economic models driving health care choices and costs, and America's health care delivery systems do not adequately foster the right incentives for American Stakeholders to (1) increase the quality of their health, (2) improve health care service to everyone, or (3) control health care costs. This reality is contributing to the rapid decline of America's pride, financial strength, and competitive advantage in a global marketplace. It is, therefore, essential for America to acknowledge, embrace, and foster The New Health Age.

We lay claim to this bold and powerful statement as the "Health Care Landscape Statement," and we use it to shape the discussion throughout this chapter. Each section in this chapter analyzes and discusses a unique component part of the Health Care Landscape Statement.

1. Who are the Stakeholders?

The Stakeholders referenced in the Health Care Landscape Statement include

- American companies of all sizes
- Individuals of every age—young, old, and in between
- Public and private sectors

- Workers and employers
- Unemployed and employed
- Patients and health care providers
- Payers and their beneficiaries
- Teachers and students
- Governments and citizens

Everyone and every entity in America is a Stakeholder in the Health Care Landscape Statement. If you care about America's soul or worry about America's fiscal strength and corresponding ability to compete in an increasingly competitive global marketplace, then you are a Stakeholder in the Health Care Landscape Statement. To stress the importance of this reference, we treat Stakeholder as a proper noun throughout the book.

As two proud and patriotic American authors, we write this book to first set the stage by describing where health care has been and where it is today. More important, in later chapters we provide a road map to the bright future of medicine and health care that lies in front of us. As Americans, we intend to alter certain negative perceptions of the changes coming in The New Health Age and replace those fears and misperceptions with confidence, knowledge, and enthusiasm.

Do not mistakenly confuse our outlook for the future of health care as a prediction that everything will be perfect. We can rarely achieve perfection in the things that we do or create. We stand firmly in our belief, however, that our current stalled progression in health care will wane and better times are before us. Our history as Americans is filled with instances of when we overcame national obstacles and challenges.

Stakeholders in America have inherited a proud history of demonstrating great courage and overcoming difficult trials. Americans alive today follow in the footsteps of the colonists who fought for their independence against the British Empire and declared our new nation in 1776. American Stakeholders follow in the footsteps of soldiers who fought in the Civil War that tore this country apart before bringing it back together as a reunited United States of America. Many Stakeholders are descendants of immigrants who entered this great nation from faraway lands through Ellis Island and made themselves into something great with no more than a single suitcase of possessions. American Stakeholders admire former war heroes, such as those who defeated the Nazis in Europe and the Japanese Empire in the Pacific. Stakeholders used their knowledge, resources, and determination to send men to the moon. American Stakeholders fought and won a Cold War, against an enemy that possessed weapons of mass destruction powerful enough to potentially eradicate all of humankind from the Earth.

If Stakeholders in this great nation have accomplished such magnificent feats, we have the ability and the will that is required to solve the health care crisis that is brewing in the U.S. today and that the Health Care Landscape Statement and this chapter enumerate. There are no outside aggressors or forces threatening us, only our own fears, uncertainty, and resistance to change—conditions that hold us back from confronting the Health Care Landscape Statement and the issues raised within it.

Next, let's survey the overall health of Americans.

2. What is the state of America's health, as described in the Health Care Landscape Statement?

"Leave all the afternoon for exercise and recreation, which are as necessary as reading. I will rather say more necessary, because health is worth more than learning."

—Thomas Jefferson

The majority of Americans still feel that this country is the greatest nation in the world, yet a growing number are beginning to question this fact. Our state of health in the United States adds to this growing pessimism and is telling about our human condition. Our state of health does not bode well for Americans who are increasingly competing in a competitive global marketplace and society. According to recent Centers for Disease Control and Prevention (CDC) statistics:

- 34 percent of Americans age 20 years and older are obese.[3]
- 20.6 percent of Americans 18 years of age and older currently smoke cigarettes.[4]
- Only 25.4 percent of American adults regularly engage in leisure-time physical activity.[5]
- 20.9 percent of American adults drink five or more alcoholic beverages a day on an annual basis.[6]
- 55.6 million Americans had ambulatory care visits (to physician offices or hospital outpatient or emergency departments) with mental disorders as the primary diagnosis.[7]

Simply focus on the obesity statistics for a moment. The rate of obesity in the United States is climbing at a rapid pace. In 1980, the CDC reported that approximately 15 percent of adults ages 20 and older were obese.[8] Today, that rate has more than doubled. A 2010 article published in *Health Affairs* concluded that health care spending linked to obesity is responsible for approximately $147 billion in health care expenditures.[9]

Let's look at what the CDC reports as the top 10 leading causes of death in America:

1. Heart disease
2. Cancer
3. Stroke
4. Respiratory diseases such as COPD (chronic obstructive pulmonary disease)
5. Injuries
6. Complications from Alzheimer's disease
7. Diabetes

8. Influenza and pneumonia
9. Kidney diseases
10. Blood poisoning through a bacterial infection

The *New England Journal of Medicine* (*NEJM*) points out that a number of these causes of deaths are preventable because they are fundamentally tied to Americans' choices and actions. The *NEJM*[10] states that annually:

- 465,000 smoking deaths could be prevented by quitting smoking.
- 395,000 deaths related to high blood pressure could be prevented through medication and lifestyle changes.
- 216,000 deaths could be prevented by reducing obesity.
- 191,000 deaths could be prevented if Americans exercised regularly.
- 190,000 deaths could be prevented by controlling diabetes.
- 113,000 deaths could be prevented by controlling low-density lipoprotein cholesterol.

The total deaths above equal 1,570,000, which is roughly the population of Philadelphia, Pennsylvania.[11] In other words, the entire population living in Philadelphia dies annually from preventable health conditions. These 1,570,000 Americans are much more than raw statistics; they are our beloved family members, neighbors, friends, and coworkers.

America's health care system cannot reverse these staggering statistics without the commitment from Americans to educate themselves better about the appropriate health choices that will ultimately lead to improvements in their own health. Americans have to choose to quit smoking. Americans have to choose to exercise regularly. Americans have to eat and drink healthier. Our lifestyles must embrace overall healthy living if we want to truly receive the most out of America's health care system.

How does America's state of health affect the nation's workforce? Kathleen Sebelius, secretary of the U.S. Department of Health and Human Services, announced at the 2011 Global Business Forum hosted by the University of Miami, School of Business Administration, that the U.S. workforce could avoid about 45 million sick days annually by improving its health.[12] This number equates to nearly 180,000 employees calling in sick for an entire year.[13]

Ask yourself: How many 75-year-olds do you know who are obese, inactive, and eat poorly? Not many, right? Do you know any?

What is the state of America's health? The data speak for themselves.

3. How do America's health care payment models and incentives impact health care costs?

The current state of American health and health care is largely a result of how health care providers are paid and the incentives, or lack thereof, related to controlling health care costs. "Follow the money" and we can understand better what made the Health Care Landscape Statement a distressing reality today. Economic motivations and incentives frequently reveal the underlying basis for an economic result.

Consider the commission based compensation model. Ask yourself whether salespeople who receive fixed salaries as opposed to commissions earn the same amount. Isn't it well known that commission sales models keep people motivated and striving for that next sale? The commission inspires a particular result— the sale.

How are health care providers paid? Are there economic incentives or disincentives behind consumer spending in health care? Are Americans rewarded for staying healthier? How do the answers to these questions impact health care costs in America?

a) How are health care providers paid?

Recall from Chapter 1 that the definition of "health care provider" for purposes of this book is all inclusive and refers to anyone and any institution involved in the delivery of health care services, including physicians, physician assistants, nurses, physical therapists, counselors, hospitals, surgery centers, long-term care providers, and others. Two basic provider reimbursement models exist today: fee-for-service and capitation. We discuss both of these models below to provide a framework for understanding how health care payment models influence the delivery of health care and the related costs.

Currently, fee-for-service is the more prevalent health care payment model in the United States. In short, this means that each unit of service or product is individually priced and paid for after the item is delivered. A patient sees a physician, the physician examines the patient, and the physician is paid for the service. The physician orders a test and the provider of the test receives payment. A physician admits a patient to the hospital and the hospital collects payment.

The more health care users consume, the more someone pays. Typically, the party paying the largest share is a third-party payer, which is usually an insurance company, an employer, or the government. Patients normally pay smaller co-pays and deductibles.

What is the process for being paid? The payers in America have established tens of thousands of payment codes and have assigned each code a dollar amount for the service provided. Health care providers provide a service, assign the service a code, and each code equates to preset dollars that will be paid for the service.[14]

Alternatively, capitation payment is a fixed fee paid per person in a defined group or population. So, for example, ABC Insurance Company might pay a physician $200 per month per member in exchange for providing care for that member. A capitation fee is paid independently of the quantity of health care services used by the member, so the physician receives $200 per member per month, regardless of whether the member visits the doctor once or 10 times in a month. In a capitation environment, the health care provider assumes risk and agrees to provide a predetermined array of health care services to members for a fixed, or capitated, rate.

Today, capitation payment models are far less common than fee-for-service models because health care providers generally fear assuming risk, even if it may result in higher profits. Health care providers base their fear on a lack of tools available to help them assess the degree of risk that certain patient groups represent.[15]

Take the ABC Insurance Company example. A physician may be able to operate a profitable practice receiving $200 per month per member, assuming that the members are generally healthy and visit the doctor a few times a year. If, however, too many members suffer from heart disease and diabetes, they will likely have more doctor visits, making the $200 fixed rate less viable economically. Unless the physician has access to information and data regarding the health conditions of patient populations (in our example, the number of members with heart disease and diabetes), how can a physician appropriately analyze the degree of risk that he or she is willing to assume in a capitated environment?

As we stated earlier, "follow the money." In today's predominantly fee-for-service payment world, health care providers of all sorts are paid more for utilizing versus preventing the need for health care services. The more health care a patient consumes, the higher a provider's revenue. The more diagnostic tests physicians order, the greater reimbursement they receive. The more procedures performed, the greater the reimbursement received. The more days a patient stays at a hospital, the greater revenue the facility receives. The more physical therapy given by a therapist, the more payments are made.

The financial incentive in a fee-for-service payment system to control or limit the provision of health care services or costs is minimal. The sicker we are, the more services and payments a health care provider receives.[16]

Under capitation, by contrast, health care providers receive the same revenue, regardless of how much care the patients consume. Providers paid by capitation have an incentive to manage costs, because they know that their revenues will be capped. They retain the downside risk when health care expenses exceed the capitated rate, and they receive the upside profit when capitation payments are higher than their costs. To oversimplify but to demonstrate the capitation model, sick patients increase provider costs and lower profits. Healthy patients reduce provider costs and increase profits.

We will further explore these payment incentives and look at the payment models of the future in later chapters of the book. Today, the fee-for-service payment model predominates American health care. Simply put, this system rewards and compensates health care providers who utilize and provide more services. Providers have little economic incentive for helping patients stay well and out of the health care delivery system because they are not paid for doing so. Don't blame health care providers for functioning in a reimbursement environment that rewards them for increased utilization. Remember, "follow the money," because it influences behavior. Change the health care system so that health care providers receive rewards for keeping patients healthier and for utilizing fewer resources.

b) What influences the health care consumer?

Most Americans have limited knowledge or awareness of their health care spending because the patients' share of the expense is generally limited. Either the government or employers pick up the largest share of health care costs while the patient typically pays only co-pays or deductible amounts.

For instance, in 2010 the average Medicare deductible amount was $1,100 per year for Medicare Part A and $155 per year for Medicare Part B.[17] For private insurance plans, co-pays averaged $22 for a primary care office visit, up from $20 in 2008.[18] Co-pays for ER visits have gone up 21 percent since 2008, to $108.[19] The co-pay visit to a specialist averages $30.[20] Private insurance deductibles averaged $1,200 for individuals, provided that that the patient remained in-network.[21]

Our perceptions are often more influential than is reality. One critical issue in America's health care reimbursement system is that the person who receives the service does not perceive that he or she is paying for it.

Imagine a retail system where the shopper's employer agreed to cover 90 percent of the purchase price, subject to a $500 deductible. Would you shop at a discount retailer or a high-end specialty store that stocks the most popular brands? Perhaps you would spend the first $500 at the discount store. Where would you spend the rest? What if you entered the store and a third-party personal advisor managed your purchase and ordered everything that the advisor "deemed necessary" (much like physicians order and prescribe services in health care). How much incentive would the shopper have in our example to control or manage the purchase price? Would such a system increase retail expenditures in the United States or decrease them?

Most Americans have limited, if any, incentive to question the cost, necessity, quantity, or quality of a health care service. Americans do not appreciate the impact of their health care spending choices. Think about it. How much in total dollars (adding up co-pays, deductibles, and all costs paid by third-party payers) did you consume and spend on your own health care last year? Do you even have access to the data necessary to answer the question? How much did you spend on housing last year? You can probably come close to answering that question off the top of mind. Why is health care spending different?

The old saying "out of sight, out of mind" is quite true. Our perception of health care cost might be limited to the co-pays and deductibles that we paid; yet, in reality, our employer, the government, or other third-party payer paid substantially more for the health care that we consumed.

When patients experience blood infections after surgery, what should normally cost $20,000 for a hospital stay can result in an additional $100,000 in hospital expenses.[22] In a fee-for-service system, minimal economic incentives exist to compensate hospitals for reducing infection rates.[23] In fact, the hospital receives more revenue when infections do occur.[24] On the patient side, although no one wants to suffer physically from an infection, economically they feel minimal pain as a result of the additional

$80,000 expense because insurance or the government absorbs most, if not all, of the extra cost.[25]

Health care consumers have little incentive to care about health care costs because they are impacted to a limited degree. If we overspend during the holidays, we see the result when our credit card bills arrive. When we overspend on health care dollars, the costs seem to disappear; yet, in reality, employers, insurance companies, governments, taxpayers, and others pay for the costs. The costs do not go away, but our perception is not consistent with this reality.

To demonstrate this point, let's examine dental care in the United States. Forty-five percent of dental care in the United States is paid for by the consumer versus the government or the insurance companies, compared to 10 percent being paid for by the consumer for physician services.[26] How does this impact consumer spending? Between 2003 and 2006, spending on dental care increased a moderate 6 percent (largely due to cosmetic dentistry) compared to an estimated 18 percent increase in other health care segments.[27] When patients have the incentive to maintain healthier teeth and to shop for appropriate and affordable dental care when needed, they become motivated to stay healthy and seek care only when needed. This results in reduced spending.[28]

In addition to health care spending, Americans have little economic reason to care about their state of health either. Regardless of whether you are an American worker who is overweight and suffering from diabetes or physically fit enough to run a marathon, for the most part, employees working for the same company pay the same amount for their health insurance. Perhaps the diabetic employee pays a few more co-pay dollars for extra doctor visits and the like, but the employee expense differential is not material. Thus, economically, why should the obese employee behave any differently than the marathon runner? Being overweight costs the same as being thin.

The same is true for Medicare and Medicaid patients. Regardless of the patient's overall health status and condition, the economic impact to the patient differs slightly. The government does not tax the Medicare patient who consumes 6,000 calories daily any more than the patient who consumes 3,000.

The CDC's webpage is full of recommendations for Americans to reduce their consumption of trans-fat foods, but what economic motivators exist to reward such behavior? If trans-fat foods are so unhealthy, should governments tax these foods like cigarettes?

Now ask yourself, does the lack of proper incentives influence health care costs? Should these incentives change? We will explore these questions throughout other chapters of the book.

Next, let's break down this chapter further and discuss the cost, quality, and service elements in the Health Care Landscape Statement. We start with cost.

4. What does America spend on health care?

a) GDP Spending

The following data demonstrate the rapid increase in health care spending in America over the past 40 years. In 2010, the United States' federal, state, and local governments; corporations; and individuals combined spent an estimated $2.47 trillion, or approximately $8,086 per person, on health care.[29] This amount represented nearly 17.4 percent of the GDP.[30] By comparison, in 1980 the share of GDP devoted to health care was 8.8 percent, and America spent approximately $1,072 per person on health care. In 1970, it was $352 per person.[31]

McKinsey & Company, a global management consulting firm headquartered in New York City, reports through its McKinsey Global Institute (MGI) that in 2006 Americans spent twice as much on health care than they spent on food and more than all of China spent on goods and services.[32] MGI leveraged and utilized health data from the Organisation for Economic Co-operation and Development (OECD) and produced an acclaimed study in December 2008 titled *Accounting for the Cost of U.S. Health Care: A New Look at Why Americans Spend More*.[33]

In the study, MGI used a proprietary measurement called the Estimated Spending According to Wealth (ESAW) that adjusts health care spending according to per capita GDP.[34] Using data from 13 OECD peer countries,* MGI concluded that $477 billion of total health care spending in the United States was above expectations when compared to peer OECD countries, even when adjusted for wealth.[35] The MGI reports that 85 percent of overspending can be attributed to hospital and physician care.[36] The complete allocation of the spending is contained in the study.

Health care spending is projected to increase 6 to 7 percent annually, well outpacing inflation in the coming years.[37] The U.S. Department of Health and Human Services (DHHS) expects that the health share of GDP will continue its historical upward trend, possibly reaching nearly 20 percent or more of GDP by 2017.[38]

Medicare and Medicaid spending accounted for 21 percent of the total federal budget and 47.8 percent of the federal budget deficit in 2010.[39] Many states also report that health care spending is a significant factor in their budget crises.[40]

Health care costs are headed nowhere but up.

b) Medicare/Medicaid and Baby Boomer Spending

One of the largest single factors predicted to raise health care costs over the coming decade is the looming entrance of the Baby Boomers into the Medicare system, starting in 2011. Nearly 80 million Americans were born from 1946 to 1964, and they will increase Medicare rolls from 45 million today to 67 million by 2020.[41] That rate will increase Medicare beneficiaries by nearly 22 million people in less than 10 years. Medicare/Medicaid costs could consume nearly half the federal budget by 2020 at the current rates of cost increases.[42] This rate of spending growth is simply unsustainable and could cripple the United States if we do not get it under control—and soon.

---

*The 13 OECD peer countries were Austria, Canada, Czech Republic, Denmark, Finland, France, Germany, Iceland, Poland, Portugal, South Korea, Spain, and Switzerland.

c) Insurance Spending

Acclaimed Princeton professor, health care advisor, author, and researcher Dr. Uwe Reinhardt states that "The issue of universal coverage is not a matter of economics. Little more than 1 percent of GDP assigned to health could cover all. It is a matter of soul."[43]

The average cost per employee for employer-sponsored health insurance hovers around $10,000.[44] Working families are experiencing annual double-digit increases in the costs of their health insurance premiums, deductibles, co-payments, and drugs.[45] In October 2003, and again in June 2007, proposed employer cuts to health care benefits for employees was the major precipitator behind a grocery union workers' strike in Southern California, during which nearly 70,000 workers protested management's health insurance proposals, which would have required employees earning slightly less than $20,000 a year to pay nearly $5,000 to maintain the same level of benefits provided in their previous contract.[46]

Some 47 million U.S. residents have no health benefits because they either fail to qualify for government support, find that health insurance is not offered by their employer, or determine that the premium costs are simply out of their reach.[47] Of the 47 million Americans without health insurance, nearly 8 million are children.[48] The number of children with no health care coverage living in America roughly equals the total number of people living in New York City.[49]

This critical state of affairs forces many Americans to avoid or delay seeking needed medical care. These scenarios create a downward spiral and actually increase health care costs long term. We get sicker and more expensive as a nation by avoiding preventative health care. Countless studies demonstrate that early intervention during illness or disease and preventative care saves money long term; yet as stated earlier, America's current health care system does not typically reward health care providers or patients for preventing poor health.[50]

d) Drug Costs

Throughout the last several decades, advances in pharmaceuticals have transformed health care. Prescription drugs help manage, cure, or prevent countless health problems. In 2007, 58 percent of nonelderly adults and 90 percent of seniors took prescription medication on a routine basis.[51] In recent years, approximately 10 percent of total health care spending in the United States has been on prescription drugs, so the cost implications loom large for America going forward.[52]

The rising costs of prescription medications impact many sectors of the health care industry, including government programs, private insurers, and patients. Recently, increases in prescription drug costs have outpaced other categories of health care spending.[53] In fact, prescription drug costs are projected to exceed the growth rates for hospital care and other professional services, such as physician care and therapy care, through 2019.[54]

In light of these increasing expenditures, should Americans question whether the continued increased use of drugs is the best approach to attacking so many diseases and health conditions? Can we obtain long-term wellness and cost control through other methods?

e) Health Care Administration and Insurance Expenses

The MGI study discussed earlier also concluded that health care administration and insurance expenses accounted for nearly 7 percent of total health care costs in 2006 and was $91 billion more than expected compared to the previously mentioned OECD peer nations.[55] Of the total costs, $63 billion was attributable to private insurance payers, in the form of profits and taxes ($30 billion) and marketing and administrative expenses ($33 billion).[56] The remaining $28 billion in U.S. spending on health care administration was derived from public programs, such as Medicare and Medicaid.[57] Although public payer administrative costs were measurably lower than private payer expenses, public administrative costs in the United States average 6 percent of public health spending, compared to a 4 percent average amongst other OECD peer countries.[58]

MGI attributed higher U.S. costs in this segment to several factors. A multipayer system and a multistate regulated insurance system resulted in extra costs and inefficiencies in the form of duplicated marketing, underwriting, administrative costs, and management.[59] How much could health care spending be reduced by simply integrating insurance companies into fewer payers and by trimming inefficiencies?

f) Medical Errors and Malpractice Lawsuits

In the *Journal of the American Medical Association* (*JAMA*) Dr. Barbara Starfield, MD, MPH, of the Johns Hopkins School of Hygiene and Public Health, reported that medical errors may be the third leading cause of death in America.[60] Dr. Starfield attributed 2,000 deaths annually from unnecessary surgery, 7,000 deaths annually from medication errors in hospitals, 20,000 deaths a year from other errors in hospitals, and 80,000 deaths per year from infections in hospitals. Medical errors alone account for an estimated $19.5 billion in added costs to the American health care system.[61] What other costs does America sustain from more than 100,000 deaths due to accident or errors?

America's tort system—patients suing health care providers for medical malpractice—also drives up health care costs. Providers often practice costly preventative medicine in order to check, double-check, and triple-check every possible scenario attributable to a potential health condition out of fear that they will be sued if something is missed.

Numerous research studies conclude that the total cost attributable to the defensive practice of medicine and medical malpractice insurance is about $55.6 billion per year.[62,63,64] Defensive medicine accounts for nearly 80 percent of that total.[65] The remaining 20 percent comes from the settlement or judgment payments made to plaintiffs, the administrative expenses incurred in handling medical malpractice claims, and the costs associated with a health care provider's lost time as result of the malpractice action.[66]

Combined, the costs of medical errors and the medical malpractice system add approximately $75 billion dollars a year to an already taxed health care system.

g) Chronic Diseases

Several key facts and stark realities demonstrate the accuracy of the Health Care Landscape Statement in the beginning of this chapter. The data related to chronic diseases in America are one of them—perhaps the most important. Consider the following:

- An estimated 70 percent of health care expenditures in the United States are attributable to people with chronic diseases, according to national health care experts, such as CDC researchers and executives like George Halvorson, Kaiser Permanente CEO.[67,68] That is worth repeating: 70 percent of health care expenditures in the United States are attributable to people with chronic diseases.

- What is even more astounding is that 10 percent of the U.S. population consumes nearly 70 percent of health care dollars.[69] Again, that is worth repeating, perhaps in a different way: one out of every 10 Americans consumes .70 cents of every $1 spent on health care.

Several chronic diseases drive a disproportionate share of health care costs at alarming annual rates:

- Heart disease and stroke: $432 billion per year[70]
- Diabetes: $174 billion per year[71]
- Lung disease: $154 billion per year[72]
- Depression: $77 billion per year[73]

High blood pressure is also an extremely relevant condition, because heart disease, stroke, and diabetes-related complications can result from high blood pressure.

The impact of comorbidities (people suffering with two or more of the aforementioned chronic diseases) generally results in the most care, and the most cost, as a result of needing numerous health care providers functioning throughout the care continuum.[74] Common diseases that give rise to comorbidities, listed in order from most expensive to least expensive, include: congestive heart failure, stroke, diabetes, cancer, dementia, chronic obstructive pulmonary disease (COPD), and hypertension.[75] A study examining the costs associated with comorbidities found that "those individuals with a comorbidity score of two or more accounted for just 26 percent of the [study] population but slightly over 50 percent of the overall costs of care."[76]

Preventing chronic diseases, as discussed later, will have a substantial effect on the lowering of health care costs for Stakeholders.

h) Bankruptcies

Health care spending forces many Americans into bankruptcy. In 2007, 62.1 percent of bankruptcy filers in the United States cited "medical causes" as the basis for bankruptcy, despite the fact that three-fourths of these filers had health insurance.[77] Even with health insurance, health care spending frequently forces Americans into economic crisis.

In summary, health care costs are wreaking painful economic havoc on our country.

5. What is the quality of health care in America?

Using five performance indicators to measure health systems in 191 World Health Organization (WHO) member states, the WHO concluded that among larger countries France provided the best overall health care, followed by Italy, Spain, Oman, Austria, and Japan.[78] The United Kingdom, which spends approximately 6 percent of GDP on health services, was ranked 18th.[79] Smaller countries, such as San Marino, Andorra, Malta, and Singapore, rated close behind second-placed Italy.[80] How did the United States fare? Shockingly, the WHO ranked America 37th in the world.

When assessing a country's health care system, the WHO considered the following criteria and rated the nations accordingly:

1. The overall level of population health [utilizing indicators such as infant mortality rate (IMR) and disability-adjusted life expectancy (DALE)]

2. Health inequalities (or disparities) within the population

3. Overall level of health system responsiveness (patient satisfaction)

4. Distribution of responsiveness within the population (how well people of varying economic status find that they are served by the health system)

5. The distribution of the health system's financial burden within the population (who pays the costs)[81]

The United States scored particularly low in the areas of IMR, DALE, and how well people of varying economic status find that they are served by the health care system.[82] Regardless of whether we doubt the accuracy of the WHO report, find it surprising, or accept it, the data imply that America has significant room to improve the quality of health care in this great country.

Many people perceive that America's health care system is the best in the world and that providers possess the most up-to-date medical data about treatments and utilize the latest and greatest medical equipment. Patients place tremendous trust and faith into their health care providers. In many cases, such trust is well deserved; however, studies demonstrate that great variations exist in the quality and standards of care across the health care spectrum. It is this variability that raises questions.

One study of 135 physicians presented the same patient to every doctor in the group. The physicians developed 82 unique and distinct treatments.[83] The percent of physicians who recommended heart bypass surgery to patients in neighboring communities varied by as much as 200 percent.[84] The rate that children underwent tonsillectomies in two adjacent communities varied from 20 percent in one community to 70 percent in another.[85] This evidence reveals the variations in medical treatments and calls into question whether the health care system effectively shares the national standards and best practice guidelines.[86]

Another study revealed that the 60-day patient mortality rate following cancer surgery can range from 5.4 to 12.3 percent depending on the surgeon providing the care.[87] Research shows that some radiologists detect 76 percent more breast cancers on mammograms than others, for no other reason than their varying skill levels.[88]

Scholars can certainly debate and challenge the data behind this research, but the point is simply that "all health care providers are not created equally." Some are simply better than others, just like in many other professions and in business. In sports, only certain players rise to the top. In accounting, some accountants understand the tax laws better than others do. In law, not every attorney becomes AV Rated by Martindale Hubbell, one of the country's most respected rating establishments. Companies have only one Chief Executive Officer. We will discuss what all this means for the future of health care in later chapters.

Even within one hospital facility, policies, procedures, and guidelines can vary by unit and floor.[89] For instance, the protocols for sharing information about patients from nurse to nurse during a shift change can vary widely within the same hospital.[90] Transferring information incorrectly and medication errors are common mistakes within hospitals, in part, because of the failure of hospitals to develop industry-wide systems and protocols related to the care process.[91]

Let's examine health care insurance and compare this segment to other industries for a moment. General Electric (GE) is so superior at developing and redeveloping production facilities and processes that the company has set a goal to achieve no more than 3.4 errors per 1 million opportunities.[92] In many GE production processes, the company actually exceeds these levels.[93] Three errors per million is no doubt impressive and synonymous with the American corporate value of producing quality products and services. Achieving such standards has helped grow America into the economic superpower that it is today.

The Healthcare Effectiveness Data and Information Set (HEDIS) is a widely used set of performance measures developed and maintained by the National Committee for Quality Assurance

(NCQA) for evaluating the health insurance industry. According to previous NCQA rankings, the number one ranked health plan in America had an error rate of approximately 11 percent for breast cancer screening.[94] This level of noncompliance with screening standards translates to 110,000 errors per 1 million patients. Compare that to GE's rate of three errors per million. What if you or a loved one were within the 110,000 errors?

NCQA also reports that health plans commit errors in 332,000 patients out of 1 million in the area of controlling high blood pressure. This equates to a 66.8 percent compliance rate for managing hypertension.[95] On average, health plans effectively manage cholesterol in heart attack patients only 50.9 percent of the time.[96] That is one out of two people.

GE would never accept these error rates. Why should health care insurance companies? Why should Americans?

This has been a quick look at health, health care spending, and the quality of health care in America. Next we explore service.

6. How is patient service within America's health care delivery system?

"In this insanity of economics of health care, the patient always loses."

—Peter Van Etten, President, Stanford Health Services[97]

Nearly every business sector in the modern world functions in an increasingly competitive environment. To succeed and get ahead of the competition, consumers are forcing companies, professionals, and institutions of various types to recognize that customer service is a critical component to their purchasing decisions. Consumers are in a constant state of measuring and comparing suppliers of products and services. They seek to purchase the "best item" for the "best price" from the "best sellers" in the marketplace.

The Four Seasons, for instance, is synonymous with providing its hotel and resort guests with impeccable customer service. From the moment of arrival, Four Seasons' engulfs guests into a culture where the employees strive to please their customers in every way possible. When a guest inquires about the location of the resort spa, it is not uncommon for a Four Seasons associate to escort the guest personally to the location to ensure that the customer reaches his or her destination in an enjoyable manner.

American consumers have come to expect, and surprisingly tolerate, a lower level of customer service from the health care sector. This is astonishing when you consider that health care consumers are often in desperate need of one the most important services needed by humankind—aid in preserving their health and well-being. The old saying "If you don't have your health, you have nothing" comes to mind. In 2009, for instance, the average wait time in an emergency room was 4 hours and 7 minutes. That time was a 4-minute increase from 2008 and a 31-minute increase since 2002.[98]

Despite these statistics, when surveyed, many Americans remain relatively satisfied with the health care they receive. In a 2008 *New England Journal of Medicine* study, researchers found that 63 percent of patients gave their hospital care a high rating (9 or 10) on a 10-point scale. An additional 26 percent rated their care as 7 or 8, whereas only 11 percent gave a rating of 6 or less. Sixty-seven percent of the patients said that they would definitely recommend the hospital in which they had received care.[99]

Think about the emergency room statistics for a moment and compare those findings to other experiences in your life. If you arrived at a Four Seasons and waited 4 hours to check-in, would you rate the Four Seasons a 7 or higher on the service scale? Why do Americans tolerate such poor service in health care and not in the hospitality industry? Perhaps it goes back to America's unrealistic perception of who is paying the bill. If a hospital bill is $20,000 and the patient only writes a deductible check for $1,000, that seems like a great deal. Even if the hospital's service was lacking, if the patient's perception is that he only paid 5 percent, how can he or she complain?

So far, we have looked at America's state of health, America's spending on health and the resulting quality, and service levels produced by America's health care system. What are your conclusions? Have we, as Americans, come to accept these findings as the norm and deem health care today as status quo? Can and should we do better?

7. In response to the conditions set forth in the Health Care Landscape Statement, the time for health care reform is now.

"Every person has the right to adequate health care. This right flows from the sanctity of human life and the dignity that belongs to all persons, who are made in the image of God.... Our call for health care reform is rooted in the biblical call to heal the sick and to serve 'the least of these,' the priorities of justice and the principle of the common good. The existing patterns of health care in the United Sates do not meet the minimal standard of social justice and the common good."

U.S. Catholic Bishops [1993] Resolution
on Health Care Reform[100]

Before concluding this chapter, let's revisit the Health Care Landscape Statement:

America's state of health, the economic models driving health care choices and costs, and America's health care delivery systems do not adequately foster the right incentives for American Stakeholders to (1) increase the quality of their health, (2) improve health care service to everyone, or (3) control health care costs. This reality is contributing to the rapid decline of America's pride, financial strength, and competitive advantage in a global marketplace. It is, therefore, essential for America to acknowledge, embrace, and foster The New Health Age.

Hopefully, you now have a deeper and more enlightened appreciation for the magnitude of this statement. The challenge now is for every American to focus on the last sentence: "It is, therefore, essential for America to acknowledge, embrace, and foster The New Health Age." If we fail to embrace this milestone in time, the consequence may be dire. America will no longer be as competitive in the new global marketplace as its health care costs spiral out of control while it provides health care that does not appear to measure up. Americans' sense of personal pride will deteriorate along their individual health.

As we saw in Chapter 3, over the last 100 years numerous presidents, congressional leaders, and some in the private sector have seen and spoken to the need for a changed health care system. With the passage of the Patient Protection and Affordable Care Act (PPACA), signed into law by President Barack Obama on March 23, 2010, the beginning of health care reform has come to America.[101] It is likely one of the most significant health care legislative initiatives in American history, standing beside the enactment of the Social Security system and the Medicare and Medicaid programs. What does it now mean for America?

As we stated earlier, we are not writing this book to take a position in the PPACA debate. We are suggesting, however, that in the wake of PPACA, many Americans of all walks of life are currently caught up in the mode of ridiculing and resistance, versus embracing the inevitable change and increasing their intelligent awareness to gain a better understanding of PPACA's overarching goals. Even if America cannot agree on all sections of PPACA and the law is eventually amended, "watered down" (which will likely occur), or even held unconstitutional and repealed, certain overall components and driving principles of health care reform have already laid the foundation for certain changes that will occur. Recall the Schopenhauer quote, which opened this chapter: "In the revelation of any truth, there are three stages. In the first it is ridiculed, in the second it is resisted and in the third it is considered self-evident."

Although PPACA can take up to 3,000 pages to print, the law can essentially be boiled down to several core initiatives, each seeking to address the issues outlined in this chapter. Let's look at the core fundamentals of this law, viewed simply as a catalyst for the coming changes that we will experience together as a country.

The PPACA's fundamental goals are as follows:

1. Increase access to health care.
2. Control health care costs.
3. Increase the quality of health.

Yes, PPACA is controversial; yes, PPACA is complex; yes, PPACA will take years to implement; and yes, Congress may amend PPACA; however, these three goals and core principles will endure.

A comprehensive presentation of PPACA is not the purpose of this book. For those readers who want to research PPACA in more detail, The Henry J. Kaiser Family Foundation's website (http://healthreform.kff.org/) contains a comprehensive and detailed review of the law and its implications. This website is a valuable resource. That said, we offer a few very brief examples of key PPACA initiatives in the following sections.

a) Access

PPACA will expand access to health care by creating new state and national health insurance exchanges through which individuals and small businesses can purchase affordable health care insurance. These exchanges seek to increase the national pools of covered lives, increase competition, and lower insurance administrative costs.

b) Costs

PPACA seeks to manage costs through adopting payment policies with an emphasis on quality and efficiency. PPACA promotes the development of new accountable care and shared savings models. Through accountable care organizations (ACOs), which we discuss at length in later chapters, providers across the care continuum will be more responsible for care and held accountable for good health care outcomes. Those who participate with ACOs will share in the costs savings if they perform care profitably and successfully (e.g., reduced hospital stays with effective post-acute care). Alternatively, health care providers will share in expenses and costs if they do not properly manage patient care or bad outcomes result, causing avoidable expenses (e.g., unnecessary hospital readmissions, infections, etc.).

c) Quality

A critical goal of PPACA is to improve health care quality through identifying gaps in care and by increasing efficiency, information, outcomes measures, and data collection through industry-proven techniques. PPACA focuses on addressing the health care provided to patients with high-cost chronic diseases in an effort to improve quality to this patient population, which currently costs the health care system upward of 70 percent of total costs.[102]

Quality goals under PPACA include

- Improving research and dissemination of strategies and best practices to improve patient safety and reduce medical errors, preventable admissions and readmissions, and health care-associated infections
- Reducing health disparities across patient populations and geographic areas
- Improving health outcomes, efficiency, and patient-centeredness of health care for all populations

So, the current landscape of health care exposes many challenges and opportunities. Yet various national health reform initiatives over the decades, such as PPACA, seek to pave the way to a new day.

The "revelation of truth" is self-evident. The New Health Age will break out of the current environment. Resistance is and will give way to self-evidency.

KEY POINTS

1. The Health Care Landscape Statement:

   America's state of health, the economic models driving health care choices and costs, and America's health care delivery systems do not adequately foster the right incentives for American Stakeholders to (1) increase the quality of their health, (2) improve health care service to everyone, or (3) control health care costs. This reality is contributing to the rapid decline of America's pride, financial strength, and competitive advantage in a global marketplace. It is, therefore, essential for America to acknowledge, embrace, and foster The New Health Age.

2. Every American is a Stakeholder in the country's health care delivery system.

3. We Americans consider our country to be the best, yet we are an unhealthy society.

4. The U.S. health care system is not ranked anywhere near the top globally.

5. Current health care incentives are procedure driven, not health driven.

6. Inefficiencies and inequalities that would be intolerable to Americans anywhere else in their lives are tolerated in health care.

7. The ever-escalating costs of health care make America increasingly noncompetitive in the global economy and the nation less fiscally sound.

5

Ages

"Civilization is a movement and not a condition,
a voyage and not a harbor."

—Arnold J. Toynbee

In Chapter 2, we mentioned that Modern Man, what anthropologists call our current iteration, has a 150,000-year history. This history can be broken down into three ages: the Agricultural Age, the Industrial Age, and the Information Age. It is important to examine these ages, because they provide a lens through which to examine how both society and health care and medicine have developed. It is through this point of view that a larger understanding of The New Health Age we are entering can be embraced.

1. The Agricultural Age—10,000 years ago

Approximately 10,000 years ago, Modern Man literally put down roots, and the Agricultural Age began. The Age of Agriculture saw the dawn of human civilizations. Agriculture created a sense of place, which led to the creation of cities and towns, which offered markets for agricultural goods. Humans started to aggregate into even larger communities. All the great civilizations we know of today occurred in this 10,000-year period. And, as you read in Chapter 2, it was also during this period that medicine began to develop as well. This age lasted for millennia, until just a few centuries ago.

2. The Industrial Age—300 years ago

The Industrial Age began with the introduction of the steam engine in the 1700s. This age saw the creation of large-scale factories and mechanized transportation, increasing urbanization, and the development of much of what we inhabit in today's societies. Industrialization occurred at different rates around the globe, leading to developed and undeveloped countries and huge disparities in all aspects of society. Some countries, certainly the United States included, created great wealth, transportation systems, cities, and scientific breakthroughs. Other countries did not progress much at all, increasing the disparity among nations that only now is beginning to change.

This was when the discoveries detailed in Chapter 2 occurred with accelerating speed. The Industrial Age saw the birth of modern medicine and its spread through expanding health care delivery systems. In fact, most of the systems of health care delivery that exist today firmly took root in this age. The philosophy, thinking, models, and marketplace structures of the Industrial Age are what are now looked at as legacy models from which legacy thinking has developed.

During the last 200 years of the Industrial Age, from the late 1700s to the late 1900s, those countries that became wealthy also had the greatest improvements in the health of their populations. This disparity became extreme, and only started to close as humanity entered the next age.

3. The Information Age—35 years ago

The Information Age began in the 1970s in the developed countries of the world. The foundations of this age in the United States were laid in the post–World War II era with the GI Bill. For the first time in our country's history, a large number of people attended college. In the mid-1950s, the number of white-collar workers surpassed the number of blue-collar workers for the first time. Other foundations of the Information Age were the invention of the mainframe computer, the rapid expansion of television, the launch of the first communications satellites, and the invention and development of the transistor.

In the 1970s, the invention of the personal computer, the increasing number of communications satellites, the emergence of cable television, and the ever-increasing power and reduction in size of computer processors ushered us into the Information Age. The ever-increasing speed of communications, computations, and electronic connectedness led to the development of an age that by the beginning of the twenty-first century had wrought havoc on the institutions and structures of the Industrial Age. The factory floor became a computer peripheral and was increasingly populated by robots not humans. The national supply chain gave way to the global supply chain. The explosive expansion of computing, with ever-cheaper hardware and software, changed the workplace and replaced human workers.

In the Industrial Age, the model structure was hierarchical, centralized, top-down, efficient, and based on economies of scale—the factory was the model. In the Information Age, the model structure became the network, the connected information networks that flattened the world and sped it up at the same time. Industrial Age inventions such as newspapers; broadcast television; and huge, cost-intensive production entities were increasingly disrupted by new technologies. Communication satellites created lower cost national television channels. Media outlets exploded in number and became available 24 hours a day. Moore's law* lowered computer costs and increased corresponding computing power, allowing smaller companies to compete successfully with the much

---

*In 1965, Gordon Moore predicted that computing power would double every 24 months and that the price of that computing power would decrease by 50 percent in the same time frame. He later revised it to 18 months.

larger corporate establishment that had used scale and economic leverage to be successful in the Industrial Age.[1]

The Industrial Age developed economies based on atoms. The Information Age developed economies based on digits. We moved from analog to digital. This ushered in a large overarching reality of the move from physical to nonphysical:

- Money moved from being physical to being digital or non-physical. Electronic fund transfers replaced physical deposits.

- All forms of content, such as music, books, newspapers, magazines, television, and radio, became digitized and available in nonphysical forms. Paper gave way to electronic digits and files.

- The 9-to-5 workplace was replaced by a 24/7 global market, where place was increasingly irrelevant as connectivity increased exponentially.

- Speed and mobility of communications increased dramatically.

- Vast amounts of data could be analyzed and searched in completely new ways.

- Power, speed, and miniaturization in computing made the vision of handheld communications and computers a reality.

This list could go on, but all readers of this book have lived through this time of revolutionary change. Just think back on what the world was like in 1975, 1985, or 1995 and compare it to what it looks like today. On almost any level and in every area, the changes to society and the speed of these changes have been unparalleled in history.

The Information Age propelled us into the twenty-first century with transformative force. The Internet 1.0 era of slow dialup connections of the late 1990s gave way to Internet 2.0 and the dramatically faster connectivity of high-speed broadband in the early part of this new century. People could shop and purchase anything in the world from the comfort of their homes. The computer screen became the portal to the global village in real time. The social and business landscapes were changed forever. Decades and even centuries' old institutions and inventions were rendered obsolete.

All aspects of society, down to the individual citizen, became computerized. The initial step of mass computerization was to get a computer or computers and use them for increased speed and efficiency in the workplace and home. This dramatically increased productivity year after year.

In the 1990s, with the introduction of the Web browser, the Internet gained widespread market acceptance, and the next stage of the computer revolution occurred—connectivity. This connectivity led to the creation and use of search engines, file sharing, video sharing, and the ability to have the knowledge of the world available at one's fingertips.

In a short decade, computers went from being restricted to a place to being globally connected—*except in the world of health care and medicine*. High-speed Internet connectivity further sped things up as vast amounts of data coursed through the information highway—*except in the world of health care and medicine*. Individuals converted to electronic banking and dispensed with paper records, as most records, documents, and files became digital—*except in health care and medicine*. Everyone became used to easily accessing information and quickly gaining knowledge of almost anything that could be imagined or that has existed in human history—*except in health care and medicine*.

Why not in health care and medicine? Until now, market and economic demands have not driven or forced change. When the first banking institution offered ATM machines, customers immediately took advantage of this convenient access to cash 24/7 and the early implementers with a competitive advantage compelled all banks to follow suit. When the first health care system in a community implements a patient health information system enabling patients to schedule their appointments online, view all personal medical records electronically, engage in disease prevention and management utilizing a smart phone, and video conference with their physician versus driving across town for an appointment, such competitive advantage will inspire competitors to follow. Patients and the competitive market place will demand it.

The Information Age was when society rapidly moved forward due to both computerization and the connection of these computers. Ultimately, this wave of rapid computerized connectivity has moved from PCs to laptops, to smartphones to app phones, and now to tablets. Everywhere in America and in the American economy this has occurred—except, for the most part, in health care and medicine. The Information Age, which began in the 1970s, was when health care and medicine in America became disconnected and fell behind the rest of the economy in terms of accessible information, data aggregation, and connectivity. At a time when the speed of communication increased, when connectivity increased efficiency, when prices fell due to consumers shopping the global economy, when one could find out about almost anything with a few keystrokes, much of the health care world stayed largely anchored in the Industrial Age.

We now take a look at the new century and new age in which we now live.

KEY POINTS

1. Modern Man has lived through three ages in the last 10,000 years.

2. The history of medicine began in the Agricultural Age and modern medicine has been developed in the Industrial and Information Ages.

3. The three-decades-old Information Age initiated a historically unprecedented amount of social, economic, and cultural change.

4. The health care sector of the American economy did not keep up with the electronic and connectivity revolution that occurred almost everywhere else.

6

The Shift Age and the Twenty-First Century

"The major advances in civilization are processes that all but wreck the societies in which they occur."

—Alfred North Whitehead

The condition of our current health care system and the state of modern medicine must be understood against the backdrop of one of the most dynamic times in human history. The future historians of 2100 will look back on the 50-year period of 1975–2025 as the time during which humanity made fundamental shifts and created new realities and levels of consciousness that did not exist prior to this period of profound change. We have already seen how rapidly much of the world has moved from the very long period of the Agricultural Age into the Industrial and the Information Ages. There will be as much change in the last 15 years of this 50-year period as in the first 35. This 50-year period of 1975–2025 began with the start of the Information Age and ends with the Shift Age. These 50 years are also half in the twentieth century and half in the twenty-first century. We now take a look at both this new age and this new century.

1. The Shift Age is here.

Everywhere there are clear signs that we have left the Information Age and entered the Shift Age, an age when we truly come to terms with what it means to be globally connected and to master the opportunities that connectedness brings. Whenever there is a transition between two ages, disruption and upheaval occur. The Great Recession of 2007–2010 represents precisely this sort of disruption and serves as the major economic signpost for the current transition. In essence, it was a reorganizational recession between two ages. Uncertainty has increased dramatically; economic schools of thought are in conflict, and, in many cases, wrong at the core. Institutions we have long lived with are crumbling before our eyes, and we are experiencing a dynamic rate of change that cannot be directed or managed with the clarity and certainty of the recent past.

It is at times such as these, when accepted constructs, ideas, and ways of looking at the world no longer seem valid, that major transitions occur. It is such times, as the Whitehead quote states, when even fundamental aspects of society begin to disintegrate and make some of us want to go back, others to wonder what lies ahead, and all of us to feel a certain level of anxiety about seemingly overwhelming change.

If you have any doubt as to whether we have left the Information Age, ask yourself this question: "Do you have enough information in your life?" Of course you have enough! In fact, you probably are suffering from information overload and are struggling to manage the incoming rush of information in our ever-more-connected world. If scarcity creates value, then information in and of itself is rapidly becoming worthless. We must now move beyond information to find real value. This value will now be based upon the analysis of the vast amounts of data that are being created to discern macro trends and patterns. We have entered the era of big data. We must assimilate the massive quantity of "content" information that is available to us and place it into the appropriate "context." The Information Age truism that content is king, now, in the Shift Age, gives way to context is king. The context in which we receive all information shapes the content as much as the content itself. Value will also now be created by attention, as attention is what creates value in this new age. Think of two websites, both with largely the same information, yet one has much more traffic—attention—than the other. The one with the most attention given and that places content data into the correct context is the more valuable website.

Embracing and rapidly managing change is fundamental to the consciousness of the Shift Age. The speed of change has accelerated so much that it is now environmental: We live in an environment of change. Change has become the context of our lives, not just one of the dynamics of it. We must always adapt. In business, 3-year business plans are now laughable, because conditions constantly change. The old phrase "standing on solid ground" no longer has merit. If people think that they are standing on solid ground and have a clear, certain view of the world, it is now a given that whether it be 6 months, 9 months, or 1 year from now that these people will suddenly realize that the world has changed while they were busy being certain.

While we have indeed experienced many periods of great uncertainty in the past, a closer examination of the three core forces of the Shift Age will make it clear that what we are now experiencing is nothing less than the global stage of human evolution. Humanity has moved from family to tribe, to village to city, to city state to nation state. At least for now, our only remaining boundaries are planetary. We have entered the global age of humanity.

2. The three forces of the Shift Age.

Every age is ushered in and shaped by a confluence of forces that disrupt and alter society. Computers, communications, satellites, a knowledge-based economy, and the move from analog to digital all helped shape the Information Age. In a similar way, the three dominant forces shaping the Shift Age are

- Accelerating Electronic Connectedness
- The Flow to Global
- The Flow to the Individual

Of course, many dynamics and influences are defining our world here in the early part of this new millennium: health care; religious fundamentalism; and geopolitical issues, such as energy, poverty, migration, resource allocation, and population growth. But these three forces—Accelerating Electronic Connectedness, the Flow to Global, and the Flow to Individual—are the underlying, essential, irresistible energy flows that announce a new age in humanity's evolution, a reorganization of global society that rivals any in history.

a) Accelerating Electronic Connectedness

In the five years from 2005 to 2010, the world experienced an unparalleled growth in connectivity. At no time in human history have so many people joined the global communications of humanity so quickly. In these five years alone, more than 3 billion new cell phone subscribers joined the existing base of slightly less than 2 billion users,[1] bringing the total number of cell phone users in the world to an estimated 5 billion.[2] Every day in the United States alone nearly 550 million Internet searches are performed.[3] Most of the communications traffic now travels at close to the speed of light through the vast networks of fiber optics that have been installed since the early 1990s.

The time difference between calling someone who is standing 15 feet from you on his or her cell phone and calling someone

12,000 miles away is negligible, perhaps five seconds or less. This means that *for the first time in human history it can be said that there is no time or distance limiting human communication*. Mobile connectivity also means that *place is no longer a limitation to human communications either*.

That is a powerful reality: For the first time in human history, time, distance, and place are no longer necessary limitations to human communication and interaction! Such immediacy is nothing less than transformational; we have reached a time when many ideas move almost simultaneously through a global population.

One powerful—and to some, frightening—outcome of this transformation is that we are becoming connected together into a global brain, a "neurosphere," that vastly exceeds the sum of the many brains that comprise it. This neurosphere is a pulsating, exploding, synaptic electronic place that is new to humanity and will transform health care. It makes possible a "global village" vastly more comprehensive and interconnected than Marshall McLuhan could ever have envisioned when he coined that phrase more than four decades ago.

Compare this current, and accelerating, connective reality to 200 years ago when the speed of human communication was however far and fast a horse could travel in a day. Even 100 years ago, when the forces of the Industrial Age were coursing through and shaping our culture, only a fraction of people and institutions, such as hospitals, had landline phones. The physical limitations of place, time, and distance no longer exist in this new connected landscape of today.

Medical cures and treatments discovered in one part of the world, which once took months or years to share through written medical journals, educational forums, and so forth, can now be published and immediately disseminated through this global connectivity. Physicians and patients can interact digitally in ways never done before, through Internet videoconferencing, e-mails, blogs, and other means. Medical centers located in remote locations simply require the Internet to connect to advanced medical institutions with highly specialized and skilled physicians who can participate during complex treatments, surgeries, and trauma cases utilizing online audio, video and data communications instruments. The examples and benefits to health care are limitless.

This accelerating electronic connectedness is both creating an alternate reality and changing our consciousness. The alternate reality is the new screen reality—our computer, phone, and tablet screens—that did not exist with critical mass connectivity until the last 10 years. The new consciousness is a global one where we are instantly sharing and experiencing events and ideas.

It is this accelerating electronic connectedness that, more than almost any other dynamic, necessitates a complete transformation of health care in the United States. As we will discuss in coming chapters, this force of accelerating connectedness, which has transformed humanity in most endeavors, is only now coming to the fields of medicine and health care delivery. This increased connectedness will create virtual health care communities, which will be as powerful and transformational as Facebook, Twitter, and YouTube have been. Electronic medical records will replace paper medical records, much like electronic banking has eradicated or minimized paper records and bank tellers. We will expand upon this discussion later in the book.

b) The Flow to Global

In the 20-plus years since the fall of the Berlin Wall and the subsequent collapse of the Soviet Union, a new global economy has come into being. The collapse of the Eastern Bloc meant that the number of potential consumers for the goods and services of capitalist enterprise literally doubled. Country after country has found its way onto the playing field of this new emerging global economy. As this change occurred, we began to move further from our past geographical orientations of family, tribe, town, state, and country (although each remains important), and more toward a global orientation that is supported by the electronic connectedness just discussed.

Historically, economics is often the initial driver of human discovery and development, followed by politics and culture. For example, Christopher Columbus did not set out to "discover" America; he set out to find a trade route to India (and Native Americans have been called Indians ever since). It was this desire for economic gain that resulted in the European discovery of America. Once America was colonized, it started to develop its own culture and, with the American Revolution, its own politics. In a similar way, the global economy in which we all now live and work will surely give birth to a global culture and politics.

The global problems humanity faces today can no longer be solved by a nation state or even several nation states. These global issues now necessitate global solutions. Nation states will continue to define the geopolitical landscape of the world, but increasingly there will be the inevitability of new regional and global entities to deal with the major issues we face as a species. Climate change, global financial connectivity, water scarcity, the development and utilization of new sources of energy, and entire new global economic behavior patterns all point to the inevitability of such entities.

Culturally, this new Flow to Global means the development of an ever-more-integrated global culture. Services such as YouTube, Facebook, and Twitter, utilizing the connectedness of the neurosphere, enable a degree of cross-cultural integration never before seen in human history. And this integration is not just happening online; the Shift Age will also be a time of great geographic migration. Whether people are temporarily or permanently settled in a country other than the one of their birth, this new migration will be numerically unprecedented. All countries of the world will experience an increasing amount of new cultural influences due to this human movement. This cross-cultural integration through electronic connectedness and through the new unprecedented levels of mass migration will have profound influences on health care and medicine.

The Flow to a Global culture will result in medical tourism rising to levels and degrees never before seen. In the coming decade, patients will travel the world seeking out the best and most affordable medical technologies, treatments, and innovations. In 2011, 6 million Americans are expected to travel to other countries in search of high-quality, yet affordable, medical care. This number is up substantially since 2007, when a mere 750,000 left America for health care.[4] In fact, some U.S. insurance plans now provide beneficiaries with the option to receive their treatment in other countries. In response, health care providers in the United States will need to adapt and compete like other businesses that have now grown accustomed to functioning in a new, highly competitive, global marketplace.

For example, consider Healthbase (www.healthbase.com), a medical tourism facilitator, headquartered in the United States, that connects patients worldwide to health care facilities and professionals on an international scope. Think of Healthbase like the new travel agent for health care services that arranges all aspects of medical tourism, including visas, travel, lodging, appointments, and interactions with local health care providers.

Dr. Devi Shetty, of Bangalore, India, for example, now owns and operates an acclaimed heart institute program, charging on average $2,000 for open heart surgery, while American hospitals charge between $20,000 and $100,000.[5] Dr. Shetty leads the Narayana Hrudayalaya Hospital, where 42 cardiac surgeons performed 3,174 cardiac bypass surgeries in 2008, more than double the cases performed at leading U.S. medical centers in a year. His pediatric surgeons operated on 2,777 children, again more than double the volume performed at nationally recognized pediatric hospitals.

Dr. Shetty did not stop his vision after building his 1,000-bed heart hospital. Adjacent to Narayana, he built a 1,400-bed cancer hospital and a 300-bed eye hospital. These facilities share laboratories and a blood bank with the heart institute for efficiencies and cost savings. Dr. Shetty's family-owned business group, Narayana Hrudayalaya Private Ltd., reports a 7.7 percent profit after taxes, which beats the 6.9 percent average for a U.S. hospital.

Soon, Dr. Shetty plans to open a 2,000-bed general hospital in the Cayman Islands, seeking to draw more Americans on a one-hour plane ride from Miami. He plans to price procedures, both elective and necessary, at more than 50 percent below what they would cost if performed in the United States.

How is the quality of care at Narayana Hospital? Dr. Shetty reports a 1.4 percent mortality rate within 30 days of coronary artery bypass graft surgery, one of the most common procedures, compared with an average of 1.9 percent in the United States in 2008.[6] Dr. Shetty claims that his mortality rates would be even lower if he adjusted the figures for risk, because his patients are often sicker than the average U.S. cardiac patient. Many of Dr. Shetty's patients lack access to basic health care and suffer from more advanced cardiac disease before they finally have surgery.

We are now clearly in the global stage of human evolution. The Flow to Global is not good or bad; it just is, and there is no turning back. This new stage demands an entirely new definition of how America's health care models should function to enable American health care providers to continue their prosperity in a global world of increased competition.

c) The Flow to the Individual

Even as humanity becomes more globally oriented, individuals have more power today than ever before in history. The changes that occurred in the world from 1985–2010 constitute the foundation for this new reality. David, in his book *The Shift Age*, coined the phrase "Flow to the Individual," and this has been embraced around the world as a fundamental reorganizational force.

The explosion of choice, the growth of free agency, the technologies and dynamics that moved us from hierarchies to networks, the ever-growing electronic connectedness, and its increasing speed have all helped to shift power from institutions to individuals. When there is a true explosion of choice, the power moves from the producer to the consumer, from the institution to the individual.

In 1985, there were three major television networks and the average American home had five television signals. Those five stations decided what we would watch and when we would watch, and none of the networks broadcasted 24 hours a day. Now the average home has anywhere from ten to one hundred times that number of television channels. Most of the channels broadcast 24 hours a day. Today, viewers can choose what they want to watch and when they want to watch it, particularly if viewers own DVRs. So, those old television networks were institutions that controlled our viewing habits. Now we control and create our viewing habits—the Flow to the Individual.

You probably have a smartphone with dozens of apps on it. You now use this app phone as your own personalized portal on the world. You find directions, select restaurants, buy movie tickets, watch videos, and read periodicals with your app phone. You have created your own unique, personalized filter through which you experience much of your life. You hold this device in your hand and carry it with you wherever you go. What used to be served up in large appliances at home or in large containers at work is now activated by a touch of your finger in a device that fits in your pocket. Such technological devices give us power as individuals in ways unimaginable decades ago. It is all about you and your view of the world.

Gatekeepers are disappearing; disintermediation and its primary agent, the Internet, have reorganized the economic landscape. The individual is becoming the primary economic unit, the micro that is combining with the macro of the Flow to Global. We are distinct individuals who are global citizens.

For many people—and perhaps even for you as a reader of this book—the full range of questions and issues that the Flow to the Individual and the other forces raise are not yet obvious, especially within health care delivery systems. Patients now have more health data available through the Internet to educate themselves and perhaps question and challenge their physician. Quality data related to hospitals, physicians, and insurance companies are now available online in many states. Health education and medical information is simply an Internet search engine away. Quest Diagnostics, one of the world's leading diagnostic testing labs, recently launched Gazelle, a secure mobile health application that enables users to receive their lab results and manage their personal health information directly from their smartphone, or other app device.

There is always a lag time in recognizing a transition as large as the one we are currently experiencing. We will see it clearly only in hindsight, but what is clear already is that the three forces of the Shift Age will have a tremendous impact on the twenty-first century. In fact, they are the beginning of the definition of what the twenty-first century will be about. It is only natural and to be expected that these forces now enter health care.

3. The twenty-first century ahead.

Although the transition to a new age can be subtle and can occur over a number of years, the numbers on our collective calendars are exact. This book is being written in 2010 and 2011, the 10th and 11th years of the new century and the new millennium. This new *century* will bring more transformational change than the last *millennium*.

A thousand years ago, Europe was medieval, living in the Dark Ages. The world was flat, the Earth was the center of the universe, and people rarely traveled beyond where they were born. Compare that reality to today. Then consider that this new millennium will bring evolutionary change at least a thousand times more transformative than the one just past.

A hundred years ago, England was the most powerful industrial country, the wonders of the Industrial Age were just becoming available to the general population in a limited way, and there had yet to be a "world war." It was also the time when, as we saw in Chapter 2, the beginning of modern medicine dawned and health care delivery systems began to take shape.

Marshall McLuhan once said "Most people drive down the freeway of life looking in the rearview mirror." What he meant was that most people can tell you about where they have been and what their story is—they carry the reality of the past forward. They do not look ahead nor are they able to articulate where they are going. Does this not describe how health care delivery in America has crept forward, by looking in the rearview mirror? Why is that? Is it fear or a lack of awareness, or both?

Fear is the only human emotion attributable to something that is yet to occur. We do not fear the past; we fear what might occur tomorrow. Some fear death because it has not happened. Some fear flying but the airplane has not crashed. Some fear change because, by its very definition, things will be different. The Shift Age and The New Health Age are about embracing tomorrow, welcoming the change because it is inevitable, and preparing ourselves for the medical miracles and new health care delivery models around the corner.

McLuhan's quote is very apropos of where we have been in the first 10 years of the twenty-first century. We basically continued with the legacy thinking of the twentieth century. Most of us have continued to view the world through the filter of the past. Sure, there have been the developing forces, described in this chapter, that have forced us to think and act differently. Yes, we have become unsettled and anxious as those great institutions of the last century, such as the newspaper, the broadcast network, and the Detroit automotive industry, have collapsed and declined. But, all said, most of our society still thinks and operates with twentieth-century constructs. That is about to change.

Living in a time when the speed of change is environmental, we must fully let go of the past except as an historical foundation. We must face the future and let go of legacy thinking. This is nowhere more important than in the area of medicine and health care delivery models.

We are now entering The New Health Age, a time of great transformation in medicine and health care. We loosely define this age as the first 50 years of the twenty-first century. The medical breakthroughs of the last 500 years will be more than matched by those in the next 50 years. The dynamics and definitions of health care delivery will also undergo the same amount of change.

The transformative New Health Age has begun. We will now look at what lies ahead. Do not fear it—embrace it—for it will transform both you and humanity.

KEY POINTS

1. Humanity has entered a new age—the Shift Age.

2. The Shift Age has now ushered us into The New Health Age.

3. The three forces of the Shift Age are Accelerating Electronic Connectedness, the Flow to Global, and the Flow to the Individual.

4. The forces of the Shift Age have radically transformed and reshaped humanity and many of its institutions and will continue to do so for the next 10 to 20 years

5. We are now fully in the twenty-first century. The first 50 years of this new century and new millennium is The New Health Age.

7

Medical Miracles
Around the Corner

*"Every great advance in science has issued from a
new audacity of imagination."*

—John Dewey

The second full decade of the new millennium, 2010–2020,
is the Transformation Decade, so named by David in a col-
umn written on 01-01-10.[1] This name has since taken root, and
David has spoken about it around the world. Why are we in the
midst of the Transformation Decade? Here is the dictionary definition of transformation: "change in form, appearance, nature, or
character."[2]

This decade, 2010–2020, will be the decade when how we
live and communicate will be transformed. It will be the decade
when most of humanity's institutions will also be transformed.
Health care and medicine will be one of the areas where the greatest amount of transformation will occur. We will think of the

Transformation Decade as the first full decade of The New Health Age. The changes in form, appearance, nature, and character of health care and medicine will be so profound in these 10 years that there will be a clear new beginning and a distinct break from the past leading up to it.

In subsequent chapters, we will deal with the coming transformation of all aspects of health care in the United States. An almost complete "change in form, appearance, nature, and character" of the health care landscape is coming in the United States. We will explain all aspects of this in the following chapters. Now we would like to present the transformation of medicine that is rushing toward us.

Simply put, the Transformation Decade will usher in The New Health Age, and with it the single most transformative period in the history of human medicine. The breakthroughs, discoveries, creations, and the moral questions they will raise will be nothing less than mind-boggling. How long we will live, how we define health, even how we define life are concepts that are about to undergo partial to full redefinition in the coming 10 years. We now examine just some of the expected breakthroughs and choices that are just ahead.

These expected breakthroughs must be viewed wholistically. We use the word *wholistic* versus *holistic* because we mean "perceived as a whole" or "perceived as a complete perspective." Each one, in and of itself, will be significant and create amazement, but their respective effects on society will also be transformative. One cannot, for example, think of a lifespan of 120 years within the current context and definitions of health, retirement, aging, and age-related productivity and activity. Because most of medicine and health care will be transformed, we must all realize that the context of our existence and the world around us will also be transformed. Humanity has almost always made the mistake of looking into the future in a linear, nonwholistic manner. We can say with certainty that such thinking is completely inadequate when looking at The New Health Age.

1. The human life span is on the rise.

In the United States and most developed countries around the world, the expected life span of humans increased by 50 percent in the twentieth century.[3] People born in 1900 had an average life expectancy of 50 years at birth.[4] By 2000, that average had increased to 75 years.[5] This percentage increase was more than that of the 3,000 years prior.[6] This again underlines the theme of Chapter 2 about how much of current medical knowledge and practice is from the last 100 years.

Numerous medical researchers, thinkers, and scientists think that a similar 50 percent increase in life expectancy will occur in the next 15 years![7,8] This means that someone born in 2020 or 2025 could well have a life expectancy of 120 years. Think about that. Someone born in 2025 will be expected to live until 2145. This of course will transform how we look at the stages of a human life. Some of the medical breakthroughs suggested in this chapter for example might point to redefining retirement age to 85 or older. This is the type of transformational thinking that will happen in The New Health Age.

To take this thinking even further, there is developing scientific thinking that aging, the actual process of growing older, is to be looked at as a disease. A curable disease!

A small but growing number of scientists and thinkers are looking at aging as something that can be cured. One of the leading life-extension researchers, Aubrey de Grey, a British biologist, views aging as a process of ongoing damage to the body. In the February 21, 2011, issue of *Time* he was quoted as saying

> People have begun to realize that the view of aging being something immutable, rather like the heat death of the universe—is simply ridiculous. The human body is a machine that has a bunch of functions and it accumulates various types of damage as normal function of the machine. Therefore, in principal, that damage can be repaired periodically. This is why we have vintage cars.

It is really just a matter of paying attention. The whole of medicine consists of messing around with what looks pretty inevitable until you figure out how to make it not inevitable.[9]

In other words, in The New Health Age we are now entering, aging might well become a treatable disease. Not only will that change life expectancy dramatically, but also it will alter the concept of aging as it has existed for centuries. Growing old might soon become treatable!

2. Low-cost genetic mapping is only a few years away.

It took some $300 million dollars of research and development invested over a period of 13 years to fully map the human genome in 2003.[10] It is now widely predicted that any individual will be able to have most, if not their entire, genetic map done in 2013 for $1,000 or less![11,12] This will transform health care in numerous ways. Consider a few examples:

- *Disease prevention.* What if a young man, age 25, had his entire genetic map done in 2015 and found out that he has a high probability of developing early stage Alzheimer's. What would he do? He would go into an active disease prevention state, doing whatever current medical science suggests might lower the risk—developing an exercise regimen; learning new skills; if right handed, use the left hand; take a lot of Omega-3 fish oil; and so on. He starts to lead a genetically driven life of Alzheimer's disease prevention.

- *Marriage.* Low-cost genetic mapping means that we can know our genetic maps, which means that we can know the genetic map of the one we intend to marry. What if it is not a good genetic match, indicating a high probability of passing on a physical malady, such as spina bifida or Down syndrome? Does knowledge trump love?

- *Insurance benefits.* What if a person has health problems due to a genetically determined physical condition that he inherited from his parents? Is that a preexisting condition? This person didn't pick his parents, so how can he be denied health coverage! It was a condition that was created at conception.

3. DNA pharmaceuticals are coming our way.

The Human Genome Project has led to individual genetic mapping, which leads to genetically specific drugs and personalized treatments. DNA is already being sliced thinly to develop drugs that treat specific diseases for those who have a genetic disposition to certain diseases. Imagine going to the pharmacy with a drug formulary prescription tailored to your individual health condition based on your specific DNA. Think of it like a tailored suit.

In just the last few years, such companies as 23andme.com have developed testing for the breast cancer gene and other life-threatening conditions. This testing leads to self-knowledge and to the desire to preventatively treat or specifically cure a disease. The pharmaceutical industry has, is, and will increasingly develop drugs, treatments, and diet plans that will address specific genetic realities.

This will be initially expensive, but one of the benefits of moving in this direction is that we will lose the death and health issues caused by "lowest denominator drugs." We have all seen the ads in magazines of some bucolic image of a cured patient having taken a general drug for a condition and then turned the page to see two pages of small print regarding what might go wrong. Yes, this drug will cure your high blood pressure, but it could kill you!

4. The bionic man and woman are no longer science fiction.

The next decade will see astounding breakthroughs in bionics. Simply put, in The New Health Age, for the first time in human history, many of our replacement parts will be superior to those that we were born with. Technological breakthroughs, unimaginable decades ago, will become commonplace.[13] In 2008, the South African sprinter Oscar Pistorius, who had artificial legs from the knees down, was initially prevented from competing in the Beijing Olympics because not having legs gave him a perceived unfair advantage over those sprinters who had legs![14,15]

5. Robotics will change humanity.

Robotic breakthroughs in The New Health Age will impact medicine and health care in three fundamental ways. First, they will allow for technological improvement of life. Second, they will dramatically expand surgical possibilities. Third, they will help to lower health care costs for the aged dramatically. Let's look at each briefly:

- *Technological life improvement.* As this book is being written, there are companies developing exoskeleton technologies, such as body suits, that will allow paraplegics and quadriplegics to walk.

- *Surgical procedures.* Today, robots are increasingly used for surgeries that are literally microscopic, utilizing precision technology that enhances significantly the precision of the human hand. Visit www.davincisurgery.com to learn more about daVinci Surgery as just one example. In some cases, the surgeon operating the robot is doing so remotely, thousands of miles away from the operating room. "Big city" health care is coming to "small town" America.

- *Lower costs for the aged.* Human care robots are coming to market that will help the aged population. The robots will remind owners to take their medicines, help with tasks around the house, and monitor the owners' medical conditions on a constant basis and relay information back to the caregivers electronically—all of which reduce the costs of human caregivers, not to mention offering peace of mind for families.

6. Tissue regeneration creates miracles.

In laboratories around the world, significant progress and success have been achieved in human tissue regeneration. For example, scientists have been successful in regenerating fingers as well as internal organs, such as bladders.[16,17,18] These early successes will quickly spread in scope and degree.

This means that the Transformation Decade will be the time when replacement body parts actually begin to enter the medical and health care arenas. Soon, organ donors will have another alternative to waiting, with both desperation and hope, for the death of someone whose organs might be both available and compatible for them. Heart bypass or transplant surgery will be replaced by a regenerated heart. This, in and of itself, is a breakthrough of historical significance. It is the early steps toward the next real possibility of medical miracles.

7. The possibility of human cloning is inevitable.

In the last two decades, humans have cloned animals successfully.[19] These breakthroughs and the success of tissue regeneration point to the real possibility of cloning humans. This is where human morals have to catch up to the speed of scientific discovery quickly. What is the definition of life? Who gets to decide who can be cloned and who does not in an overpopulated world?

The history of medical science is one of trial and error and constant recalibration. How do we deal with the mistakes and failures on the path to perfecting human cloning? Will the failures be considered humans? What do we do with them?

We could all decide that we do not want to have cloning be socially acceptable or legal.[20] If so, that does not mean that someone, somewhere, in some country might not go ahead with experiments.

Think for a minute how you might feel if your loved one were sick or dying. Might you not want to gather all necessary DNA to clone that person perhaps? Obviously, this will be incredibly expensive, but there will be eccentric and wealthy people willing to pay for this. As history indicates, successful use of a new medical breakthrough at the upper end of the social strata usually becomes ever more affordable and trickles downward.

How do we think about this? What do we do? These are questions that we will have to answer, and soon.

8. Creation of artificial life will change the world.

We are now beginning to create artificial life. Standing in 1818, who would have imagined that Mary Shelley's Frankenstein could one day be possible? Shelley wrote,

> I succeeded in discovering the cause of generation and life; nay, more, I became myself capable of bestowing animation upon lifeless matter. The astonishment which I had at first experienced on this discovery soon gave place to delight and rapture. After so much time spent in painful labor, to arrive at once at the summit of my desires was the most gratifying consummation of my toils.[21]

In May 2010, *Science* reported that humankind took a significant step toward actually creating artificial life. The lead scientist, Craig Venter, named this new life form and synthetic cell "Synthia." The *Economist* proclaimed, "In the end there was no castle, no thunderstorm, and definitely no hunchbacked cackling lab assistant. Nevertheless, Craig Venter, Hamilton Smith, and their colleagues have done for real what Mary Shelley merely imagined. On May 20th, in the pages of *Science*, they announced that they had created a living creature."[22]

Creating artificial life is now a reality. What implications will this have for medicine, health care, and other aspects of society? The definitions of life, forged over several millennia of human science and religion, must now be expanded. Can we alter our belief systems to embrace this? How do we guide this new transformative breakthrough to serve humanity best and the planet on which we all live? Lieutenant Commander Data from the television series *Star Trek: The Next Generation* may not be science fiction for much longer.

9. Socially engineered health will become an essential part of health care delivery.

Socially engineered health is a very significant area of health care as we plunge into the transformation of the health care delivery system in America. In order to lower our health care costs, we must have better education about health. This must occur within medical education and society as a whole. We must implement socially acceptable methods, processes, architectures, systems, and incentives to change behavior to promote and to actually increase health for all Americans. In short, we must take our knowledge of health and embed it into our education, culture, our habits, and our landscape.

Lifestyle medicine will become a foundational principle in The New Health Age. Organizations such as the Institute for Functional Medicine (www.functionalmedicine.org) are actively training and teaching forward thinking doctors that twenty-first century medicine must migrate from the prevailing acute-care model to a far more effective chronic-disease management model, which focuses on the underlying drivers of America's health problems—the complicated lifelong interactions among genetics, environment, and lifestyle.

Healthier lifestyle changes will occur in everyday living too. In the United States today, thousands of suburban housing developments have no sidewalks. This sends the socially embedded message that you have to drive your car; you are not supposed to walk. This is just an example of how we have inadvertently increased health care costs by promoting less exercise, which, in turn, contributes to obesity and all the maladies that come from being overweight.

We must lower our health care costs. As we discuss in the dynamic flow chapters later in this book, a number of transformations, flows, and forces must be understood, embraced, and acted upon if we as Americans want a healthier country with lower health care costs.

Here are just a few things we as a country can introduce into our society that will actually lead to a healthier nation and lower our overall health care costs. A few of these may be controversial to some, but all must be considered if our goal is to improve health and lower costs:

- We must think about the building and construction of living and work spaces with health in mind in a fashion similar to how we have brought environmental, or green, thinking into our homes and workplaces. Corporate campuses should have walking trails and fitness centers. Even small businesses can promote the use of stairs over elevators. Urban planners should design bicycle lanes across cities in America to encourage more physical activity and exercise.

- We must work as a country to eliminate or lower the consumption of foods and ingredients that we know cause conditions that lead to higher health care costs. We must incorporate nutrition, diet, and fitness counseling into all employment and health care delivery models. This will be controversial, because vested interests will fight this and consensus might be difficult to achieve.

- We must create economic incentives to change behavior. Such incentives could offer positive or negative reinforcements:
  - *Positive.* When obese adults lose weight, they are rewarded with credits that reduce health care spending. When children complete courses in healthy eating and exercise, they receive a small contribution to their college fund.
  - *Negative.* Tax products that have been proven to lower health and therefore increase overall health care costs,

such as cigarettes, foods with trans-fats, and products with lots of sugar or cancer-causing chemicals.[23] This has proven successful with cigarettes; the decline in the percentage of adult Americans who smoke has been in lockstep with increasing "sin" taxes on cigarettes.[24]

Socially embedded health is simply bringing what we know about health, diet, exercise, and lifestyles and integrating it into our country. This will not be easy, but if the goal is to lower health care costs in America this is a key component. We will discuss socially embedded health ideas, concepts, and predictions throughout the coming chapters. We conclude the book with a charge to all Americans that we join the Race to a Healthy America, which you will learn about in Chapter 16.

This chapter has presented just a brief discussion of all that can and will happen in the Transformation Decade of 2010–2020. We must rise up to face, embrace, and integrate these medical and health developments to create a healthier nation and lower overall health care costs. We need to get ready to act, because this is all part of The New Health Age.

KEY POINTS

1. 2010–2020 is the Transformation Decade.
2. The definition of transformation is "a change in form, nature, appearance or character."
3. This decade fully starts The New Health Age with medical breakthroughs and cultural changes that will transform humanity, health, society, health care costs, and even our definitions of life itself.

‹ CHANGE VISION ›

Dr. Robert S. Epstein is a physician with more than 30 years of experience in health care with experience as a treating physician, a public health official, and an academic at a medical school. Since 1995, Dr. Epstein has worked for Medco within the private sector, currently directing 2,000 researchers around the world investigating a range of issues, including personalized medicine, drug safety, health economics, and outcomes research. He has published nearly 100 medical papers on these topics and is frequently quoted in the Wall Street Journal, USA Today, *and the* New York Times *and has appeared on CNN,* Dateline, *PBS, and a variety of other television stations and programs. Medco Health Solutions is a publicly traded company whose mission is "to make medicine smarter." Medco is the world's largest advanced mail service pharmacy, filling more than 100 million prescriptions annually and serving more than 65 million people. The company is global, with operations in the United States, Europe, and Asia.*

Medical Breakthroughs Ahead

By Dr. Robert S. Epstein

Over the past 25 years, we have witnessed the launch of an unprecedented number of treatments for diseases heretofore either untreated or inadequately cared for. This has produced amazing results, such as reducing the mortality rate for a particular form of leukemia from 50 percent at 5 years to 5 percent; changing HIV/AIDS from a frequently fatal and devastating disease to a chronic and controllable illness; restoring function for those suffering from some rare diseases, such as the "bubble boy," or severe combined immune deficiency syndrome; and providing hope for a halt in the decline for those afflicted with multiple sclerosis or osteoporosis. Yet not all interventions work for all people with these and other conditions. Additionally, people with conditions like Alzheimer's disease, many types of cancer, stroke, spinal cord injury, or those afflicted with the nearly 4,500 rare diseases still struggle to find anything that can help them.

Advances in science in recent years provide hope for even more dramatic and rapid advances for those in need. Recent advances in biotechnology hold part of the key. The biotechnology revolution began in earnest in the 1980s with the production of products enabled by the science of recombinant DNA. The initial breakthrough was when scientists figured out that they could recombine DNA from humans and bacteria, inject this new DNA into the nucleus of yeast cells, and the yeast cells would then become mini-factories, churning out what the instruction manual from the DNA told them to make (e.g., the first marketed biotechnology drug was for human insulin, which was produced in vats of these types of yeast cells. Prior to that, insulin was obtained from animals like pigs or even human cadavers, and terrible injection site side effects could occur). In the 1990s, the concept of monoclonal antibodies was developed when biotechnologists reasoned that they could attack targets within the body utilizing created clones of specific targeted antibodies—the way we take flu shots to develop antibodies to attack the flu should we be exposed. This provided breakthrough drugs like Enbrel and Humira for rheumatoid arthritis and psoriasis, whereby injected monoclonal antibodies attack the overzealous immune system, thus decreasing the consequent swelling, deformity, or dysfunction associated with these conditions. Today, 29 monoclonal antibodies are on the market for a wide variety of conditions, but with the recent and improved understanding of new disease targets and mechanisms more than 130 are in development for a wide range of conditions, including Alzheimer's disease, which hold promise for market launch in the near term.

The mapping of the human genome in 2003 provided another extraordinary range of possibilities to be realized in the next 5 to 10 years. Beyond learning the basic genetic building blocks of what causes many health problems, we have also learned and can now measure our personal genetic variation as it relates to treatment response. For example, the oral lung cancer drugs that target those people with the particular gene (EGFR) fueling their cancer can in some cases completely resolve the cancer or at least slow its progression. For those who do not test positive for this gene, other drugs about to launch can attack another mechanism (ALK). The same is true for the treatment of colon-rectal cancer; those 40 percent with K-RAS mutations respond to drugs like Erbitux, whereas those without the mutation should try another therapy. Most drug companies today are biobanking DNA from all their drug development programs, and we will be witnessing an unprecedented number of drugs codeveloped with companion diagnostic tests over the next decade. This should sharpen the effectiveness and reduce safety problems and take us deeply into personalized medicine, where each of us receives drugs that we know will stand a stronger chance to help us.

Nanotechnology (a nanometer is 1/50,000th the diameter of a human hair) has just started to produce amazing breakthroughs. Take, for example, the marketed drug Abraxane, which is an infusion chemotherapy for the treatment of some forms of breast cancer. At its core is an older drug called paclitaxel. In order to make that drug in a form to be infused, developers had to attach a solvent to the drug, which then caused hypersensitivity reactions during the infusion administration.

To minimize this, patients were given steroids in advance, but also had to have the drug infused slowly over 3 hours. Finally, like many other chemotherapy agents, the drug worked on all fast-growing cells and not just the cancer cells, causing a myriad of side effects, such as hair loss and gastrointestinal discomfort. A drug company felt it could replace the solvent with nanoalbumin (a form of protein), and what resulted was quite astonishing. This more "natural" drug no longer caused the hypersensitivity reactions, so patients did not have to undergo precautionary steroid infusions, and the infusion could occur over 20 minutes rather than 3 hours. The nanoprotein acted like a Trojan Horse in that the cancer cells grabbed the protein and inadvertently got a heavy payload of chemotherapy dropped right inside. This resulted in a near doubling of treatment effectiveness and also a reduction in side effects. Today, this drug accounts for over $300 million in revenues.

Aside from providing advances in the route of administration, nanotechnology as a device for cancer treatment is under study, and one version was approved in Europe in 2010. Here, patients with solid tumors undergo infusions filled with nanoparticles of substances such as gold or even nanomagnets. After 24 to 48 hours, these particles fall out of leaking blood vessels, which generally are only those that support fast-growing solid tumors. A form of ultraviolet light is irradiated over the tumor area, and the nanoparticles heat up and sizzle the tumor. Mouse studies have shown 90 percent cure rates with prostate cancer, and ongoing studies at MD Anderson and elsewhere will be the substrate for a whole new era of diagnostics and therapies we didn't even conceive of in the twentieth century.

As for other new sciences yet to have marketed products, our understanding of stem cells provides a lot of excitement for an actual cure and not just conversion to chronic disease for conditions as diverse as diabetes or even spinal cord injury. Stem cells are essentially healthy baby cells that are unclear as to what they are destined to become—hair, skin, nail, heart tissue, whatever. The notion is that the placement of these stem cells in damaged organs may stimulate regrowth to normal tissue and essentially restore function. There is some evidence to this. For example, an uncontrolled study in Brazil published in the *Journal of the AMA* in 2007 demonstrated that 14 of 15 newly diagnosed insulin-taking patients who underwent stem cell transplant did not need insulin at an average of 18.8 months after their treatment. In this case, the stem cells were harvested from the patients themselves, so there was no need for the controversial fertilized egg. Human studies are currently underway to see if stem cells injected at the site of spinal cord injury can help regrow the neural pathway, something again inconceivable in the previous century. Other studies are ongoing for a wide range of treatments, and the FDA has developed a pathway for approval.

Regenerative medicine is likewise moving quickly. The idea is to literally regrow your own organs outside the body and then implant them back inside once fully mature. This would be an enormous benefit to society, because there are more than 100,000 people on the organ transplant waiting list, and even those who successfully survive a transplant face a lifetime of anti-organ rejection medications that have their own set of side effects. Today, Tengion is in Phase II trials of regrowing patients' own bladders in the laboratory within 30 days of harvesting their normal cells and, with a surgical procedure, replacing their faulty organs and restoring normal function. Others at the VA are working on regrowing limbs. The NIH has successfully funded a study at Columbia University in which they literally regrew the bone of those afflicted with temporomandibular joint syndrome. It is anticipated that the first of these products could hit the market as soon as the next 2 to 3 years. Oddly, the first marketed product might be cosmetic in nature, as one company has already applied for FDA approval for a product that injects skin fibroblasts into facial wrinkles to enable patients to regrow younger and more natural-looking skin folds.

A technology that is expected to start penetrating the marketplace in the next 5 years is gene therapy. Here the notion is that if we were to drop a virus that has a curative gene embedded within it into a part of the body that is by birth missing an important gene a complete resolution of the gene-mediated ailment could result. A recent publication in the medical journal *Lancet* provides some hope that this will actually bear fruit. The authors described a single injection of a virus containing a particular gene into a 9-year-old legally blind child's eye (in which he did not have the gene by birth). As a result of this treatment, the child can now see stars at night and is looking forward to playing Little League baseball. Clinical trials for such disparate conditions as Parkinson's and congestive heart failure are underway in humans. These therapies hold the promise of cure and not just symptomatic improvement.

Although there are many ways to bend the health care cost curve, scientific advancement is moving swiftly to provide yet another pathway for hope. Hope not just for patients and families with these conditions, but hope that this level of treatment for unmet needs will result in overall health care cost reductions. This can only be determined through a rational framework for the evaluation of these versus existing treatments (comparative effectiveness), a robust and transparent system of the generation of the evidence of both the risks and benefits, and an informed and wired health care system ready and able to quickly take up these potentially transformative solutions where and when the evidence appears it is appropriate.

80 Percent Accepted, 20 Percent to Go

"No country can be strong if its people are sick and poor."

—Theodore Roosevelt

W e have all experienced an amazing amount of change in the last 30 years. The way we conduct business, live our lives, communicate with each other, and depend on connectivity and technology have all changed dramatically. The current evolution into the Shift Age, and into the early beginnings of The New Health Age, has been nothing less than transformative. The amount of change that society has experienced needs to be put into perspective, as we have become so accustomed to it that we forget how much has happened in such a relatively short period of time.

It was only approximately 30 years ago that the personal computer (PC) was introduced into the marketplace. It was some 25 years ago that the fax machine and the cell phone became available. It was in 1995, 15 years ago, that the Internet browser introduced us to the

World Wide Web and the online world. It was less than 10 years ago that the smartphone started to work its way into the hands of business-people. At the turn of the century, music became available for digital download. The Human Genome Project published a complete draft report, mapping the entire human genome, in 2003. It was in 2007 when the first iteration of the app phone, the Apple iPhone, entered the market. The Kindle launched the age of eBooks in 2007. Apple struck again with the iPad in 2010, initiating the age of the tablet.[1] The era of mobile computing is now upon us.

In the last 10 years, many of us have moved our banking services online. In the last 10 years, we have fully integrated the use of Internet search engines into our lives. As we already mentioned in Chapter 6, every day in the United States alone, nearly 550 million Internet searches are performed.[2] We have developed the sense that all the information that we could ever want or need to find is just a few keystrokes away. We have entered a world of information access that is unmatched in human history. A 10-year-old today has access to more information and knowledge within seconds than the greatest scholars had merely 20 years ago.

The words "Google it" and "search" are now completely active verbs, something that we do daily. If information and data are not easily available to us online, it is of less value in our minds. All businesses know that having a robust website, providing full access to information and products, is "a must" for doing business today. We scoff at people who are not connected as being behind the times. Great fortunes have been created in the last decade by the creation of businesses that are only available to an online customer base (i.e., Facebook, YouTube, Twitter, iTunes, etc.).

Desktop PCs have given way to laptops, which are now giving way to netbooks, tablets, smartphones, and app phones that have more computing power than most laptops had merely 10 years ago. The science fiction dream of carrying a computer in our pocket is now a reality. Everything is moving to the mobile platform. E-mails, text messages, calendars, to-do lists, address books, media, and tools to access all of the world's information can now be held in our hands.

The "paperless office" is not quite a reality, but it is closer. In fact, when computers came to market, copy paper sales (the paper that fills copiers and laser printers) actually increased by nearly 5 percent per year. Then something profound occurred. For the first time in nearly 25 years, in 2000, North American copy paper sales started to level off; and beginning in 2006, actually started to decline.[3] What does this trend imply? More computer users are finally getting comfortable reading data and information through a computer screen versus needing to print what they need from the computer. The human ability to read and comprehend information through computer and smartphone screens as opposed to paper is manifesting itself.

(During the writing of this book, we never once printed a draft of the manuscript. All writing and editing was done on our laptops. As co-authors, we e-mailed digital versions of our draft chapters all over the world as David completed an acclaimed global speaking tour and Jonathan advised North American health care clients regarding the future of medicine.)

One of the high-level macro trends of 1975–2025 is the move from a physical to a nonphysical reality. In 1975, the word *file* denoted something physical—a physical folder of paper documents. The notion of a *file* today is more of an electronic concept. This move toward virtual has transformed many business sectors, including financial services. In the 1970s and 1980s, money lost much of its physicality with the electronic storage of account information and the increasing use of electronic fund transfers, ATM cards, online banking, credit cards, and, most recently, debit cards. In 1995, Americans wrote 49.5 billion checks.[4] In 2009, that number had dropped to 27.5 billion. Why? Americans were utilizing many new forms of electronic payments.[5]

There are young people today for whom music has never been a physical object to purchase. They have never used a camera with film. They read periodicals and massive amounts of information online, never thinking that there is a need to print the material in physical form. They watch video on screens that are not televisions.

Ten years ago, you would have laughed aloud if you were told that you would, in a matter of years, be able to carry 2,000 "albums" or "CDs" in your pocket on an electronic device and that you could electronically carry a library of 3,500 books in your briefcase or purse. Now you live with that reality and are likely growing to depend on it as a critical personal and business resource. The phrase "the computers are down" or "I've lost my cell phone" instantly throws us into complete panic and elevates stress and blood pressure.

Many thriving businesses no longer require a physical office. In 2010, IBM announced for the first time in its corporate history that more of its employees worked from home than in a physical office.[6] IBM's move toward a distributed workplace based on cloud computing would not have been possible but for the ability to communicate through technology as effectively "out of the office" as "in the office."

Connectivity, mobility, miniaturization, more powerful and smaller computers, full information access, and ever lower costs for all of these is a reality that we completely embrace and expect to continue in both our professional and personal lives. This is the new reality—*except in health care.*

U.S. GDP data from 2010 reveal that 17.4 percent of GDP spending is on health care and 82.6 percent is not.[7] To make this point easier to describe, let's round health care GDP spending to 20 percent and other GDP spending to 80 percent for the purposes of this book. That 80 percent has, is, and will embrace the "connected electronic community" just described. It is now time for the reality of that 80 percent of the economy to move into the 20 percent that has yet to manifest it, yet alone embrace it.

Here are some questions for you to answer about your own life and current life experiences:

- Do you expect to find information when you want it—24/7?
- Are most of your documents kept electronically, in electronic files for access anytime you want them?

- Do you keep information, pictures, or any type of content (such as your Facebook account) online or in the "cloud"?
- Do you have easy access to all your personal information?
- Do you conduct business online from wherever you are, such as online banking or online shopping?
- Do you communicate with important people in your life via text messaging or e-mails?
- Have you experienced an ever-lowering of the cost of technology and the connectivity that connects us to it?

We suspect that you answered at least some of these questions in the affirmative. If not, you are part of a very small minority of Americans.

Okay, now go back to these questions again. This time think about your current experience when dealing with today's health care system. For example, take the questions above and ask them now in this manner:

- Do you expect to find your medical information when you want it—24/7?
- Do you have easy access to all your personal medical information?
- Do you communicate with your health care provider via text messaging or e-mails?
- Have you experienced an ever-lowering of the cost of technology and connectivity relative to your health care?

Simply stated, the realities that you now accept as the "new normal" and the current reality in the rest of your life you cannot experience in the medical and health care part of your life. What you accept, and often in fact demand, in the 80 percent of the economy that is not health care and medicine, you accept in the 20 percent that is, but you will not for long.

All of the massive, destructive, creative, reorganizational change that we have lived through in the last 30 years is now coming to health care. Nineteenth- and twentieth-century businesses and institutions either have disappeared or have been dramatically altered. Recall the dictionary definition of the word *transformation*: "to change in nature, shape, character, or form." Media, communications, computing, automotive, and financial institutions are radically different in their nature, shape, character, and form than they were 30, 20, even 10 years ago. Health care delivery systems? Not so much.

The New Health Age now upon us will bring about the time when the 20 percent of the economy will catch up to the 80 percent that is far ahead and has already raised the bar.

The following statistics, both real and estimated, further amplify this viewpoint:

- Estimate of how many paper record systems remain in the 80 percent: Very few, not even published according to our research.

- Estimate of how many paper record systems remain in the 20 percent: 88 percent.[8,9]

- Estimated number of smartphones used in the United States in 2010: 61,500,000.[10]

- Estimated number of smartphones used in the U.S. health care sector in 2010: 3,000,000, approximately 5 percent of the total market.[11]

- Approximate percentage of online travel reservations made in the United States in 2009: 81 percent.[12]

- Approximate percentage of health care appointments made online in the United States in 2009: 3 percent.[13]

- Estimated number of paper drug prescriptions and renewals written in the United States in 2009: 1,440,000,000.[14]

- Estimated number of electronic drug prescriptions and renewals made in the United States in 2009: 190,000,000.[15]
- In 2010, the health care sector spent $88.6 billion on information technology.[16]
- In 2010, the retail sector spent $149 billion on information technology.[17]
- In 2010, the banking and financial sector spent $396.9 billion on information technology.[18]
- Percentage of revenue spent on IT in the financial service industry in 2010: 6 percent.[19]
- Percentage of revenue spent on IT in the health care industry in 2010: 3.2 percent.[20]
- In 2007, 39 percent of adult Americans maintained their bank accounts online.[21]
- In 2008, 2.7 percent of adult Americans maintained a personal health record online.[22]
- Percentage of U.S. hospitals using computerized physician order entry (CPOE) for medications in 2008: 17 percent.[23]
- Percentage of U.S. hospitals using electronic physician transcription technology in 2008: 12 percent.[24]
- Some physicians still use beepers. Do you remember those?
- Some physicians still submit insurance claims on paper.

Do you get the picture? While technology and the corresponding efficiencies have subsumed nearly every business sector in America today, health care providers have been slow and resistant to invest in technology and to incorporate technology into the fabric of their businesses. Why? As mentioned previously, the lack of market forces and incentives have never compelled health care providers to do so.

As demonstrated in the Health Care Landscape Statement in Chapter 4, remaining in an archaic era of the past (e.g., paper medical records) is no longer an option if the United States wants to compete as a great nation, improve the health of Americans, and provide the best quality health care in the world.

Get ready 20 percent, here comes the 80 percent.

KEY POINTS

1. Amazing change has occurred in the last 30 years through increased connectivity and technology.

2. Health care spending approximates 20 percent of GDP. GDP spending in other areas approximates 80 percent.

3. The 80 percent world of non–health care has embraced and utilizes technology and connectivity much more than the 20 percent world of health care.

4. The 80 percent world is coming to the 20 percent world, and fast!

◀ CHANGE VISION ▶

Glen Tullman *is an Oxford-educated social entrepreneur who focuses on issues that are personally important to him as well as pressing for our communities and our country— health care, energy, and education. After leading two previous public companies, Glen currently is Chief Executive Officer of Chicago-based Allscripts (NASDAQ: MDRX), a company centered on fixing health care from the inside out. Joining in 1997, Glen led Allscripts growth from a $100 million niche player to a $1.3 billion leader in providing electronic health records and other clinical and financial technologies to the largest client network in health care— 180,000 physicians, 1,500 hospitals, and 10,000 post-acute care organizations.*

Glen graduated from Bucknell University magna cum laude with a double degree in economics and psychology. After working at the White House, he accepted a fellowship to study social anthropology at Oxford University. His passion for education has resulted in a number of business ventures and led to his serving as guest lecturer at Harvard Business School. He currently teaches entrepreneurship at the University of Illinois Chicago's Institute for Entrepreneurial Studies.

A strong proponent of "giving back," Glen serves on the International Board of the Juvenile Diabetes Research Foundation (JDRF), where he initiated and personally funded a program to develop an artificial pancreas. His own foundation contributes to both educational and inner-city diversity programs as well as many other charities.

The Future of Health Care: A Radical Shift to a New Operating System for Health

By Glen Tullman

The future is often hard to predict, both in terms of what will happen and when it will happen. However, every so often forces conspire to give us a clearer picture of what we can and should expect, and such is the case in health care today. Government, market forces, technology, consumer demand, and the cost, or the inability to continue to pay for the cost, of health care, have all guided us to a clear vision of what we can expect in the future. And, the future is coming fast.

Before we discuss both the picture of that future and what it will feel like, let's spend a moment on the reason change is so necessary today and the forces that are driving the change. Today, there is more controversy around health care, both in political and social circles, than ever in our history. Health care is front page news for economic and equity reasons. The simple fact that we can all agree on, however, is that we spend more and have less to show for it than anywhere else in the world. And, we, as individuals, as businesses, and as an economy, can no longer afford it. So, the underlying change driver, as is often the case, is economic in nature.

But a number of other factors have appeared to accelerate what was already a necessary change. The Government HITECH stimulus is pumping over $30 billion dollars into the primary technology necessary to effect the change—electronic health records (EHRs). This stimulus, which is a 10× multiplier, will cause the single fastest transformation of an industry in history. Never before has the government invested so much in such a targeted fashion to fundamentally change an industry. And, just while the government is investing, the technology, both in terms of mobility and usability, has taken a giant step forward, with the appearance of smartphones and tablet computing. And patients, who are bearing an increasing percentage of the cost of health care, are beginning to act like consumers and demand quality at affordable cost, along with traditionally consumer-oriented services that have been long absent from health care.

So, what should we expect given all of these factors that are creating the perfect information storm? Nothing short of a fundamental shift in how we experience our health care and how we manage health. I like to describe the times as BMU (before meaningful use) and AMU (after meaningful use), because we are remaking health care into the information business it is destined to be.

The federal government's incentives and the follow-on payer and employment payment strategies will drive virtually 100 percent adoption of electronic health records in a variety of formats, including traditional desktop-hosted environments, cloud-based virtual systems, mobile and tablet formats, and the like. Federal standards will also drive the connectivity between those systems and set the stage for both broader and more robust connectivity with other industry stakeholders and with a series of new devices that monitor patient health.

The challenge, of course, will be that once we automate all of the paper and results and connect all of the information, we'll quickly move from not enough to too much information. So, the stage following EHR adoption and connectivity will be to extract the information contained in these systems, making it readily available to patients and the physicians who treat them, eliminating reentry of information and often duplicate tests and labs. That is where many European and Scandinavian countries are today.

That is, however, not the end of the story, but rather the beginning of a "Connected Community of Health." A

Connected Community of Health is the future of what we today call health care. Communities that share information with each other will find ways to collaborate, innovate, and create new knowledge. The key to our future in health care, both from a quality and cost standpoint, is turning "Information into Insights™" that physicians use to actually improve the care they are providing at the point of care.

Often we hear about outcomes, but outcomes are like telling a football coach on Monday what plays he should have called on Sunday. They are after-the-fact measures—a score-card—but the patient may already have expired. This is not a game—it's about patients' lives—so we need information that "informates" the physician-patient experience, in real time. Think of this as "Bloomberg for Health Care," a reference to the real-time information system that traders use to buy and sell stock.

In five years, health care will look very different. First, it's not about a visit to the doctor's office, because much of it will be done remotely. Physicians around the world will interact in real time over telecommunications devices on tablets that we all carry. Much of the basic information will be available to us at the touch of our fingers on self-help tutorials by avatars who know us and our allergies, medications, and even sleeping and eating habits. Health care will feel more like "take two of these pills and don't call me in the morning" than anything we know today. Many people with chronic diseases will wear electronic, connected monitors that submit and monitor their vital signs, blood sugar levels, and other critical body indicators and notify their physician or other caregivers if they are not headed in the right direction. Remote care teams will proactively monitor your health, providing "suggestions" on how to live better; suggestions that, if not followed, will drive up your health insurance rates.

And how will health care "feel" in the Connected Community of Health? Managed care will, perhaps for the first time, live up to its name, because your care will truly be managed proactively by someone who has an incentive to keep you healthy. Think of this person as a life coach, but it may not be a person at all. It will be an avatar with a name who knows exactly what you like and how to talk with you. Let's bring the example to life.

Diane is a 47-year-old mother. Her day begins at 6:30 a.m. with a wake up voice from her smartwatch that sits next to her bed. A device turns on her favorite show and has already brewed her green tea. The voice announces that she needs to get up and eat in 30 minutes because her artificial pancreas (a combination of a continuous glucose monitor and an insulin pump) has already been giving her insulin for the day. It also notifies her that her dosage was remotely changed by her life coach, who has studied her blood glucose levels over the past 15 days and determined that this is the healthiest choice. Given that she is vacationing in the Swiss Alps, her dosage was also adjusted for altitude and for her activities for the day, including rigorous skiing. Unfortunately, Diane's day is cut short by a bad fall. Taken to the hospital, Diane gives permission to scan her retina, and her medical records from Raleigh, North Carolina, appear instantly on the screen, including allergies to the pain medication about to be given. The physician stops the nurse, changes the medication to an acceptable one, and then asks Diane if she would like to have a quick teleconference with her physician in Raleigh to discuss options. She agrees, and instantly a familiar face appears and a three-way conversation begins. Her personal physician also adds a surgeon, who looks at both the X-rays and the actual sprain and consults with the local physician. As a team they agree on how to proceed. The physician calls the next day and suggests, having reviewed Diane's chart, that she also do her routine testing and mammogram while she is stuck in the hospital.

Everything just described in our future scenario exists today. As William Gibson said, "The future is here; it's just not evenly distributed." The Connected Community of Health is functioning on service like FaceTime from Apple (on the iPhone) or, more robustly, on Cisco's Telepresence. The artificial pancreas is in clinical trials and being worn by patients today, courtesy of research funded by the Juvenile Diabetes Research Foundation. People who run every day are "coached" by an avatar's voice on a joint service provided by Nike and Apple, and their results are remotely sent, tracked, and monitored on a website. That virtual community even allows "running clubs" to exist, courtesy of Garmin.

As our troubled health care system of today moves to the Connected Community of Health in the future, we'll see the quality of life and the quality of care dramatically improve, and although costs won't come down, we'll feel better about the investments we make in our health and attribute real value to the services we are provided. Today, as patients, consumers, and citizens concerned with the health of our country and our loved ones, the best way to help bring on the future is to demand it. As Charles F. Kettering said many years ago, "My interest is in the future because I am going to spend the rest of my life there."

Our goal is make it a healthy one.

PART II

The Dynamics of The New Health Age

The Dynamic Flows of The New Health Age

*"Healing is a matter of time, but it is sometimes
also a matter of opportunity."*

—Hippocrates

The New Health Age will be defined by fundamental flow dynamics that will usher us into the coming future of medicine and health care. It is vital in order to understand the monumental shift that is about to occur to understand each of these extremely significant dynamic flows that will come to define the transition to, and beginning of, The New Health Age.

Massive change is ahead. A new age is beginning. We are at an inflection point in the history of medicine and health care. Such times are triggered by multiple dynamics and forces that occur simultaneously to birth us into a new place, a new time, and a new reality. The most important thing to realize is that it is not just one force, but many at the same time that are converging with historical imperative to move us all into the new landscape of medicine and health care.

We are entering a significant shift in the landscape of health care in America. It is clear to most Stakeholders that major change is and will be taking place. Humans react to such transformative changes in different ways. The majority of humanity gets uneasy when confronted with change. It is human nature to identify with the way things are. So change, in and of itself, creates a sense of anxiety. This is accentuated when the direction and shape of the change is not readily apparent. If we all knew that The New Health Age will be better for each of us and for the benefit of America, we would excitedly anticipate it. If we all knew for sure that the coming changes will reduce health care costs in America, promote high-quality patient-centered care, and improve the health of Americans, we would largely support this change. This is not the case, as we have already pointed out. The discussion about changing health care delivery in America has been largely shaped by fear, uncertainty, misinformation, and resistance.

Those who expect to benefit embrace the change. Those who fear that the change will hurt them economically resist it. Both of these positions, although understandable, are way too narrow to have any accuracy or depth. Self-interest has always been a primary driver in human endeavor. The problem with looking at the impending shift from a narrow point of view or through the lens of legacy thinking is that this huge historical shift encompasses a multitude of converging forces that transcend simple self-interest.

We are not just speaking about legislation, politics, insurance changes, lifestyle choices, and altered care; of course all of these are involved. We are not just talking about change for change's sake, though that is part of what is involved. Almost every category of Stakeholder in the American health care delivery system agrees that at least part of the current system is broken, expensive, inefficient, and in need of some type or amount of change. Where there is large disagreement is with regard to what should be done. The only way to find agreement, to reach deeper understanding, is to really look at all the forces and flows that are in play. We are going through an historical transition, moving from an established way of doing things to a new way of doing things. A new era is now upon us.

The reason health care and medicine are undergoing the change that they are and will be for the next decade is due to a confluence of dynamic flows. It is important for all Stakeholders to have at least a passing understanding of these dynamic flows. Each dynamic flow describes in a succinct and understandable way where health care has been and where it is now going. The flows on the left side reflect notions of the past. The flows on the right indicate concepts that will exist in the future.

The flow dynamics of The New Health Age are the following:

How we THINK about health care

Sickness → Wellness

Ignorance → Awareness/Understanding

Opposition → Alignment

How we DELIVER health care

Treatment → Prevention

Reactive → Proactive

Episodic → Wholistic

The ECONOMICS of health care

Procedures → Performance

Isolation → Integration

Non-efficient → Efficient

We will now look at each of these dynamic flows. We will examine each one and then tie them all together as they collectively are and will shape The New Health Age.

10

The Dynamic Flows in How We THINK About Health Care

"Without changing our patterns of thought, we will not be able to solve the problems we created with our current pattern of thought."

—Albert Einstein

How we think about "our health" and the way that health care providers deliver "health care" will undergo a huge transformation in the next decade. We will have to completely reshape fundamental concepts and definitions of what health care is in the United States and how it should be delivered. Such alterations to our thinking and thought processes will be dramatic and profound; however, Americans have experienced great change before. Adapting to change and using it to make us stronger is what makes us the greatest nation on earth.

In Chapter 5, we explored how America seized the Industrial Age and used such change and opportunity to transition and grow

America into the wealthiest and strongest nation on the planet. More recently, America led and guided the world into the Information Age, through great companies like IBM, Apple, CNN, Microsoft, and Google. Now, we enter the Shift Age, of which The New Health Age is an integral part.

Like the proud American companies and individuals that have come before us, Stakeholders in the United States of America should grasp and embrace the incredible shifts and changes that are occurring in health care today, resist their fears, and use today's change to make the twenty-first century and the new millennium one of the most remarkable periods in human history.

Consider how Americans shifted their way of thinking about transportation after the automobile was invented and mass-produced. Prior to the automobile, the predominant modes of transportation included the horse, carriage, and train. When automobiles came along, individuals and families altered their perspectives related to travel and transportation in enormous ways. Such change in thinking was incredibly profound and significant for the time. People could travel longer distances in shorter periods. Cars were personal, like the horse, but did not require food, water, or rest, so the notion of enhanced personal convenience entered the world of transportation. Americans experienced a sense of freedom and independence that they had never comprehended or experienced prior to the automobile's arrival. Our ideas, perspectives, and thoughts about transportation changed with the advent of the car, and the car led Americans into a new era of movement that today we take for granted and assume always existed; yet it has not. One's cognitive perspective toward transportation in 1900 was completely different from the perspectives that existed in 2000. The world of transportation fundamentally changed over a period of 100 years.

The shifts and changes in our ideas, approaches, and beliefs about health care will occur on an even a grander scale than the thought changes that occurred when the means for human transportation moved away from legacy modalities of the past to the automobile. The scale of change in The New Health Age will be massive, and the change will occur incredibly fast, particularly over the next 10 years. The reorientation in our thinking about health care has already begun; however, many of us are not cognizant yet of the transformation taking place. It will take far less time than in the century past for the new dynamic flows of The New Health Age to be embraced and become the "new norm."

The pace of change to our thinking will occur quickly for several reasons. First, as outlined in Chapter 4, the current landscape underlying America's economy reveals that our health care spending is out of control and it must be contained to avoid a financial disaster. Spending and costs related to government and private health plans alike are increasing at alarming rates. Second, American businesses are competing in a new global marketplace, and these businesses must find ways to be more competitive and profitable in this contemporary cutthroat environment. American employers are increasingly demanding healthier and more productive employees in order to retain or reclaim their competitive advantage. Third, because of the poor health of many Americans, our nation is losing its sense of pride and well-being. Fourth, medical advancements and discoveries are occurring at an accelerating pace.

We start with the following dynamic flows because the first step in understanding The New Health Age is to reorient one's thinking. The three dynamic flows in how we THINK about health care are

Sickness → Wellness

Ignorance → Awareness/Understanding

Opposition → Alignment

We will now look at each one first from a general point of view and then with some detail and specificity.

1. Sickness → Wellness
We Will Change Our Thinking
Americans have spent their lives thinking about health care providers as people or institutions that find solutions to health care

problems. Through analysis and diagnosis, health care providers treat our symptoms, injuries, and physical and psychological problems or diseases. In other words, the way that we think about health care is that it exists to help us when we are sick or injured. We do not think about health care when we feel good. Until there is a pain, a fever, an injury, or a developing condition of concern, we do not interface with a health care provider, such as physicians, nurses, hospitals, urgent care centers, or therapists. Today's health care model does not motivate Americans to seek out health care providers to find ways to stay well and prevent disease, nor does it currently pay providers in any meaningful way to focus on wellness or disease prevention.

Medical conditions fuel and energize health care delivery systems today. Sickness is a very large and integral component of health care. Dealing with sickness and illness will, of course, always be a significant part of health care, but in The New Health Age, treating sickness and poor health will become a declining percentage of the total practice of medicine and revenues within the health care sector. This fact is critical to understand and acknowledge if you practice and work in the health care space, so we will repeat it: Treating sickness and poor health will become a declining percentage of the total practice of medicine and revenues within the health care sector.

As advisors, we are stressing to our health care clients that any professional or business that fails to embrace this new flow during The New Health Age will very likely go out of business at some point. Consider this warning your "canary in the coal mine," and the canary is flying toward the new future of wellness.

The thinking process within the health care establishment and for all Stakeholders will shift toward promoting, achieving, and maintaining health and wellness. If we want to lower health care costs, we must reengineer our thinking, focus, and practice toward wellness and prevention ideals. Through this mode of thinking, we will ultimately drive down the number of Americans currently suffering from chronic health conditions that cost more to treat than to prevent. Through this mode of thinking, we will make the American workforce more productive, reduce absenteeism, and thereby preserve the economic foundation of the U.S. economy. Through this mode of thinking, Americans will regain a sense of pride in how they look, feel, and function on a day-to-day basis.

Recall from Chapter 4 that 10 percent of the U.S. population is responsible for nearly 70 percent of health care dollars.[1] Americans with chronic diseases, including diabetes, heart disease, lung disease, and depression, represent this 70 percent of our total health care costs.[2]

While it would be wonderful if *every* American embraced wellness, history demonstrates that such a goal is unlikely, nor is it necessary to achieve significant and positive results. If we simply focus on making the 10 percent class referenced above well or healthier, America's spending will decrease exponentially. If 30,000,000 out of 300,000,000 people are responsible for 70 percent of the total health care dollars, simply reducing this group by 3,000,000 people cuts total costs by 7 percent. Said another way, deal effectively with 1 percent of the total population and receive a sevenfold return. Imagine if a stock investment returned your money back seven times over! Tremendous amounts of money will be saved and generated by simply focusing on and managing chronic diseases during The New Health Age.

In order to reduce the number of Americans afflicted with chronic disease, we will move toward a new era of thinking about wellness and prevention. Wellness and prevention will become "hip" and "cool" in The New Health Age. As discussed in Chapter 4, health care is delivered and compensated through thousands of billing codes, most of which are focused on sickness as opposed to wellness. This archaic payment and incentive system is about to change dramatically because American businesses and policy makers realize that "follow the money" rules the day. If we want America to focus on wellness, we must put the right incentives into place.

Take asthma as an example. If we prevent an asthmatic from having an asthma attack through better monitoring, inhalers, and nebulizers, the patient stays well and the costs are dramatically less, both in the short and long terms. We can reduce costs, avoid lung damage, and improve the quality of life for asthmatics by lowering or eliminating the frequency of emergency room visits.[3]

Many Americans can prevent coronary artery disease simply by changing their thinking about the need for wellness and better lifestyle choices. Nine risk factors account for 90 percent of the risks attributable to having a first heart attack (which is often fatal):

1. Cigarette smoking
2. High blood cholesterol levels
3. High blood pressure
4. Diabetes
5. Obesity
6. Lack of physical exercise
7. Low intake of fruits and vegetables
8. Alcohol overconsumption
9. Psychosocial factors[4]

Now ask yourself, how many of these nine factors are in Americans' total control? Smoking, physical exercise, diet, and alcohol consumption are completely within our power to address through behavioral change. That takes care of four out of the nine. If we address these first four, several of the other factors can be reduced as well. By controlling diet and increasing physical activity, we reduce obesity, blood pressure, and bad cholesterol. We can also address many psychosocial factors (i.e., depression, anxiety, stress, anger) through exercise and weight loss.[5]

How will this dynamic flow to wellness occur and who will drive it? What will motivate Americans to skip the double-stacked hamburger with cheese and fries on the menu and order a turkey sandwich on whole grain bread with fruit salad instead? How will the approximately 75 percent of Americans who rarely engage in exercise, as discussed in Chapter 4, be encouraged to take the stairs versus the elevator or walk a mile through a park as opposed to sitting in front of the television or computer at home? The answer is through incentives and awareness (i.e., education), in that order of priority.

Both incentives and awareness have the power and ability to bring about massive cultural and behavioral changes toward wellness. Let's focus on incentives for a moment.

Create the Incentives to Achieve Wellness and Prevent Disease

New incentives to facilitate the flow toward wellness will soon begin to surround us as we enter The New Health Age. Certain Stakeholders will champion these initiatives, such as employers and government payers of health care. Newly designed and reengineered corporate America employee wellness programs are being developed and implemented in ways never effectively utilized before. Entitlement programs, such as Medicare and Medicaid, are moving toward wellness models, too.

Let's start by looking at American businesses. Employer-sponsored health plans will integrate insurance benefits and health management through a comprehensive approach, utilizing behavioral health as the foundation for success. Health plan advocates with behavioral health backgrounds will work closely with employees through coaching and advocating to bring about better life choices. Healthy diets, exercise, and smoking cessation programs will be integrated into corporate health plan models across America. Well-designed employer wellness programs will incorporate a team of professionals, including employee advocates, dedicated to fostering "people-to-people" interactions, leading employees to making improved health and lifestyle choices.

It will take more than lifestyle coaches, though, to change American behavior. Only through monetary incentives will Americans change their behavior toward wellness. We will continue to explore this concept in the chapters ahead.

Having healthier employees reduces the utilization of expensive health care services, decreasing employer health plan expenses, and increasing corporate profits. Having healthier employees also reduces absenteeism, resulting in more productive employees through both increased days at work and improved productivity while on the job. Increased productivity leads to increased profitability in corporate America, leading to greater economic prosperity for all Americans and increased global economic competitiveness.

Government benefit programs, such as Medicare and Medicaid, will also incorporate wellness and better lifestyle awareness initiatives. Because of PPACA's health care reform laws, starting in January 2011, for the first time Medicare beneficiaries can receive covered annual physical exams that are designed to develop wellness and prevention plans based on each individual's risk factors and history. This benefit was designed, in part, to elevate awareness and educate Americans 65 years and older that much can be done to achieve wellness and prevent disease.

Medicare will compensate physicians to work and collaborate with beneficiaries to

1. Develop appropriate screening schedules based on the patient's medical history.
2. Establish a list of risk factors and conditions (including any mental health conditions) for which interventions or preventive measures can be taken to avoid disease.
3. Furnish personalized health advice and referrals to health education or preventive counseling programs, including those targeted at weight loss, physical activity, smoking cessation, fall prevention, and nutrition.

Primary care physicians and their allied health professionals, such as nurse practitioners, physician assistants, and dieticians, will become the cornerstone Stakeholders to drive these new wellness models within employer and government programs. Primary care providers are in the best position to effectively manage patient care because they typically see their patients more frequently and are trained to take a wholistic perspective (view the complete picture) when analyzing and diagnosing health care conditions.[6]

Make no mistake, paying doctors to achieve patient wellness and prevent disease will create incentives and cost money in the short term. Americans will not change decades of thinking and poor lifestyle habits overnight. Recall, however, the sevenfold return on investment if only 10 percent of the chronically ill Americans improve their health. In the long term, such investment will more than pay off by reducing overall costs and by living and working in a healthier nation.

As we write this book, Drs. Mehmet Oz, Mark Hyman, and Ann Kulze are a few of the most amplified doctor voices in America promoting wellness and lifestyle change. Their messages regarding how to live and move toward better life choices are model examples for the physician of the future. Visit www.doctoroz.com and enter Doctor Oz's world of wellness. Go to www.drhyman.com and learn about functional medicine models of the future. Visit www.drannwellness.com and see how she educates about wellness purely and simply. If you have any doubt that this flow toward wellness is occurring, these physicians will change your perspective.

2. Ignorance → Awareness/Understanding

The *Merriam-Webster's Dictionary* defines *ignorance* as one's "lack of knowledge, awareness, or education." Ignorance is usually more expensive and more limiting on human lives than awareness and understanding. Ponder why inventors created paper maps and modern GPS systems. Before maps, people were ignorant about where they were going and the best route to reach their destination. Shipping companies cannot afford to be ignorant about the shortest and fastest route from one destination to another. Longer routes lead to lost time and increased transportation costs. In the shipping and transport sectors, the shortest time from point to point is critically important and linked directly to profitability.

Lowering health care costs, currently at approximately $2.47 trillion in annual spending, will necessitate the lessening of ignorance at multiple levels. In America, the level of ignorance about good health is high among all Stakeholders. We need a clear map, education, knowledge, and awareness to show us how to get healthier as a nation. Health care delivery systems need more knowledge, awareness, and education to promote greater efficiencies with technologies that other business sectors have seen as a necessity for years, such as electronic records. Health care providers require enhanced knowledge, education, and awareness related to preventing and managing chronic diseases and must learn how to operate profitable businesses while doing so. Let's expand on each of these ideas.

Employers Will Become Aware That Employee Health Is Critical for Business Success

Bringing more knowledge, education, and awareness to corporate America about wellness is one of the best ways to improve the health of America quickly. Employees get healthier and happier and employers get more profitable as a result.

As mentioned earlier, a critical component of The New Health Age will include employer health plan benefit design, utilizing employee health data linked with disease management information, as well as effective employee wellness and disease prevention programs. Astounding and profound increased corporate profitability will result from employers being more aware of how critically important it is to their bottom line to have a healthy, happy, and productive workforce. A day will come when stock analysts investigate companies' employee wellness programs and use that data as a factor in valuing corporate stock. Companies with healthy employees will be worth more, no doubt.

For instance, take a manufacturing company that employs 5,000 workers in a metropolitan city. This model employer health plan will provide employees with powerful online resources to enhance their health knowledge. Employees will receive economic incentives (i.e., cash cards, discounts on insurance premiums, etc.) to take online health risk assessments by answering questions and entering their personal health data. Do you have a family history of heart attack? How many fruits and vegetables do you consume per day? Do you smoke? And so forth. Once completed, automated systems will calculate health scores and provide comprehensive analysis of key health categories, such as heart health, nutrition, stress, fitness, weight management, and cancer risks. Health plan designers and coaches will utilize the results of employee health risk assessments to provide them with tailored recommendations and monitoring tools to achieving better health. Vast educational information will also be available through these wellness coaches and online wellness resources.

By analyzing their employees' prior health insurance claims data and gathering employees' health information, including family history, genetic information, and other health risk data, employers can tailor and design health plan offerings that will be specific to the health needs of their employees. Employers and health plan administrators must protect the employees' health information under numerous state and federal laws. Employers simply want the overall health data and employee grouping information, not the employee names. This information will lead to better health plans that employers tailor and customize to employee health needs.

For instance, the employer's awareness that certain classes of employees are at high risk for developing chronic diseases will enable the employer to develop targeted and focused wellness plans, reducing costs among the high-risk employee segments of the health plan. If the employer in our example learns that 40 percent of its workers are obese, it becomes abundantly clear that the company's wellness and prevention plan should establish weight loss goals as a primary objective to reduce employee weight and health plan costs. Health plan coaches and caregivers can get to work on that tailored and targeted goal.[7]

Let's take diabetes to demonstrate how all this will work. Studies have shown that only 37 percent of type 2 diabetics stay in compliance with their recommended diet protocols and that 24 percent either never self-monitor blood glucose or do so fewer than 12 times annually.[8] Helping diabetic employees stay in compliance will increase their health and productivity while also reducing the employer's health care costs. Remaining ignorant and uninformed as to the horrific consequences that diabetes can cause, such as heart attack, stroke, blindness, and kidney failure, will not be part of corporate cultures during The New Health Age.

Employer health plans will implement awareness initiatives for diabetic employees and implement automated monitoring systems that notify employees if they go out of compliance. For instance, employer health plan administrators will be notified by pharmacy networks or electronically connected pill bottles that are linked to the Internet if an employee fails to refill a prescription for insulin or refuses to follow a required drug protocol. Noncompliance will automatically trigger an e-mail or a phone call to the employee reminding the person that drug compliance is critical to his or her health.

Employers will reward compliant employees. Noncompliant employees will not receive preferential treatment. Ignorance will wane; understanding and awareness will flourish.

Recall the 10/70 statistic: 10 percent of the population is responsible for 70 percent of the cost. By focusing on reducing chronic diseases among that 10 percent, employers will receive massive returns on their investment through wellness programs. The goal will obviously be to reach larger numbers of people, but simply focusing on the 10 percent responsible for the bulk of the costs will produce outstanding results.

No initiative should be more important in corporate America today than increasing shareholder profits by implementing effective employee wellness programs. If this goal is not part of every company's strategic business plan, the company is leaving shareholder dividend dollars on the table, not to mention C-level executive bonus money.

We will dedicate many sections throughout the remainder of the book to employee wellness programs, such as the one described above, because workplace wellness is critical to The New Health Age and to America's future as a nation. In fact, as strategic advisors to health care companies, health care providers, consulting firms, and corporations all over the globe, we have developed a brand name for these new models—Employer Accountable Care Organizations (EACOs), which we will present and define with more clarity later in the book.

Medicare and Medicaid Patients Join In

Bringing about lifestyle changes, education, and awareness to the older Medicare population and to younger groups who participate under state Medicaid programs is also critically important to improving health and reducing health care costs. That is why PPACA's health care reform laws added annual physical exams to the Medicare program, as we discussed earlier. This new benefit aims to elevate awareness and educate Americans 65 years and older to learn that much can be done to achieve wellness and prevent disease.

On the Medicaid side, PPACA contains numerous new programs focused on expanding community health center services offered within the underserved areas of American cities and rural communities. A great number of the 10 percent population that costs 70 percent of health care dollars lives within underserved communities. Increasing awareness and education within these groups will be part of The New Health Age. We present several examples and models targeting the Medicaid population later in the book.

Americans Have Lost Sight of Their Most Important Possession—Their Own Health

Americans, as a Stakeholder group—employees, the Medicaid population, the Medicare population, and others—have unsuspectingly allowed the forces of advertising and marketing of food to become more powerful than the forces of informed education about the ways to eat in a healthy manner. Consumer culture, habit, lower food costs, and immediate gratification are powerful forces that can lead people to make both immediate and long-term decisions that adversely affect their health.

Fast-food restaurants, for instance, which blanket the United States, enable Americans to purchase an entire meal and a drink, albeit unhealthy, for less than $5.00. With the American unemployment rate hovering around 10 percent, and the underemployment rate likely higher than that, a $5.00 meal is extremely tempting and understandable. Yet, ignorance and denial promote Americans to make these decisions with a great lack of understanding and acknowledgment that many citizens are in fact very unhealthy. We are currently facing a tsunami of chronic diseases that will greatly damage us and, in turn, our great nation.

Time reported in its January 17, 2011, edition that 89.7 percent of people in the United States describe their diet as healthy; however, close to two-thirds of Americans are overweight or obese. Few people seek to harm themselves consciously with their daily decisions, yet that is what millions of Americans do every day simply due to ignorance of the health consequences of their actions.[9]

Thankfully, as we enter The New Health Age fast-food restaurants are beginning to embrace this flow to awareness and wellness by offering healthier meal choices and options for smaller portion sizes for many meals. McDonald's, for instance, is one of the largest buyers of apples in the United States and is developing new innovative menu selections geared toward greater nutrition and healthy eating.[10,11] Americans, however, still have the freedom to choose from unhealthy restaurant menu items, and a greater understanding of the consequences of poor dietary selection is coming as part of this dynamic flow to awareness and understanding.

As we hinted in Chapter 7, in Chapter 16 we propose something radically new for the United States—The Race to a Healthy America! As part of the race, we develop a plan that will place one of the best guides about eating correctly in the hands of every American. *Eat Right for Life*, written by Dr. Ann G. Kulze and published by the Wellness Council of America, is a "must read" and represents a cornerstone principle of The New Health Age. Dr. Kulze's book contains powerful tips and strategies for eating the foods that will keep Americans healthy and happy. Topics include how to choose the right fats, which carbs will keep us moving forward, the wonderful world of fruits and vegetables, how to eat the right proteins, and how to select the right beverages. Dr. Kulze filled her book with eye-opening facts. Consider this one: Americans drink approximately 20 percent of their calories! If we simply change what we drink, we change our life. That fact is just the beginning. *Eat Right for Life* will become your blueprint for healthy eating to create a more productive and happier life.

The Wellness Council of America is currently the exclusive publisher of *Eat Right for Life*, so the book cannot be purchased through traditional retail outlets. Dr. Ann's home page at www.drannwellness.com includes all the information needed about her book.

Ultimately, knowledge will provide people with greater understanding. This greater understanding will promote healthier choices and thus lead to happier Americans and lower social health care costs in The New Health Age.

Health Care Providers Will Gain Access to and Knowledge about Health Information as They Have Never Experienced Before

The New Health Age will bring about the proliferation and integration of information technology tools that will increase health care providers' access to data and information across the entire health care spectrum. Health care providers will function in an environment where greater information about health will surround them, and this new awareness will be empowering and enlightening.

Patient electronic medical records (EMRs) will be accessible through secure web portals to all physicians, nurses, and other caregivers who require patient information to provide health care. An emergency room team treating a person from out of town will be able to gain instant access to the patient's medical records from across the country within seconds. Diagnostic test results, whether sophisticated three-dimensional images or simple CBC results, will be transmitted anywhere in the world to the most qualified and skilled physicians for their superior interpretation and analysis.

This new era of increased health information will enable physicians to access instantly the latest medical research, news, and advancements in medicine. Doctors will quickly source electronic clinical guidelines and protocols that have proven to be successful. This will enable doctors to deliver needed care faster and better.

When a patient presents to a physician in The New Health Age showing unusual and complex symptoms, the physician will have faster and increased access to global and national disease registries. These electronic registries will create collective knowledge databases that link complex symptoms to diagnosis information and treatment options instantaneously.

As we discussed in Chapter 7, with genetic data becoming commonplace, physicians will be able to practice "personalized medicine," tailoring treatment plans based on an individual's genetic makeup to improve outcomes. Take, for instance, the use of drugs to treat and fight certain diseases. The Wall Street Journal reports that many drugs are ineffective in up to one-half the people who take them. Personalized medicine incorporates genetic information to target specific drug formularies for people on whom the drugs have been proven effective.[12]

Utilization and value associated with sophisticated diagnostic tests performed on continuously advancing equipment will flourish as clinicians incorporate the test results into wellness, prevention, therapy, and monitoring programs. For instance, three-dimensional body part image reconstruction is currently being used to further enhance CT and high-speed MRI scans, making these studies faster, more efficient, and easier for physicians to interpret than in years past. Today, advanced radiological technology produces images that nearly replicate a person's actual organ on a high-definition monitor for the physician to study and analyze. With new imaging technologies, doctors can rotate, slice, and manipulate digital images to enhance data for diagnosis and to simulate an organ or other body area in preparation for the actual surgery.

The practices and technologies applied to aircraft flight simulators are coming to health care education, diagnostics, and practice in a major way. Medical Education Technologies, Inc. (METI) is an industry leader in developing advanced health care learning tools, including a complete line of human patient simulators. METI's simulators and training center save lives by providing a "close to real life" learning platform that allows students and practitioners to practice on simulated human bodies without harming real patients. These simulated human bodies replicate vital signs, body temperatures, organs, and more. By offering a variety of simulators that meet the exacting needs of METI's clients, the company is able to provide a higher level of measurable skill acquisition for health care professionals.[13]

As we mentioned in Chapter 7, the Institute for Functional Medicine is bringing awareness, understanding, and education to physicians and teaching twenty-first century medical methods that migrate doctors away from the prevailing acute-care model to a far more effective chronic-disease management model, which focuses on the underlying drivers of America's health problems—the lifelong interactions among genetics, environment, and lifestyle. Ignorance gives way to awareness and understanding. Health, happiness, increased productivity, and profitability result.

3. Opposition → Alignment

Three principal groups of participants dominate the current landscape of health care today: suppliers, payers, and patients. The relationships between and among these participants currently exist in opposition. Such antagonism is destructive, costly, and will soon change.

For purposes of this discussion, we use the inclusive word "suppliers" as any person or entity who supplies a health care product or service, including, among others, physicians, nurses, therapists, hospitals, long-term care organizations, other caregivers, medical device companies, pharmaceutical companies, and pharmacists. "Payers" include patients as well as public and private entities.

Payers in the Health Care Marketplace Set the Prices, Leaving Little, if Any, Room for Suppliers to Negotiate

Unless you are a massively sized supplier with significant market power, such as a national or large regional hospital chain, insurance companies rarely negotiate their fees. If a major hospital system threatens to cancel its contract with an insurance company to leverage a particular payer for higher rates, the insurance company will likely pay attention; however, if a smaller hospital attempts this posturing, it will have much less of an impact.

On the public payer side, the primary method of "negotiating" with government payers is through lobbyists. Again, major players have greater resources to lobby government payers for increased reimbursements. Small providers do not.

The resistance by insurance companies to negotiate and the imbalance of power between providers and government payers create significant negative posturing between payers and suppliers. They stand in opposition across the health care battlefield.

Patients Have Had Very Little Influence over Health Care Prices and Little Motivation to Impact Prices

Historically, patients have played a minimal role on the health care pricing battlefield. Patients covered by insurance or government entitlement programs have little incentive to influence health care prices because few dollars come out of their wallets. That said, as Medicare and Medicaid make eligibility more difficult, as more Americans become uninsured, and as employers continue to raise co-pays and deductibles and reduce covered benefits, patients are "waking up" to the reality that they *should care* and that they *need to care* about their health care costs.

Patients are feeling more in opposition to the current health care pricing system and questioning the value that they are receiving for health care services. Patients perceive a $300 doctor visit charge or a $1,000 diagnostic test very differently if they pay for it out of their own wallet. Patients are quickly entering the battlefield.

From the Payers' Perspective, Suppliers Possess Much of the Power Today

Suppliers of health care products and services have long stood on the battlefield. Hospitals, nursing homes, hospices, home health agencies, and physicians own one critical prerequisite to providing health care that payers do not. Suppliers control the legal license to perform a particular health care service; payers do not. Individuals cannot practice medicine without a license. Hospitals require a license to function. Nursing homes, hospices, and home health agencies require licenses, too.

With the license comes power—power that payers and patients do not possess. Suppliers hold the power to diagnose, perform a procedure, order a test, prescribe a drug, and so forth. No others do.

Payers, Patients, and Suppliers Are at War

The inability to meaningfully negotiate health care prices places payers at significant odds against suppliers and patients. This may come as a shock to many, but the United States has effectively already adopted a single-payer model, because most private insurance companies tie their reimbursement rates to Medicare reimbursements. When Medicare cuts provider reimbursements, most private insurance rates decrease, too. America's existing single-payer system increases economic volatility, risk, and uncertainty for health care suppliers. One significant Medicare cut in reimbursements can have a catastrophic ripple effect across the entire supplier side of health care.

When the Deficit Reduction Act (DRA) was signed into law by President George W. Bush in 2006, the federal government slashed Medicare reimbursements for diagnostic imaging tests by as much as 30 percent. Imaging companies, hospitals, and physician medical practices went into an economic tailspin because these groups did not have adequate time to adjust operating budgets to accommodate such drastic and immediate revenue cuts. Many imaging companies sold, went bankrupt, or restructured following the DRA. A single-payer model amplifies the opposition between payers and suppliers because suppliers need more revenue consistency and reliability from their payers.[14]

Payers possess the power to reject a supplier's claims for payment for a variety of reasons. In some cases, payers deny patients' benefits coverage, leaving patients to fight with payers to cover the claim. The definition of "loss ratio" actually means the amount of money that an insurance company pays out divided by the total premiums. Payers consider paying a patient's claim as a "loss" versus an insurance benefit paid.

Payers regularly deny suppliers' claims for reimbursement, arguing that the suppliers failed to process the claim correctly. A supplier may inadvertently submit a claim with incomplete patient demographic data or transpose a patient's Social Security number, resulting in the claim's denial. The payer often asserts that a service is not "medically necessary," thereby challenging the physician's clinical judgment. The fight to get benefits and services paid for is an ongoing war in health care today.

Patients in the mix have very little influence because they rely on and trust educated medical professionals to provide the necessary and appropriate care to fix their health care problem. Payers may control prices, but suppliers drive most health care utilization and resulting expenditures.

Think of the concepts presented in Chapter 8—80 percent accepted, 20 percent to go. In the U.S. economy, the 80 percent of the GDP that is not health care fully accepts that demand from customers—the ones who pay—drives supply. If customers do not choose to pay for a product or service, that product or service goes away. If there is no market demand for goods or a service, the producer will likely cease production. In fact, some producers who delay responding to marketplace failures might even go out of business. The history of business is littered with products or services that were brought to market but failed due to a lack of demand, too high a price, or bad timing. We accept that fact as the dynamic within a supply-and-demand-based economy.

Now think of America's health care establishment as it has existed in recent decades. A medical practice or hospital buys an expensive piece of diagnostic equipment. That decision drives the entity to promote the usage of that equipment to justify the decision to buy and to cover the cost of the purchase. This drives the health care supplier to create the demand for that product. In some cases, the health care entity did not purchase the equipment based on traditional supply-and-demand economic principles. In fact, in communities across America there is an oversupply of medical equipment because health care providers each want the latest and greatest technology. Yet, how many patients walk into a health care provider demanding that the health care provider upgrade the MRI machine? Does a community need numerous MRIs operating at half capacity or should the market eliminate redundant machines to gain greater economies of scale? The current health care system encourages health care providers to purchase new technology and then seek reimbursement from the payers and the patients, without prior dialog regarding the need, desire, or demand for the service. This is simply the way that the health care market has functioned in America for years.

Think about that concept. In the non-health-care parts of your life, would you allow yourself to be told that you needed something from a store because the seller bought a product that you had to buy? Would you allow a seller to tell you how much you had to pay and that you had no choice but to purchase it? What would you do? Likely walk out of the store and do some comparison shopping. When have you ever walked out of a hospital or doctor's office? Why not? Because payers and patients have grown to accept that suppliers wield the power to drive demand. Suppliers possess the medical license and knowledge "to know what is best" in terms of health. If a doctor orders a test, we assume and trust that we need it. If a hospital upgrades its equipment, we assume and trust that it is necessary.

The system and such blind acceptance, however, now place payers and patients in opposition to suppliers. With patients and payers paying more for health care year after year, they are now questioning the value that suppliers offer and are demanding measurable results on money spent.

Payers', Patients', and Suppliers' Interests Come into Alignment

In The New Health Age, payers', suppliers', and patients' interests and incentives flow from being in opposition to functioning in alignment. New ways of thinking and approaches will come about, bringing payers, suppliers, and patients to the same table.

In some communities, suppliers and payers will merge into united and integrated organizations. Kaiser Permanente and the University of Pittsburgh Medical Center (UMPC) have owned and operated health insurance companies or divisions for years. The trend will accelerate in the future.

New care models will be centered on the concept of providing accountable care. Under unified accountable care models, payers and suppliers will negotiate collaboratively regarding the value of health care services and determine the best jointly desired outcomes for patients. The full spectrum of payers and health care suppliers will take ownership in accountable care models, including physicians, hospitals, post-acute care providers, and so on.

We will explore accountable care models throughout the remainder of the book. As an introduction, think of accountable care models as the instrument that will bring patients, payers, and suppliers all together in one conference room. Whiteboards cover the walls to develop ideas and plans, with the goal of providing high-quality health care services for the lowest cost. A payer might propose a goal to provide open heart surgery, from beginning to end, for $40,000. Suppliers agree to accept that rate for all open heart surgeries. If they provide the service for less, suppliers keep the profit. If the service costs more, the suppliers lose money. Shared risk and shared savings. The payer might be a government entity or an employer. What would that goal take to achieve and what would the process look like to achieve it?

The participants in the conference room would determine how to best integrate and collaborate to achieve the goal. A team approach will be vitally important. Participants will analyze how to collaborate with the best doctors who produce the highest success rates. The team will examine the cost of all medical devices to match the patient's needs with the right device. Participants will work to shorten the length of hospital stays because receiving care in a hospital is very expensive. They will develop ways to minimize the opportunities for a patient to get an infection, because complications lengthen hospital stays and increase costs. Hospitals and physicians will develop coordination of care plans with the post-surgery care team, including rehabilitation facilities and home care agencies to facilitate a fast and high-quality recovery. The longer it takes to recover, the less profit from the $40,000 payment.

In The New Health Age, this is just one example of how previously opposed parties in the health care delivery process will come together in alignment and think about how to provide care in an accountable, coordinated, and integrated manner. Doing so will lead to better quality care for less cost. Unlike many other markets, in health care, high quality can coexist with less cost.

How we think about health care in The New Health Age will assuredly change. Societal wellness, citizens assuming more personal health responsibility, and enlightenment through our greater awareness will take place. Alignment of previously opposing interests will come into being.

KEY POINTS

The three dynamic flows in how we THINK about health care are

Sickness → Wellness

Ignorance → Awareness/Understanding

Opposition → Alignment

1. Americans have lost sight of the most important possession they have—their own health.

2. We will change our thinking about health going forward.

3. Our thinking about health will move toward achieving wellness and preventing disease.

4. Employers will come into great awareness that employee health is critical for business success. Employees will follow incentives and get healthier.

5. Bringing about lifestyle changes, education, and awareness to the older Medicare population and to younger groups who participate under state Medicaid programs is also critically important to improving health and bringing down health care costs.

6. During The New Health Age, health care providers will gain access and knowledge to health information as they have never experienced before.

7. Payers', patients', and suppliers' interests come into alignment in The New Health Age.

11

The Dynamic Flows in How We DELIVER Health Care

"Any serious restructuring of business must directly attack the organization and the entire system of power based on it."

—Alvin Toffler

C hange in thought eventually brings about change in action. When people's thinking and thoughts change, their actions and behavior change in response. This chapter examines how health care delivery will change because of the changes in our thinking about health care.

How America delivers health care is about to be fundamentally reorganized. The process of this reorganization has already begun and the pace of this change is accelerating. This reorganization will be the manifestation of the dynamic flows in thinking described in the previous chapter. The landscape of the health care delivery system in the United States is about to undergo as much transformation as has already occurred in the delivery systems of most other businesses in the last 25 years. Health care delivery is simply catching up to the rest of American business. The New Health Age will shed the health care delivery systems of the Industrial Age that are largely still in place and replace them with models and approaches that fundamentally redefine the entire landscape of health care as we know it today.

As Stakeholders' perspectives flow from sickness to wellness, from ignorance to awareness, and from opposition to alignment, Stakeholders will require health care delivery systems that function in harmony with this new reality. Old delivery models will not work after massive change of thought occurs. New delivery models will evolve to provide health care around our new thoughts effectively.

Consider again, as we did in the prior chapter, the progression of the automobile over the centuries. When the initial mass production of the automobile began in the early twentieth century, it was perceived, in its narrowest form, as merely a new mode of transportation. No one pondered the numerous ways that automobile accidents and collisions would place new risks and dangers into our world. As people became aware that cars created new perils, governments, manufacturers, and insurance companies fostered new car designs with safety in mind. Turn signals, bumpers, seatbelts, and airbags came about as society gained awareness of the need for car safety. Over many years, the car industry improved automobiles by incorporating safety features into the design process. New awareness led to change of thought and change in action, resulting in entirely new systems and products.

As The New Health Age brings about wellness, awareness, and an alignment of Stakeholders' interests, health care delivery systems will be reengineered, just as the automobile was transformed following society's desire to make the car safer.

The three dynamic flows of change in how we will DELIVER health care in The New Health Age are

Treatment → Prevention

Reactive → Proactive

Episodic → Wholistic

We will examine each of these flows and how they will influence health care Stakeholders.

1. Treatment → Prevention

Treating sick and injured patients has always been at the core of America's health care delivery system. The vast majority of efforts, costs, processes, and payments in the U.S. health care delivery system go toward treatment. Good treatment should always be a cornerstone of any health care delivery model. People get sick or suffer from injuries and, as a result, they need quality care. In The New Health Age, however, the focus on treatment will nonetheless be overshadowed by a concentration on preventing sickness and disease and, therefore, preventing the need for treatment from occurring in the first place.

America has experienced significant changes in its thinking regarding health care issues before. We touched on this nation's history with tobacco products in Chapter 7, but let's revisit that point in detail. In 1965, roughly 42 percent of Americans smoked cigarettes.[1] In 1964, the U.S. Surgeon General announced that smoking was linked to cancer.[2] As more Americans became aware of the dangers surrounding smoking, and as governments raised taxes on cigarettes, the percent of American smokers declined. By 2010, 21 percent of Americans smoked.[3] Public awareness, combined with government intervention, led to a change in thinking, and thereafter changes in actions and behaviors.

In The New Heath Age, individual Stakeholders will become enlightened with new perspectives regarding their health, and corporate as well as government Stakeholders will implement new incentives, such as wellness programs, to change thought and promote new actions.

Remember the old saying "An ounce of prevention is worth a pound of cure"? Today, our health care delivery systems are based on paying for the "pound of cure." And, quite frankly, numerous costs associated with "cures" do not actually cure anything. Many "cures" simply treat the condition rather than eliminate its cause. Obese Americans suffer from high blood pressure. Beta-blockers may control high blood pressure, yet the "cure" is losing weight in many cases. So, we know this old saying and have accepted it as true, yet in our health care delivery systems we embrace paying for the pound of cure, which is often questionable and of limited long-term value.

The following are just a few cases that point to the financial benefits for prevention versus treatment, not even accounting for human pain and suffering.

Consider diabetes, heart disease, asthma, bone problems, and several cancers, such as breast, colon, and kidney cancers. Studies show that a medical relationship and correlation exist between obesity and each of these health problems, yet the girth of America continues to expand.[4] Obesity, directly and indirectly, is attributed to approximately 10 percent of health care spending in the United States.[5] On top of all these direct costs, if all employee sick days, productivity issues, disability costs, and, yes, the cost of lost years due to an early death were added to the costs of treating the diseases associated with obesity, the causal effect of obesity is disastrously expensive, painful, and now, in The New Health Age, unnecessary.

Obesity is a major contributing factor to diabetes, which is a crisis chronic disease in America today. In 1980, 5.6 million Americans had diabetes.[6] That number reached 18.1 million in 2008.[7] Diabetes is the number one cause of kidney failure.[8] Each year between 12,000 and 24,000 adults go blind from diabetic retinal disease.[9] At least 80,000 people have lower limb amputations as a result of diabetes.[10]

The direct and indirect cost attributable to diabetes in the United States is approximately $174 billion.[11] Nearly one-third of all the monies spent by Medicare are in some way related to diabetes.[12] If Stakeholders do not focus on treating diabetes, America's health deterioration will continue. In The New Health Age, prevention will become the focus, and we will reverse the downward trend. Studies show that if Americans were simply 5 to 10 percent thinner and walked only 30 minutes a day, the incidence of type 2 diabetes could be slashed by more than one-half.[13] This could potentially save America $87 billion.

This new flow toward preventing diseases in The New Health Age will foster and encourage lifestyle changes for Stakeholders at risk for diabetes. Stakeholders, including employer and government health plans and health care providers, will develop targeted programs to help people effectively make life choices to avoid diabetes. Prevention will reign over merely treating the disease.[14] Again, health, happiness, productivity, and longevity will increase with this "ounce of prevention."

In the United States, 38.4 million people suffer from asthma, and these numbers are growing, especially in children.[15] Asthma accounts for over 2 million emergency room visits, 500,000 hospital stays, and an estimated 5,000 deaths each year.[16] When a patient suffers from an asthma attack, an emergency room visit can cost on average $2,000 to $4,000.[17] Subsequent hospitalization of the asthma patient can cost an additional $10,000 to $40,000 or more.[18]

Compare those treatment costs to the average cost of prevention, which might be $100 for a doctor visit and another $200 plus or minus for an inhaler as a prevention device.[19] We can prevent the acute episode from occurring in many cases by spending $300 compared to spending upward of $44,000 on treatment during a crisis. Asthma sufferers also miss school and work. In 2003, asthmatic children lost more than 14 million days of school and asthmatic adults missed almost 12 million days of work.[20] Calculate the math on the economic impact of those lost-productivity days.

Stakeholders will witness tremendous decreases in absenteeism as prevention infiltrates our society and culture in The New Health Age. Clearly, preventing chronic asthma versus treating acute asthmatic situations will save us money and lead to higher quality lives.

High blood pressure increases an American's risk of experiencing a heart attack by 69 percent and a stroke by 77 percent.[21] Controlling high blood pressure reduces those percentages by 50 percent. Preventing heart attacks and strokes not only saves lives but substantial dollars as well.[22]

The Department of Health and Human Services (DHHS) announced on April 12, 2011, a new "Partnership for Patients" initiative that brings together the government with hospitals, employers, health plans, physicians, nurses, and patient advocates to improve care and lower health care costs. DHHS predicts that the Partnership will help save 60,000 lives by stopping millions of preventable injuries and complications in patient care over the next three years and has the potential to save up to $35 billion in health care costs, including up to $10 billion for Medicare alone. According to DHHS, more than 500 hospitals, as well as physicians and nurses groups, consumer groups, and employers have pledged their commitment to the new initiative. To launch the Partnership, DHHS announced that it would invest up to $1 billion in federal funding made available under PPACA's recent health care reform laws.[23]

These are but a few examples of how focusing on prevention will yield tremendous benefits to health care and why this dynamic flow change will have a great impact in the future for all American Stakeholders.

Health Care Delivery Models Will Be Progressive in the Future

Today, many urgent care centers, emergency rooms, hospitals, medical clinics, physicians, and other traditional health care delivery institutions are narrowly focused on treatment. Tomorrow, these establishments will let go of the historic traditions of yesterday and work to liberate the health care delivery system to bring about a fundamental shift toward wellness and prevention.

New organizations of a different genre will emerge, with a focus on preventing illness and disease. As shown already, significant data support the fact that the cost of preventing disease and illness is less than the cost of treating these ailments.

It will be the Stakeholders currently paying for health care services that will ultimately drive this unified movement toward prevention in the future because prevention will save these Stakeholders literally billions of dollars and will improve the health and happiness of Americans.

Here is an introduction to a few examples of new delivery models that will come about. We will discuss each of these fully in Chapter 14, "The New Structures of Health Care."

Medical Homes

The "medical home model" has existed for years without getting much attention but will finally become a reality in The New Health Age. The model will be an integral component of preventing many illnesses and diseases. We discuss this valuable concept here because the model will be critical to the prevention flow. The notion of a medical home is confusing to some. Medical homes are not physical structures. Medical homes are not "nursing homes." The medical home model is a philosophy about how to deliver health care more effectively. Medical home models transcend the limitations of any physical office or infrastructure.

Physicians lead medical homes and create a symbiotic and balanced relationship among the entire patient care team, the patient, and the family. Medical homes will function as the center and catalyst for community-based collaborative care networks, which will expand people's access to primary care and general health care services.

To physicians who currently fear that their role in health care will somehow diminish in the future, review the prior paragraph a second time. "Medical homes will be led by physicians." What will be different, however, is that physicians will perform more coordination of care versus delivering care personally, and physicians will rely more on other professionals to step in and assist where appropriate.

The model facilitates collaborative and shared decision making among patients, physicians, and other caregivers by increasing and enhancing communication. Medical homes will emphasize the incorporation of patients' preferences and values into their medical plan, with a focus on using educational tools or decision aids to help patients and their representatives understand treatment options and communicate their beliefs as to which care is best for their particular case.

Through interacting with patients in a proactive manner, medical homes will drive patients to comply with their treatment plans through medication monitoring initiatives, therapy compliance plans, diet, and so forth. Physicians and other caregivers working in medical home models will concentrate on identifying patient health trends, such as changes in blood pressure, fever, or blood counts, so that the care delivery team can address any material variation in a patient's health sooner as opposed to being reactionary—true prevention.

In 2007, various leading primary care physician organizations in the United States, including the American Academy of Family Physicians, the American Academy of Pediatrics, the American College of Physicians, and the American Osteopathic Association, issued the Joint Principles of the Patient-Centered Medical Home. It sets forth the following principles:

- Each patient has an ongoing relationship with a personal physician trained to provide first contact, continuous, and comprehensive care.
- The personal physician leads a team of individuals at the practice level who collectively take responsibility for the ongoing care of patients.
- The personal physician is responsible for providing for all the patient's health care needs or taking responsibility for appropriately arranging care with other qualified professionals.

- Care is coordinated and/or integrated between primary care physicians, specialists, hospitals, home health agencies, and post-acute care providers, such as hospice and nursing homes.

- Quality medicine and patient safety are promoted through the care-planning process, including adopting (1) evidence-based medicine, (2) various clinical decision-support tools, (3) performance measurement, (4) patient participation in decision making, and (5) information technology.

- Access to care will be expanded and enhanced, including open scheduling, expanded hours, and new instruments for communication utilizing technology.

- Payment for services must "appropriately recognize the added value provided to patients who have a patient-centered medical home." For instance, payment should reflect the value of "work that falls outside of the face-to-face visit," "support adoption and use of health information technology for quality improvement," and "recognize case mix differences in the patient population being treated within the practice."[24]

Patient centered physicians, employers through their health plans, and government payers, such as Medicare and Medicaid, will be the Stakeholders ultimately driving and promoting the growth of medical home models. These Stakeholders will embrace medical homes and use them as a key instrument to move America toward positive lifestyle choices, leading to wellness and prevention, versus focusing narrowly on sickness and treatment.

Employer Health Plans and Employer Accountable Care Organizations

Recall from Chapter 4 that with the average cost moving upward of $10,000 per employee for employer-sponsored health insurance, American companies can no longer sit idle on the sidelines while their employees' state of health deteriorates in this great country.[25] The health issues crippling American workers, as outlined so far in this book, are expensive, debilitating, and stunning to say the least. Employer and employee Stakeholders must immediately grapple with their response.

As discussed in the prior chapter, successful employer health plans will offer health and lifestyle management, prevention initiatives, and wellness programs. Whether employers contract directly with outside health care providers for managing new corporate medical home-based programs or hire medical home physicians directly through employment models, corporate America, not the government, will be a driving force toward employee disease prevention initiatives. This will be free enterprise, without any government intervention, working at its best toward the endgame of making American businesses stronger and more competitive.

Employers will reward their medical home providers and employees for improved employee health status and good health care outcomes. We stated earlier that the brand name for this exciting new model is EACOs, which stands for Employer Accountable Care Organizations. EACOs will incorporate medical and disease management and offer employee assistance and behavioral health programs, including smoking cessation plans, pharmacy advocacy, diabetes care management, nutritional programs, weight management, and fitness education to employees.

A new era of good health is coming to employer health plans through EACOs. EACOs, incorporating medical homes into their models, will offer the right incentives to employees and health care providers to drive accountability across the spectrum of these Stakeholders, thus bringing about the flow toward prevention and reducing costs.

The significant beneficial economic components of EACOs will be discussed in Chapter 12, "The Dynamic Flows in the Economics of Health Care," and in subsequent chapters.

Prevention

Imagine the benefits that humans can derive from living out healthier lives. In the rest of our world, we live by the rule of prevention. We know that if we take our cars to the mechanic for regular maintenance, we decrease the need for major repairs later. Entrepreneurs have created an entire industry around drive-up oil and car filter change stations, and most American car drivers know that they should replace their oil every 3,000 to 5,000 miles.

We know that good preventive maintenance will keep our automobile maintenance costs down and increase the number of years that we can drive a car. Why would we treat our cars better than we treat our own bodies? We can buy another car, but our bodies—not yet.

In The New Health Age prevention will become the new norm and treatment will no longer be the full definition of health care as it is today. In fact, treatment will, in many cases, be seen as the failure of the health care system and the people within it. The time will come when days or even hours in a hospital will be viewed as a circumstance when the system failed in one form or another. Although a profound statement, that day is indeed coming.

So, as America sheds pounds as a result of our flow toward wellness, we also pick up valuable "pounds of cure" through the prevention flow.

2. Reactive → Proactive

This dynamic flow is closely tied to the prevention flow, but it has its distinctions. Treatment is reactive; prevention is proactive. Going on a diet is a reaction to being overweight. Eating a healthy diet and exercising regularly is a proactive way to prevent becoming overweight. Spending $25 dollars on a flu shot is proactive. Avoiding the shot and later suffering from a longer bout of the flu, which costs more for treatment and incurs additional lost productivity, is reactive.

In the United States, we have largely viewed medicine as being reactive to a condition or ailment. We wait until we are sick, overweight, depressed, or have some other preventable condition before we seek medical advice. We are a very reactive society and culture, because that is how Americans have been conditioned. We think of medicine largely as treatment, as discussed in the earlier flow. In The New Health Age, we will look at medicine as a force to create a proactive approach toward obtaining and maintaining better health. We will be healthier and happier people, while simultaneously lowering health care costs.

The following are several illustrations of changes that will occur within health care delivery systems as proaction replaces reaction.

The New Health Age Will Bring about a Focus on Patient Risk Stratification

Approaching health care proactively requires identifying and stratifying patient Stakeholders who are at the highest risk to developing chronic disease. Once identified, health care providers and payer Stakeholders can better control or eliminate the risk for developing these costly diseases. Doing so will lower costs and foster better quality lives.

Information technology tools in The New Health Age will be used to identify patients who are at high risk for developing chronic disease. For example, advanced analytics software programs will examine employee health claims data and process data that employees provide to EACOs through health risk assessments (HRAs). Employees will complete HRAs online. EACOs will also incorporate health information gained through employee diagnostic testing, including genetic testing, into the employees' HRAs. These advanced and powerful software analytics programs will then be able to produce meaningful health scores and place employees on a predicted risk stratification scale for developing certain diseases. This same approach will work with patients under government welfare programs, too, such as Medicare and Medicaid.

After discovering where certain patients or employees fall on the risk stratification metric, medical homes will develop more effective intervention and preventative actions utilizing evidence-based medicine and clinical pathways models. Patients who are at high risk for developing breast cancer, for example, will likely participate in programs that increase the number and quality of mammograms. Perhaps they will be placed on diets that are proven to reduce breast cancer. This will be another example of how patients will enjoy more personalized medicine in The New Health Age. Pharmacists will tailor medicine to individuals based on their medical history, genetic makeup, and other factors.

Other applications for risk stratification include identifying patients who are at high risk for hospitalization or readmission to a hospital following an acute episode, such as a heart attack. Using heart failure as an example, health care providers will follow certain guidelines following a heart attack to better monitor and control these patients, thus reducing hospital readmission rates.

The primary goal of risk stratification and disease management is to bend the spending curve in health care and improve people's quality of life. The overarching mind-set in health care will migrate toward providing proactive health care versus responding to acute situations. Wellness care will replace much of what exists today, which is a system that is focused on treating chronic health care conditions.

High-Risk Clinics

Once new information technology tools and systems develop in the coming New Health Age to help identify individuals who are at greater risk for disease or illness, high-risk medical homes will emerge. These clinics will focus on targeted populations, such as patients who are post-acute, chronically ill, or who have had multiple hospital admissions in one year. High-risk clinics and medical homes will incorporate proactive medical models to prevent acute and high dollar episodes from occurring among high-risk patients.

Patients with chronic diseases will be closely monitored and treated, to better control their illness or disease. Diabetics, heart failure patients, asthmatics, and the clinically depressed, to name a few, will receive special attention. Medical homes will implement proactive care plans focused on monitoring and controlling the health of geriatric patients as a high-risk group. Geriatric patients will receive more comprehensive evaluations to determine high-risk areas and health conditions. Older patients will be given tools to assist them with advanced care planning, prior to the development of an acute situation. Health care providers will work with individuals and their families to assess when life-saving treatments are desired and when they are not. Medical decision makers in the absence of a patient will be identified so that people's preferences and wishes toward the end of life can be fulfilled.

Health care providers will incorporate behavioral health assessments into treatment models so that care plans can maximize patient compliance, such as implementing medication reminders. The day will come when patients receive e-mails related to their personalized treatment plans. As highlighted earlier, diabetics will receive an e-mail or phone call if they forget to refill insulin prescriptions. EACOs will be notified as well, so that employee case managers can communicate with employees to determine the reason for an employee's noncompliance.

High-risk medical homes will offer disease education and connect community health resources with high-risk patients. Diabetics will link with dieticians. Heart disease patients will connect with fitness centers. Community educational programs will take place, and so on.

New regionalized systems for delivering emergency and trauma care will emerge.[26] In an emergency health crisis, the time between the occurrence of the event and receiving care becomes the enemy. For every minute that a patient goes without care after suffering a stroke, the chance of a full recovery declines. Cardiac arrest can be reversed if it is treated within a few minutes.[27] Health care delivery systems will develop new and more powerful models that fight against this time-enemy.

More trauma centers will open near higher density population centers. When a trauma patient receives proactive, fast, focused, and specialized care soon after the event occurs, the patient's chance to improve increases, thus saving health care costs and improving recovery rates.

Retail-style urgent care centers (UCCs), open 24/7, will continue to expand. UCCs will be strategically located away from hospital campuses and will be positioned within communities to provide convenient access to mid- and low-level emergency care providers. The goal of UCCs is to be proactive and treat minor emergencies faster and cheaper than hospital emergency rooms. UCCs will be better suited for treating flu; minor broken bones, burns, and cuts; and less acute injuries.

By focusing on improving care to high-risk patients, the resulting benefits will be substantial on both the cost and the delivery side of health care.

Hospitals

Even though hospital care by its nature is generally reactive versus proactive, numerous proactive systems and developments will emerge within hospitals throughout The New Health Age. As discussed in the next chapter, hospitals will increasingly receive more and more payment incentives to reduce patient length of stay and to improve quality outcomes. Hospitals will naturally have a driving motivation to move toward being proactive and less reactive. The following are a few cutting-edge examples.

Physicians known as "hospitalists" will continue to expand their roles within hospitals and will become a critical element to the prevention and proactive health care flows. Hospitalists will be dedicated to treating hospitalized patients and working with the patients' care team to manage all aspects of health care within a hospital and to better transition care at discharge. In 2007, approximately 20,000 physicians in America were hospitalists. That number will continue to grow over the next decade.[28]

Primary care physicians and specialists cannot reside within a hospital at all times. Once a patient is stabilized, the patient may remain in a hospital for several days, but 24/7 physician care is seldom needed. However, a patient's attending physician needs to stay abreast of a patient's condition and rate of recovery, which is what led to the practice of "physician rounding." Most physicians round in the early morning and in the evening, before or after office hours.

Being disconnected from a hospital makes providing physician care more challenging. Hospitalists, focused and located at the hospital at all times, can better coordinate with a patient's care team, enabling hospital care to be provided in a more effective and timely manner. Because hospitalists are focused on maximizing quality care within the hospital, hospitalists will reduce unnecessary admissions and readmissions, decrease average length of stay, assist with emergency room intervention and triage, and enhance education and communication among patients, families, and clinical care teams.[29] The primary goal for hospitalists in The New Health Age will be to provide proactive patient care, laser focused on hospital patients who are in higher risk situations.

Hospitals will utilize newly developed advanced medical equipment and technology, better enabling physicians and hospital staff to provide proactive care to prevent unnecessary complications, thus improving hospital care and outcomes. For instance, newborn beds will be equipped with special tools to resuscitate babies in emergencies so that clinicians do not have to waste precious seconds wheeling in rescue carts and equipment in pediatric emergency situations.

Emergency alerts in hospital room systems will no longer require a patient to hit a button or pull a string. Bracelets, necklaces, and other devices will contain self-activating features that sense when a person falls or if vital signs drop, alerting the nurses' station automatically.

Body sensors and high-definition video cameras in hospital rooms will connect physicians and nurses to their patients instantaneously, regardless of where the caregiver may be physically located. A physician can be at his medical office seeing patients and immediately connect to a hospitalized patient's room to monitor the patient's progress and to check for potential complications. Physicians will be able to see and interact with their patients through video conferencing and have vital health information on the computer screen simultaneously, enabling the attending doctor to make more informed and faster clinical decisions. This technology—known as telehealth—will also enable rural hospitals to connect with metropolitan health systems and highly specialized physicians in patient crisis situations, such as stroke, heart attack, and traumatic injury.

Today, the CDC estimates that 1 out of every 20 patients acquires an infection while in the hospital, at a human cost of 99,000 deaths a year and an economic cost of between $28 billion to $34 billion a year.[30] Hospitals will increasingly implement more proactive and preventative measures to reduce hospital infection rates. Not doing so will put them at huge financial risk.

One example includes the use of new privacy curtain systems in emergency rooms and operating rooms that change out, similar to automated paper towel machines, to ensure that bacteria do not remain within fabrics. Today, studies show that health care workers wear gloves only 82 percent of the time when necessary to prevent germ transfer, don gowns only 77 percent of the time, and wash their hands only 69 percent of the time.[31] In the future, hospitals will focus more and more on preventative measures that will increase hospital staff compliance rates to avoid infections.

The Department of Veterans Affairs reported a 62 percent decline in VA hospital intensive care unit infection rates over a 32-month period simply because the VA focused on measures that targeted infection control, such as screening patients for infections at admission and requiring more use of gloves and gowns by hospital staff.[32] Increasing the frequency that workers washed their hands was also a part of the VA's successful initiative.[33]

These advances are only a few examples demonstrating how proactive approaches to hospital care will expand in the future because of this flow change.

Home Health Care

As discussed in other chapters, patients must avoid hospital care altogether or be discharged from hospital care as quickly as possible, because receiving health care within a hospital setting is one of the most expensive options available. In The New Health Age, the home health care model will play a crucial part in providing stepped-down care for patients who need more focused health attention but do not require hospitalization.

Providing care in one's home, by its very nature, will save money. Home health care companies incur minimal facility costs because the patient owns the physical structure where caregivers provide the service. Imagine that. You operate a home health business and require few physical locations.

The Florida Trend reported in March 2011 that Florida's Medicaid program would save an average of $60,000 annually per person if these patients were transitioned out of nursing homes and into home care, if clinically appropriate.[34] With Florida's Medicaid spending up by 36.4 percent in just the last three years, Florida's governor and legislature are examining many new alternative models to control state spending, home health care being one of them.[35]

On the delivery side, home health care providers will focus on taking proactive measures with patients to better monitor and improve their health. Home health care will continue to grow rapidly in The New Health Age, as preventative and proactive medicine expands. Caregivers in the home, both family and health care workers, are in the best position to serve as the patient's daily "eyes and ears." When patient symptoms and conditions change, being proactive with early intervention is critical and saves downstream costs by avoiding costly acute episodes and treatments.

Consider the costs of post-surgery infections. If a home health care provider spots a fever and delivers an antibiotic early in the progression of the infection, the patient's recovery occurs faster, complications are likely avoided, and the system saves health care costs as a result.

Home health caregivers can easily focus on a patient's personal goals, living conditions, social and financial needs, and foster quality-of-life discussions with patients and family members.

Each of these factors can and should be incorporated into treatment plans, so that care can become more personalized in a home environment. Focused care, tailored on a patient's individual needs at home, will result in more cost-effective care and produce better outcomes.

Telehealth—remote patient monitoring and mobile health devices—will explode in the home health care market. Home monitoring devices have become more sophisticated, providing physicians and other caregivers across the continuum with additional and enhanced information in a timely manner so that they can be proactive with their treatment regimen. The healthier a patient remains at home, the more likely he or she is to avoid costly facility-based care, such as hospitals, assisted living, or rehabilitation centers.

Telehealth devices will range from widely used technologies, such as glucose monitors for diabetics, to advanced telemonitoring equipment that allows nurses and doctors to electronically gather and transmit daily information regarding a patient's weight, blood pressure, oxygen saturation, wound healing, heart conditions, and lung function. Telehealth will help physicians and other caregivers spot subtle changes early, enabling nurses to transmit that information to physicians quickly. When necessary, physicians can intervene before complications turn more serious. Smart medicine bottles will transmit alerts electronically to nurses and case managers when medications run out and patients fail to refill their needed prescriptions.

As the average age in America increases with the Baby Boomers moving into their senior years, people will wish to age independently at home for as long as possible. Home care advances and emerging technology will enable this to occur in The New Health Age. Telehealth devices in the home will enable an 80-year-old to receive medication reminders straight to a beeping wristband. A 75-year-old with a new hip will have body sensors to track his movement patterns. If a patient's mobility worsens post-surgery, physicians and other caregivers will be notified quickly so that they can intervene to avoid more serious complications, such as infection or device failure.

Live, interactive videoconferencing technology, so common in the non-health-care part of our society, will be of great value, at little cost, to home health and elsewhere across health care. How much less would it cost to have a daily video Skype interaction between a doctor and patient than to have the patient drive to the doctor's office, leaving work or family? Millions of us do this every day as a way to stay in touch and keep the costs down in other aspects of life. Why not in health care?

These technologies will have wide application within home health, physician offices, hospitals, skilled nursing facilities, hospice houses, and other facilities, promoting better care with fewer human resources.

In The New Health Age, reactive health care transitions to proactive health care. This shift will be profound and empower patients and health care providers to gain more control over health to improve quality and outcomes, while reducing costs in the process.

3. Episodic → Wholistic

Much of health care today occurs in episodes. When you get sick, you go to the doctor for treatment. When you are injured, you go to the emergency room. When you get a disease, you seek a cure. We think about health care episodically and the system itself functions as such. Americans rarely associate their daily lifestyle choices to their long-term overall health. We do not think expansively or connect the dots between diet and nutrition and heart disease. Health care tomorrow will become wholistic, both in thinking and in delivery. Let's explore what all this means for the future of health care.

We Will Think About Health Care Wholistically

In The New Health Age, Stakeholders will think about health and how to deliver health care in a macro versus a micro sense. People's genetics, environment, and lifestyle all combine and affect our health, and each aspect of a person's condition will be considered within the health care system. Health care delivery will incorporate all of the necessary component parts and people needed to provide comprehensive care, wholistically. Identified leaders in health care will be managing it all, such as a primary care physician operating a medical home oriented practice, as just one example.

Health and health care will be seen and lived as a life experience, not in episodes or segments as it is today. Long-term wellness, prevention, and medical treatments will become part of our everyday life.

Physicians who view patients wholistically and deliver corresponding care as such, will emerge in the coming years as the leaders in medicine. In The New Health Age, primary care physicians, through the medical home model, will be empowered and rewarded to manage the complete health care of their patients. Physician specialists will continue to be an important part of the patient care team, but they will be viewed as supportive partners rather than the ones "in charge." America will need more internal medicine and family practice physicians going forward. Physician extenders, such as nurse practitioners and physician assistants, will also contribute to this coordination effort.

Physicians will be paid in The New Health Age for preventing chronic disease. An example of how wholistic medicine will operate in the future includes physicians collaborating with diet and nutritional counselors to promote healthier eating within patient populations to reduce their heart disease rates. Orthopedic physicians will partner with massage therapists and incorporate massage therapy into a preventative aspect of their specialty practice. All of this wholistic delivery of medicine and more is coming, if not already occurring within pockets of health care.

If you are not familiar with Planetree Hospitals and affiliated health centers, we suggest that you learn more about the model to prepare for The New Health Age. More hospitals will be adopting

Planetree systems or similar philosophies.[36] Planetree founder Angelica Thieriot, while fighting a rare virus in the hospital, became disenfranchised with traditional Industrial Age hospital care after staring at the cold, blank walls of her hospital room for days. She was disheartened to find a lack of personalized care in the midst of her hospital's high-tech environment. After recovering, she created a unique type of hospital where patients could receive care in a patient-centered, healing environment. Planetree Hospitals move away from the institutional hospital stereotype and engage with patients to become active participants in their own care and well-being.

The name *Planetree* was taken from the tree that Hippocrates sat under as he taught some of the earliest medical students in ancient Greece. Planetree is an internationally recognized new leader in patient-centered care, with facilities ranging from small rural hospitals with 25 beds to large urban medical centers with over 2,000 beds. The organization has received recognition in numerous publications, including the *New York Times*, *JAMA*, *Prevention*, *Healthcare Forum Journal*, *Hospital & Health Networks*, *Nursing Times*, the *Quality Letter for Healthcare Leaders*, *Health Facilities Management*, and *Newsweek Japan*.[37]

The faith-based Bon Secours Health System, led by CEO Peter Bernard, builds hospitals with light-filled lobbies, waterfalls, chapels, and meditation gardens that are designed to incorporate hospitality strategies gleaned from the likes of The Walt Disney Company and The Ritz-Carlton Hotels.[38] Bernard rightly concludes that Americans will soon begin to demand better access, greater convenience, and top clinical results from their hospitals, so he is building and operating Bon Secours' facilities with the future in mind.[39]

We Will Deliver Health Care Wholistically

Health care providers today typically function in separate silos while their patients move throughout the health care system across a continuum of care events. Patients encounter a specific health episode with one provider and then move to the next provider, often without effective coordination or transition of care along the way. The process and each event are episodic and isolated in nature. Rarely is one physician or other caregiver "in charge" and coordinating all the care wholistically.

A patient may be experiencing abdominal pain, so she visits her primary care physician. The primary care physician refers the patient across town to see a gastroenterologist. The gastroenterologist orders diagnostics tests and refers the patient to another location with a diagnostic imaging center and blood lab. Each component part of this experience is episodic, without a wholistic sense of cohesion or collaboration.

In large part because medical records remain paper-based, many physicians and other types of health care providers are usually segregated and isolated from each other when they make clinical decisions. Many physicians do not practice in large medical groups, so they cannot easily walk down the hall to collaborate with a colleague regarding a treatment issue. Few physicians and health care systems have implemented technology such as videoconferencing to support communicating remotely because no incentive for doing so has existed in the past. Such a disconnect leads to physicians making many clinical decisions in a vacuum, versus reaching decisions with a broader and cohesive perspective. Health care efforts are often duplicated inadvertently, leading to increased expense and patient inconvenience, because one caregiver is unaware of another caregiver's treatments or the diagnostics performed. Through no fault of their own, physicians and other health care providers often lack the tools and technology required to give them the "whole picture" surrounding a patient's condition.

In The New Health Age, health care providers will utilize twenty-first century technology to better coordinate care wholistically. Clinicians will possess, at the touch of a button, complete patient information for better treatment and decision making through electronic health and medical records (EMR). A patient's EMR will play a much broader role than simply serving as electronic storage space. EMRs will be dynamic and changing as clinical care teams from across the patient's health care experience access a patient's health record and interact with it, giving providers a complete and up-to-date picture of a person's health status.

In the wholistic era of medicine, patients will be transported to a hospital emergency room by ambulance for chest pain. The emergency room team will conduct a diagnostic imaging test, and the cardiologist located across the hospital campus will have instant access to the patient's heart images via a handheld tablet computer. Results from tests that may have been performed on the patient a few days earlier across the country at another health care facility will be immediately accessible and will provide the treating physician and care team with the patient's complete health picture.

Through tablets and online EMR systems, the care team will gather and analyze the patient's entire medical history and use this valuable information to develop an immediate treatment plan. When the patient's primary care physician receives an e-mail on her smartphone notifying her that the patient has been admitted to the hospital, she can instantly access the patient's progress report and provide meaningful contributions to the hospital care team's plans. The primary care doctor may have years of relevant medical history and perspectives related to the patient that a cardiologist should be aware of during an acute episode.

Recall the neurosphere concept from Chapter 6. The new neurosphere electronic place will create a "global information village" with comprehensive and interconnected health information available to health care providers in a millisecond. Increased information when and where it is needed the most will enhance and improve health care delivery in countless ways.

The overarching flow of this experience in The New Health Age will be wholistic. Gone will be the days when emergency room physicians and cardiologists were forced to make instant medical decisions "in the moment," without possessing all of the patient's medical information required to make fully informed decisions.

In The New Health Age, Wholistic Models and Structures Will Grow and Expand to Support End-of-Life Care

As futurists, we can make one prediction with 100 percent total accuracy: we are all going to die, someday. In The New Health Age, health care providers will continue with their mission of preserving and prolonging meaningful life, but health care providers and society as a whole will confront the *degree of care* that is actually needed to extend quality of life *relative to the cost*.

The discussion and debate surrounding end-of-life care will not be an easy one to have, because humans possess an innate desire to live and prolong life at any cost. The medical profession strives to do everything possible to cure the patient. Although the average age of Americans will increase because of the medical breakthroughs discussed in Chapter 7, humans cannot evade death, and questions must be asked about when "enough is enough" toward the final days of life.

Consider the following data related to spending on end-of-life care:

- Nearly one-third of terminally ill patients with insurance use up most or all of their savings to cover uninsured medical expenses such as home care.[40]
- Forty percent of Medicare dollars cover care for people in the last month of their life.[41]
- In 2009, Medicare paid an estimated $55 billion just for hospital and doctor charges during the last two months of patients' lives. This amount of spending is nearly equal to the annual budget for the federal Department of Homeland Security.[42]

Data related to spending on end-of-life care must be examined in relation to the value that patients receive for such cost. A reported 75 percent of Americans die in a nursing home or hospital, yet a vast majority of Americans express that they would prefer to die at home.[43]

Dr. Elliott Fisher, a researcher at the Dartmouth Institute for Health Policy, analyzed Medicare records for patients in the last two years of their lives and reports that more patients die within institutions not because they must but because it is easier and more efficient for physicians and other caregivers to manage patients who are seriously ill in a hospital situation. Dr. Fisher also questions whether the expensive care that patients receive during their final days of life actually enhances a patient's quality of life.[44]

According to Dr. Fisher, up to 30 percent of hospital stays in the United States are probably unnecessary. After end-of-life patients are admitted to a hospital, Fisher states that they are treated by numerous specialists who conduct a variety of expensive tests and utilize tools available to them with modern medicine to maintain people on the cusp of life for days, weeks, even months, but at what quality of life?[45]

Various studies have concluded that many patients and their families are not aware of end-of-life options or the importance of living wills, hospice programs, or palliative care, which includes pain management options.[46] In The New Health Age, Americans will become more aware of the emotional and economic price surrounding the dying process and Americans will confront what is the appropriate and humane course of treatment during one's final days of life.

In Chapter 4, we cited numerous instances where we consume health care service without appreciating the relative costs. In fact, the former head of the federal General Accounting Office (GAO), David Walker, reports that 85 percent of health care is paid by either the government or private insurance, leading to a disconnect between the consumer and the payer of health care services. Nowhere within health care is this disconnection more pronounced than during the dying process.[47]

During The New Health Age, new models will emerge to help us cope with the social and economic issues surrounding dying. Hospice and palliative caregivers will pilot American health care through this innovative and transformative period. Hospice physicians and other medical professionals have spent decades developing caring and suitable treatments for their patients. Hospice focuses on giving treatments and care that is appropriate during each phase of the dying process. The hospice philosophy incorporates these ideals with the patient and family to enable joint decisions to be made regarding when it is best for the patient to be allowed to die naturally and peacefully.

Our approach to dying will be viewed from a wholistic perspective in The New Health Age. Too many people today resist hospice care until their final few days, if not hours of life, even though many payers, including Medicare, cover hospice care for up to 6 months. Society, physicians, and other caregivers often view entering hospice care as "giving up on life" versus extending life through a wholistic process that is focused on end-of-life treatment.

Studies show that patients actually extend their life by an average of 2.7 months if they enter a hospice program early enough.[48] Hospice specializes in end-of-life care and focuses on treating dying patients in a manner that enables patients to maintain quality of life throughout the dying experience.

All of us will die. The question that is often ignored today but that will be asked tomorrow is when do patients, families, physicians, and other caregivers acknowledge death and seek out a hospice treatment plan that enables patients to die compassionately, without spending resources needlessly for no quality of life? As America confronts these realities, hospice institutions will expand going forward and will become increasingly valuable providers in The New Health Age.

The three dynamic flows of change in how we will DELIVER health care in The New Health Age are

Treatment → Prevention

Reactive → Proactive

Episodic → Wholistic

1. "An ounce of prevention is worth a pound of cure."

2. Progressive and proactive health care delivery models, such as medical homes and accountable care organizations, which are designed around prevention and wellness will evolve in the future.

3. Health care delivery systems will design and implement proactive initiatives in order to increase health care quality and to reduce costs.

4. The practice of medicine and delivery of health care will become wholistic.

5. In The New Health Age, wholistic models will expand and support end-of-life care.

‹ CHANGE VISION ›

David Steinman is a business strategist, an attorney, and a health care management consultant with over 30 years of experience in the public and private sectors. He has held a variety of line, staff, and consultative positions, including Vice President and Senior Vice President positions at three Fortune 500 companies: IBM, Computer Sciences Corporation, and Ceridian. He is currently working as a Director at Navigant Consulting, where he focuses primarily on physician-hospital integration transactions. During his career David has designed, developed and implemented strategic programs to dramatically improve client performance through joint ventures, human resources benefits and administration, technology, and outsourcing. His clients have ranged from the Ohio Bureau of Workers Compensation and the Cleveland Transit Authority to numerous health care payer and provider organizations. He is a graduate of Hofstra School of Law and graduated first in his MBA class at the Johnson Graduate School of Management at Cornell.

The Market of One:
Delivering Value One Person at a Time

By David Steinman

In the last decade, new technologies have transformed our ability to tailor individual products and services to better meet consumer needs and preferences. We are coming to expect "mass customization" as a routine part of American consumerism. Information gathered from and about each of us is being used by businesses to identify our tastes and target our personal requirements. We are seeing the "mass market" which drove (and was driven by) the production line in the Industrial Age being replaced by technology-enabled economies of individualization and giving way to "the Market of One." Americans are already conditioned to expect our financial products, our clothing, and our personally designed homepages (on social networking and other websites) to be structured to meet our individual preferences and interests.

Over the next 10 years, we will see individualization extend to every aspect of health care, from prevention to intervention, from clinical to financial, from the mediums through which we send information to our service providers, to the modalities in which we receive services and support. The transformation from today's fragmented, provider-centric delivery system to tomorrow's integrated, consumer-centric support and service systems, will fundamentally change the roles, goals, and values of American health care.

We are at the very beginning of this exciting change. New and emerging technologies are being introduced to improve the quality of both health care resources and the patient/provider interactions that shape patient satisfaction. For example, the government (along with private health insurers) and health care providers (doctors and hospitals) are investing enormous time and resources in the creation and adoption of information technology tools, particularly Electronic Medical Records (EMRs). While the primary objective of investments in EMRs is to reduce unwarranted duplication and variation in treatments, which can lead to adverse outcomes and avoidable costs, there is an even greater potential for improving the effectiveness of clinical interventions by scientifically customizing them based on our individual biochemistries and genetic compositions.

For years, doctors have wondered why certain treatments, both pharmaceutical and other interventions, are highly effective for some patients, less so for others, and completely ineffective or even counterproductive for yet other patients. Genetic science is providing critical tools for understanding those individual differences and matching treatments to particular conditions, and to specific patients suffering from those particular conditions. In the coming years, genetic testing and profiling will become routine components of an individual's health record. These profiles will guide the selection of the treatment(s) best suited to the particular patient presenting the specific conditions.

The completion of the mapping of the human genome in 2003 has provided both genetic information and scientific processes which allow us to match and/or design pharmaceutical and other treatments to our unique individual compositions and conditions. This customization of treatments promises to both increase the success of interventions while dramatically reducing the frequency of adverse drug reactions which researchers estimate to account for millions of incidents and approximately 100,000 fatalities per year in American hospitals alone.[49,50]

While the most frequently touted example of the new capabilities flowing from the Human Genome Project is the creation of individually tailored "designer pharmaceuticals" that particular capability may remain one of the most economically elusive benefits to capture on a grand scale. As the industry continues to advance the research and production methodologies required to make these customized pharmaceuticals affordable to the population as a whole, other applications of genomic research are already delivering benefits to large patient populations. For example, the use of genetic markers to identify which existing treatments are most likely to have a positive impact on an individual patient, or which treatments are most likely to trigger adverse reactions on a particular patient's biochemistry, is already impacting treatment selection. This is particularly true of cancer treatments, where genetic indicators are already becoming a major consideration in treatment selection.

Other areas of particular focus for genomic research include heart disease, diabetes, and kidney disease. Over the next 10 years this research is likely to transform how medical science is used to identify "at-risk populations," improve the targeting and impact of preventative measures, produce different categories of both interventions and maintenance drugs tailored to different genetic predispositions, and reduce or eradicate medical errors.

Clinical customization or personalized medicine may be the most dramatic application of individualization in health care, but it is far from the only application. In the area of health care finance, "customer-driven health care" is creating a Market of One generation of insurance products aimed at creating incentives for individuals to take a more active and informed role in health care decision making. Frequently called "high deductible plans", these programs are currently attracting over 10 million consumers, with enrollment growing at approximately 25 percent a year for the past several years.[51] While the pace of growth is likely to slow, these plans are particularly attractive to young, healthy people, providing greater choice and flexibility in how their health care resources are deployed.

Customer-driven plans come in many different shapes and sizes, and may be tailored to fit individual (or individual employer) preferences. Some plans encourage members to utilize prevention services by providing payment on a "pre-deductible" basis. Other plans maintain incentives for the use of "in-network" providers (doctors and hospitals). Virtually all plans include "Health Savings Accounts (HSA)," which allow customers to set aside pretax dollars (usually matched in whole or in part by employer contributions) for use in future years, or even "cashed out" at retirement. While many of these HSAs are very conservatively invested, financial giants like Fidelity and Wells Fargo offer HSA products that allow for investment in stocks and bonds, based on the individual risk preference of the enrollee.

As the market penetration of these insurance products increases, new innovations to address catastrophic care, encourage healthy behaviors and preventive care, and to help individuals make informed decisions about their health and health care choices will need to be routinely designed into the offerings. New professional "guides" or coaches will emerge to help consumers navigate the increasingly complex systems of both delivery and finance, and assist each of us to capture the benefits of innovation and individualization.

Pharmaceuticals and finance are not the only areas where customization is reshaping our health care system. As the unsustainable cost of the American health care system becomes of increasing concern to business leaders, policy makers, and individual consumers, there is growing appreciation that those costs are largely driven by a subset of the population: those suffering from one or more chronic diseases. New and existing technologies (applied in new ways) promise to improve our effectiveness at identifying "at risk" individuals, as well as at managing those conditions to reduce the frequency of the acute episodes that drive the overwhelming majority of the costs associated with those diseases.

As we learn to customize clinical and financing vehicles, we will also learn to customize our support for those suffering from chronic diseases. Recent advances in tools and educational materials to help those suffering from chronic diseases monitor and manage their conditions (like telephone-based devices for monitoring blood pressure, blood sugar, respiration, and other functions) are the leading edge indicators of what will become standard over the next 5 to 10 years. To list just of few things that will become commonplace in the coming Market of One:

1. Telemedicine capabilities connecting individual patients directly and conveniently to physicians and other provider resources with access to global data, without the requirement and attendant expenses of in-person visits and interminable wait times

2. New and different information channels which will allow us access to those resources through whatever modalities best suit our individual needs and preferences

3. Individually designed incentive programs, to motivate compliance with treatment and to lower costs

4. Social networking groups to provide ideas, support, reinforcement for those struggling to maintain or overcome challenging conditions

5. Directories and/or message boards, with information about new programs, clinical trials, patient and/or provider networks in specific geographic regions, relevant to specific clinical conditions

The Market of One will transform the U.S. health care market on all dimensions, dramatically improving the value available to each of us: personalized and convenient delivery of customized products and services, allowing each of us to improve our health while reducing the financial burdens and routine inconvenience of care we currently face in our provider-centric delivery system. And it will do so by extending one of the most time-honored of American traditions: individualism.

The Change in the ECONOMICS of Health Care

*"If you want to teach people a new way of thinking,
don't bother trying to teach them. Instead give them a tool,
the use of which will lead to new ways of thinking."*

—Buckminster Fuller

In the prior two chapters, we looked at the dynamic flows regarding how we think about and deliver health care and medicine in the United States. These discussions greatly affect health care economics because how we think about health care and deliver it has an associated cost.

In this chapter, we look at the three dynamic economic flows of health care. In many ways, understanding these three flows can lead to a general understanding of the coming health care transformation. The reason for this is obvious. The health care debate, the recent passage of PPACA's health care reform laws, and all the calls for change have largely been driven by the increasing cost of health care combined with no parallel increase in health.

The three dynamic flows of the ECONOMICS of health care are

Procedures → Performance
Isolation → Integration
Nonefficient (Passive) → Efficient (Active)

We now look at each one.

1. Procedures → Performance

American Health Care Functions as an Event-based Payment System, Regardless of the Outcome

This flow, in and of itself, will trigger significant change to how medicine is conducted and will have massive impacts on health care expenditures in the United States. Markets and marketplaces have always had economic structures and dynamics that shape the economic activity of those who practice within those markets. The current 20 percent of the United States' GDP that is called health care is no different.

The existing primary economic driver of U.S. medicine is payment based on events, such as doctor exams, procedures, tests, surgeries, therapies, and so forth. Doctors, hospitals, long-term care providers, clinics, and the vast majority of medical institutions are paid today based on one or more of these events.

Today, U.S. health care providers use some 18,000 diagnosis and procedure billing codes, most of which are "event driven."[1] That is generally how Stakeholders in the 20 percent of the American economy are paid—per event. When a person visits the doctor's office because of some health problem, the first thing the doctor does is examine the patient, order tests, or schedule procedures—each one of which costs money. So the health care marketplace functions extremely well based on the underlying construct of an "event results in payment."

The fundamental problem with this marketplace dynamic is that there are few billable codes for obtaining overall and daily good health—the primary purpose of health care. For the most part, a doctor is not paid for healthy patients, the desired outcome of health care. A doctor, hospital, or diagnostic laboratory cannot be paid for a "cure." Think about that for a minute. There are limited economic payments for keeping patients healthy. Most payments are for conducting exams, tests, or procedures on patients. Within the health care delivery marketplace, there is minimal economic motivation for coming up with a cure, because it is not a billable event.

Take this point one step further. When health care providers perform one of these 18,000 procedures and treatments, few payments are tied to outcomes or appropriateness. A cardiologist can place a stent into a heart artery and get paid, but that payment is not adjusted if known, preventable complications follow or no measurable benefits result. An orthopedist can replace a knee and get paid the same amount regardless of whether the knee performs optimally or not post-surgery. A 90-year-old patient may receive the same knee replacement device as a 50-year-old, both costing the same, yet these patients' mobility needs are likely very different.

In most areas of our economic lives, we pay or are paid based on performance and value. In sports, in business, and in service industries, it is the performance that counts. We accept that fact without questioning it. How one performs a job is closely tied to one's compensation. The amount that we pay for a product or service is directly correlated to the value that we expect to receive back—but not necessarily in health care.

Recall the data cited in Chapter 4. The 60-day patient mortality rate following cancer surgery can range from 5.4 percent to 12.3 percent depending on the surgeon providing the care, yet all surgeons get paid the same amount.[2] Some radiologists detect higher percentages of breast cancers on mammograms than their peers, but they all get paid the same.[3] Name one other industry that compensates in such a fashion. As we stated previously, the results and aspects of these studies may be challenged, but the point of raising this information and how it relates to the future of health care delivery remains the same. Not all physicians, hospitals, nurses, hospices, therapists, pharmacists, and other professionals are equal. Some professionals and health care organizations are simply better than others.

In The New Health Age, American health care will move into a payment system that reward health care providers for higher and better performance. Health care practices and thinking will change when payment systems compensate based on a multitude of outcome measures, including the resulting health status of the patient and the procedure's relative cost and value. This new payment approach will change health care delivery to its core, so understanding it, preparing for it, and beginning to participate within it is critical. Fighting against it is futile and counterproductive.

We will now examine the groundbreaking performance-based payment models that are coming in The New Health Age. Preparing for and adapting to these new systems today, will give health care providers a competitive advantage tomorrow.

New Payment Models Will Be "Evolutionary" Not "Revolutionary"

In Chapter 4, we noted that most of health care economics currently revolves around the fee-for-service payment model. In a fee-for-service world, the more services that a health care provider performs or provides, the more revenue that a health care provider receives. In the prior chapter, we presented the episodic to wholistic flow, which has applicability in this chapter too.

Currently, most health care payment systems compensate providers for performing as many episodes of care as possible in a single day. Health care providers are rarely paid based on outcomes, prevention systems, or wellness initiatives. Providers are not paid to prevent the need for further treatment or to prevent people from requiring any treatment to begin with. Have you ever heard of a health plan that actually pays a physician to keep the patients healthy and out of their medical office or hospital? These health plans are coming in The New Health Age. Why? American business is now demanding such plans because business requires healthy and happy employees to compete, expand, and remain profitable. Government entitlement programs, including Medicare and Medicaid, are now demanding such plans because taxpayers are no longer willing to subsidize the current models, with costs going up year after year.

This approach to payment will infiltrate every sector of health care, including doctors, hospitals, long-term care providers, ancillary providers, and others. This principle and approach, however, is not completely new. It is evolutionary but not revolutionary. Examples of this economic structure already exist, yet seem to have gone unnoticed until PPACA and other recent health care reform laws. Let's look back in time for a moment so that some of these new payment changes can be put into perspective.

The hospital diagnostic related group (DRG) payment model is a micro example of where all of health care payment models have been headed for the past several decades, but in small steps. Under the DRG model, hospital patients get classified or grouped based on their diagnosis, which is then matched with an average length of hospital stay and therapies received. The result is used to determine how much money the hospital will be given to cover the inpatient care. The amount paid is generally fixed, based upon the applicable DRG. If a patient's length of stay extends beyond the cap established by the DRG system, the hospital picks up the unreimbursed cost. The hospital, therefore, should be motivated to provide quality care, produce good outcomes, and control a patient's length of stay if the organization wants to operate profitably—a performance based economic driver.

The DRG system, also known as the prospective payment system, came about in the 1980s under the foresight and leadership of the Reagan administration. In 2007, author Rick Mayes looked back and described DRGs historically as

> the single most influential post-war innovation in medical financing…. Inexorably rising medical inflation and

deep economic deterioration forced policymakers in the late 1970s to pursue radical reform of Medicare to keep the program from insolvency. Congress and the Reagan administration eventually turned to the one alternative reimbursement system ... prospective payment with diagnosis-related groups (DRGs). Rather than simply reimbursing hospitals whatever costs they charged to treat Medicare patients, the new model paid hospitals a predetermined, set rate based on the patient's diagnosis. The most significant change in health policy since Medicare and Medicaid's passage in 1965 went virtually unnoticed by the general public. Nevertheless, the change was nothing short of revolutionary. For the first time, the federal government gained the upper hand in its financial relationship with the hospital industry. Medicare's new prospective payment system ... triggered a shift in the balance of political and economic power between the providers of medical care ... and those who paid for it—power that providers had successfully accumulated for more than half a century.[4]

Nearly 30 years ago, the Reagan administration designed the DRG economic instrument as the initial performance based health care payment model (designed to control cost and reward health care providers) that could succeed under the system. In The New Health Age, this type of economic model will evolve and expand rapidly throughout all of health care, at rates much faster than ever before.

New performance based models will compensate newly integrated care teams and pay them for coming together to provide care in a high-quality, yet economically efficient, manner. The team providing care will be paid based on outcomes and their level of performance. If the team does a good job, it is paid more money. It will be as simple as that.

Let us look at an example. It takes numerous health care providers to replace a broken hip and nurture the patient to a complete recovery. Providers include the surgeon, hospital, pharmacist, rehabilitation facility, home health agency, and physical therapists, to name a few. Each of these participants is involved, in one form or another, with replacing a hip.

Today, each of these participants receives payment under a fee-for-service system in a frequently uncoordinated and disorganized manner. The surgeon submits a claim for payment separately from the other providers. The hospital, rehab facility, and home health provider seek their separate payments, too, and so on. For the most part, the payment system for the episode of care is divided into numerous component parts, and all the participants are paid separately, regardless of inefficiencies, outcomes, appropriateness, or costs.

The surgeon may perform beautifully, but if the hospital fails to supervise the patient during recovery and the patient falls from the hospital bed, all of the surgeon's brilliance may be for naught. The surgeon may not select the hip implant based on the actual physical demands or age of the patient, resulting in unnecessary and added costs. (A 90-year-old patient may not require the same device as a 50-year-old patient.) Currently, care teams with low infection rates and high recovery rates receive the same dollar amounts as care teams with high infection rates and lower recovery rates. (In fact, teams with low infection rates are paid less, because treating infections actually increases a care team's revenue.)

In The New Health Age, providers will be held accountable to provide the highest quality care possible and will be paid relative to their performance and outcomes. Those care teams that perform to higher standards and produce better outcomes will share in higher profits and savings. Care teams that utilize resources less effectively and produce lower quality results will make less money.

Public and private health plans will offer physicians, hospitals, and other health care providers monetary incentives and bonuses based on a number of quality-oriented goals. Such pay-for-performance based compensation models in The New Health Age will be clinically oriented. The programs will set targets or objectives that define what will be evaluated and then establish measures and performance standards for achieving the target criteria.

Health plans will allocate higher payments among those who meet or exceed the reward threshold and reduce payments to health care providers who fall short. A significant area of focus for these systems will be on preventive care delivery and disease management for chronic illnesses. Plans will pay physicians bonuses for following clinical practice and disease guidelines to reduce the long term cost curve. They will be paid for prevention as well as performance.

Payers will link payments to how well physicians reduce hospitalization rates. Health plans will also offer financial incentives to hospitals for achieving high quality results. Hospitals that reduce infection rates, medical errors, and length of hospital stays will receive higher reimbursements. Those who perform to the established standards and produce good outcomes will receive more money going forward.

ACOs Will Reign in The New Health Age

Accountable care organizations (ACOs), discussed in earlier chapters, will be used as one key force to promote new pay-for-performance models. ACOs will become one of the new economic engines within health care, seeking to drive higher quality for less cost. Let's examine how ACOs will change much of the economic underpinnings in health care.

ACOs will be separate legal entities that contract with private and public health plans to provide comprehensive and wholistic health care services. ACOs will partner with all the numerous groups of health care providers in the marketplace required to provide wholistic health care, including physicians, hospitals, skilled nursing facilities, pharmacies, therapists, hospices, and other ancillary professionals.

ACO partners will collaborate with each other and agree on how to best coordinate and provide health care to achieve higher outcomes, while also producing profits for the ACO and its partners. Those who participate with ACOs will agree how to divide the payments and profits at the end of the day. Those who do not

participate with ACOs will be left out of the new pay-for-performance reimbursement era. Learning how to function and thrive
in an ACO will be critically important in The New Health Age.
Health care providers should begin the learning and preparation
process now!

ACOs will exist as a separate provider of service and enter
agreements to provide a full range of health care services. ACOs
will contract with payers and offer payment models for managing
the overall health of certain patient populations, such as a group
of employees or Medicare patients in a community. The payment
system for managing patient lives may be capitated, fee-for-
service, or, more likely, some combination of the two, with a slant
more toward capitation. There will be a great variation in how
ACOs are structured.

ACOs will agree to accept fixed payments associated with
certain episodes of care, such as orthopedic replacements, heart
procedures, and other isolated events. The fixed payment will include performance-based criteria and requirements to receive the
full payment.

Continuing with the example above, an ACO will agree with
payers to replace a hip and nurture the patient to recovery in exchange for a certain dollar amount. Performance bonuses will
be built into the potential payment. The ACO will contract with
Medicare and private health plans to perform hip replacements
for, let's say $40,000, with add-on bonuses for fast recoveries with
reduced length of hospital days and reduced numbers of infections. In cases where the opposite outcome results, the care team
will not share in savings and will receive a reduced amount.

Health care payment models and incentives will move toward
such performance-based models in every respect—managed and
coordinated by ACOs and other health care providers. High-
quality outcomes will equal cost-effectiveness and higher profits.
Providers across the spectrum of health care delivery systems will
be paid based on their performance. The Reagan-era DRG model
matures and expands going forward.

In Response to Rewards for Wellness and Prevention, Patients' Views, Behaviors, and Actions Will Change in The New Health Age

Changing health care provider payment models from fee-for-service to performance-based plans will be one element to controlling health care spending. In the future, patients' views, behaviors, and actions will also change toward wellness and disease prevention.

Altering our thinking and behavior patterns toward wellness and disease prevention will not happen, however, without intervention through motivation and incentives. Left alone, America's current declining state of health, as discussed in Chapter 4, will likely continue.

We have already stated that it will take new economic incentives and rewards to modify human behavior. Behavioral change will be critically important in The New Health Age. On the employer health plan side, we have shown how employees will be induced to embrace wellness. One example will include developing employee wellness programs, such as smoking cessation programs and nutrition and exercise plans, where employees receive economic benefits for participating that can be applied toward lowering their health care costs in the form of reduced co-payments, reduced deductibles, and, in some cases, cash. Employees who refuse or fail to perform under this model will ultimately pay more for their health insurance. Smoking, overeating, refusing to exercise, and other harmful habits will always be permitted in America as a free country, but these choices will come at a higher price tag.

Numerous studies show that disease management and prevention programs for simply four conditions—asthma, congestive heart failure, chronic obstructive pulmonary disease, and diabetes—generate potential annual savings in the tens of billions of dollars.[5] Reducing people's need for the health care system leads to health benefits, but we can also anticipate reduced absenteeism in the workplace and in school. The societal benefits will be enormous.

Government health plans will eventually adopt these incentive-based models, too. Medicaid and Medicare patients will be required to participate in wellness and disease management and prevention programs if they seek to maintain full benefits. As a current example, beginning January 1, 2011, Medicare pays for wellness visits to encourage doctors to offer wellness and preventative services. Certain secondary-coverage Medicare insurance plans offer reduced rates to Medicare beneficiaries who utilize Medicare less and embrace wellness.[6]

Government entitlement programs will also start looking at ways to tax and collect reimbursement for unhealthy lifestyle choices, such as smoking, overeating, or refusing to exercise. In April 2011, the State of Arizona proposed legislation that would charge obese Medicaid beneficiaries $50 annually unless they agree to follow a doctor's weight loss program. Medicaid would charge smokers a similar fee.[7]

Health Care Providers and Patients Will "Follow the Money"

Regardless what type of Stakeholder you are—physician, hospital, employee, employer, Medicare patient, Medicaid patient, or otherwise—changing incentives to performance-based models will alter behaviors to ultimately bring down health care costs by improving health and health care in America. People will not change their behavior, however, simply because someone asks them to. Incentives or disincentives, as the case may be, are the key.

For health care providers to change, it will take economic incentives, such as receiving more money for better outcomes and being paid for providing wellness and preventative services to foster change. Good doctors will do very well in these models. Bad doctors will not do as well. The same will be true for hospitals, nursing homes, hospices, home health agencies, pharmacies, and others. Those who produce high-quality results will receive higher dollars. Those who don't, won't.

As discussed earlier in the book, even when the U.S. Surgeon General proclaimed that smoking tobacco products caused cancer, a surprising number of Americans refused to quit. It took the substantial raising of taxes to get people to change in a meaningful way. Eating healthy diets, exercising, losing weight, complying with medication instructions, or remembering to use an inhaler regularly when asthma kicks in will not "just happen." Governments and private payers of health care benefits will initiate performance incentives in The New Health Age to foster and promote such change.

As governments and employers begin to pay for wellness, Americans will change their thinking about its economic value. In the same way that consumer rewards points and airline frequent flyer programs motivate customer behavior and loyalty through incentives, similar techniques will be implemented in The New Health Age to foster choices that will lead American Stakeholders toward thinking about and embracing wellness and performance-based payment models.

In a July 24, 2011, *New York Times* op-ed article, Mark Bittman advocated for taxing unhealthy foods and subsidizing healthy foods in America to motivate Americans to eat and drink healthier. Bittman reported that at least 30 cities and states have contemplated excise taxes on soda or sugar-sweetened beverages. The articles confirmed that health-related obesity costs are projected to reach $344 billion by 2018. According to Bittman's research, a 20 percent increase in the price of sugary drinks nationally could result in about a 20 percent decrease in consumption. The effect of these changes in consumption could prevent 1.5 million Americans from becoming obese and 400,000 cases of diabetes, saving Americans billions of dollars, not to mention improving lives.[8]

In The New Health Age, doctors will be paid for keeping patients well, patients will get paid for staying well and Americans will pay more if they elect to remain unhealthy. Follow the money. It usually tells a good part of the story, and sometimes all of it.

2. Isolation → Integration
Health Care Delivery Functions in Silos

In America today, many health care providers function in isolation. Health care delivery is not a connected or integrated system. Care occurs across a vast continuum and unfortunately all the participants in the delivery chain, hospitals, physicians, therapists, pharmacists, home health, and others, do not have easy means or methods to collaborate, coordinate, or come together as one enterprise. Under the current health care system, it is often difficult for health care providers to function as a team.

Let's continue with our hip replacement example. Consider each critical health care provider involved with providing care following a patient falling and breaking a hipbone. The team may include the paramedics, emergency room caregivers, radiologists, operating room staff, surgeons, implant and medical device suppliers, intensive care unit staff, pharmacists, physical therapists, rehabilitation providers, physical medicine physicians, and home health agency providers.

Most of these participants are not part of an integrated system. Hospitals generally function independently from physicians. The rehab providers are separate providers from the hospitals and doctors. Health care providers often purchase medical devices from separate companies, and the hospitals and physicians rarely coordinate purchasing decisions to achieve the greatest discount. Home health agencies are typically independent businesses. Across these numerous silos, few economic incentives exist to provide and coordinate care as efficiently and effectively as possible.

Each silo often duplicates efforts and expenses. For instance, every provider submits a separate claim for payment. What if a doctor orders a test that a patient has already recently had? What if one doctor prescribes a medicine that has contraindications to another medicine that the patient is already taking, unknown to the physician? Is it the responsibility of the patient to connect all of these isolated health care providers? Who is responsible for providing that information? Currently, the patient is responsible because health care providers are typically isolated from one another.

On the operational side, each business has its own management, administration, liability insurance, policies, procedures, strategic plans, and marketing and technology costs. In some cases, providers share facilities and campuses, but in many cases providers are physically distant from one another, adding logistical and communication challenges because providers are not connected by offices or through technology.

This isolation and duplication creates frustration, health risks, and added cost.

Other Businesses with Multiple Service Lines Have Integrated—Health Care Providers Will Do the Same

Health care is not the only American industry that requires multiple service lines to deliver a service. Consider the airlines. Airline travelers require a plethora of service providers, including reservations, ticketing, check-in, flight crews, aircraft, air traffic control, mechanical support, airports, food services, and baggage claim.

Imagine a traveler's experience if each business unit had limited integration or inefficient means to coordinate the service. How would airline consumers react if reservations and ticketing were not integrated? Imagine if passengers made their online reservations, but learned at airport check-in that none of the information was accessible to the airline through integrated technology.

Thankfully, independent reservations and ticketing companies integrate with the airlines; yet in the health care industry, silos exist across a spectrum of providers. Each caregiver operates largely in isolation from the rest of the medical world. This makes communication among health care providers incredibly inefficient. Medical records are not generally electronically accessible among care providers. Many medical records remain on paper. Even those few records that are now electronic cannot be accessed across the health care system, nor are they accessible to the patients. That is why we typically fill out new medical history forms each time we go to a new physician or hospital. How many times in your life—heck, in the last year—have you filled out the same basic forms on a clipboard at a doctor's office or a hospital?

In health care, the patient receives separate invoices from all the providers along the care continuum. The physician sends a bill. The hospital sends a bill. The rehab provider sends a bill. That lack of coordinated billing does not exist in the airline industry. Imagine getting separate bills from the flight check-in department, the aircraft department, the fuel supplier, the flight crew, ground transportation, and the airport.

In The New Health Age, health care will function as efficiently and effectively as the airline industry, or better. Both industries have tremendous operational challenges and safety issues to overcome, so health care delivery systems are up for the task. The airlines deal with weather, unions, travelers, equipment, fuel, and airport logistics. Few industries seem as complex. Health care perhaps is, but if the airlines have figured out how to integrate across multiple service lines, so can America's health care system, and it will, soon.

We now live in a connected, integrated society. As we explained in the early chapters of this book, society, business, communications, and most parts of the economy have become ever faster, ever more connected, and ever more efficient as a result. Data from around the world can be retrieved in milliseconds. The accelerated connectedness of the planet allows us to work with people, to collaborate in real time, anywhere in the world, 24 hours a day.

Data mining is routine today. Collaboration in the "cloud," including blogs and e-mail, is now standard procedure in today's fast-paced collaborative world. Social media sites, including Facebook, LinkedIn, and Twitter, will play a significant role in health care moving forward. While health care providers will need to be aware of patient privacy and confidentiality issues, at some point, patients will expect to have social media relationships with their physicians and other providers.

Remaining isolated is not a state to be in if one seeks economic success in an integrated world. Yet that is largely how health care is currently functioning. Nevertheless, all that is changing as we enter The New Health Age.

Health Care Delivery Providers Will Integrate in The New Health Age

Isolation in health care is ending and ending fast. A sports team cannot score points to win a game functioning with players who are disconnected, noncommunicative, and unorganized.

America likes to win. Let's be blunt. America loves to win. That is who we are as a nation. We are a competitive people, always striving to be best in every aspect of our lives. Regardless what you believe personally about the state of health care in America today in terms of quality, cost, and service; in America, we can always do better. With this mind-set, it is time for the health care delivery system in the United States to do better. Why? Because Americans never stop getting better, stronger, and more prosperous as a people. America's health care team needs every player on the field, off the sidelines, and engaged to win.

The time for health care providers to integrate, in one form or another, is now. We will outline specific health care integration models in Chapter 14, but we will "tee up" the discussion here. Many Stakeholders delivering health care today will come together in The New Health Age through various means and to varying degrees.

Numerous respected integrated health care systems exist today, and they will serve as models for others.

Consider just a few models:

- Cleveland Clinic
- University of Pittsburgh Medical Center (UPMC)
- Mayo Clinic
- Geisinger Health System
- Kaiser Permanente
- HealthCare Partners Medical Group

In short, integrated health care delivery systems will arise in The New Health Age as networks of health care providers that provide or arrange to provide a coordinated continuum of health care services. Integrated delivery systems will be clinically and fiscally accountable for the clinical outcomes and health status of the patients and populations that they serve. As we discussed in Chapter 10, some systems will incorporate insurance health plans into their service lines and either own or closely align with them. Payers, providers, and patients will align and integrate. As demonstrated by these great health care systems in America, integration is not just coming; it is here.

Integration to the magnitude and effectiveness of the institutions just listed will not happen overnight across a nation as diverse as America. It will clearly take time to evolve. In some communities, integration to this scope and magnitude will not be possible, either because of a lack of resources or other factors. That said, at least some of the characteristics attributable to these organizations can be embraced in every health system in America. Small hospitals in rural communities can collaborate with physicians to function more like a "team" through local ACOs or similar joint ventures. In larger communities with numerous competitive forces in play, it may be more difficult to achieve full cooperation and integration, but systems can still embrace many of these ideals.

Players on the health care team need to get onto the field if America is to win. Stakeholders who do not embrace integration to some degree will be at an extreme competitive disadvantage in the future and will ultimately be fighting for their survival. Why? The American drive to succeed will leave them behind.

3. Nonefficient (Passive) → Efficient (Active)

While America continues to make tremendous strides through medical innovation, much of the data presented in this book substantiate that the U.S. health care delivery system, from getting insurance claims paid to receiving chronic or acute care services, is one of, if not the most, inefficient business sectors in America. Patients waste time in waiting rooms. There is endless duplication of paper records, few of which are electronic. The lack of connectivity between health care providers prevents efficient information transfer. The billing and collections process is a nightmare for providers, patients, and payers. Out of the 18,000 billing codes we discussed, many are rejected by payers, misposted, or not posted correctly, all of which leads to nonpayment causing providers and patients to fight with insurance companies and Medicare or Medicaid bureaucracies. Avoidable medical errors occur too frequently.

In The New Health Age, however, efficiency across the board will become the norm and the standard behind how we access, utilize, and choose our medical care. Any organization, whether a physician practice, hospital, nursing home, hospice, pharmacy, or other entity that remains inefficient will either fail, go out of business, or be forced to sell at reduced valuations. Inefficiency will simply not be tolerated in The New Health Age. Americans would not accept an airline that functioned in the disorganized manner mentioned earlier in this chapter. They will not accept health care providers that function inefficiently in The New Health Age either.

The New Health Age will bring about unprecedented new efficiencies to medical practice. Many of the tools and technology are currently available. The business models outside medicine are numerous and can be easily replicated. Profits can increase and costs can decline at the same time when efficiencies of operation and documentation are implemented.

Information Technology Will Revolutionize Health and Health Care Delivery

The necessity to embrace, implement, and utilize technology has been a constant theme, with numerous examples identified throughout this book. It is in this flow that all of the health information technology (HIT) discussion comes together and into one simple statement:

In The New Health Age, patient health information will be accessible, yet protected, across America's entire health care system, during the time when health caregivers need the information the most, and it will be in a form that is most useful and helpful to all Stakeholders.

This fact alone will serve as a primary catalyst for the start of The New Health Age. The growth and increased utilization of HIT over the next decade will be one of the many visions unveiled in this book, demonstrating why the years ahead will be full of some of the most incredible events in American history.

During the time of writing this book, our American economy needs a spark (okay, a lightning bolt) to get us back on track, so that this great nation will again be the force behind new technologies and jobs in the emerging global marketplace. In preparation for The New Health Age, the HIT space will be one of the fastest—if not the fastest—growing economic markets in the United States. The following are the reasons why.

Patient Health Information Must Be Accessible Throughout America's Entire Health Care System When Health Care Providers Need it the Most

Thanks to HIT, no greater power will result from The New Health Age than the ability to preserve and extend human life through a gained awareness. During this new era, medical records and health information will no longer reside in a file or stay saved on PCs. Medical records will no longer rest in a dormant and inactive state. Health information will "come alive" and "get active" for the first time in human history.

Think of light. One candle alone in a dark room brings about light, but it is weak. One million candles together can be seen from miles away. When we unite knowledge and information, we create great power. Within the context of health care, through the connectivity and marriage of people's health information utilizing HIT, such uniting force will lead to better treatments, faster and better cures, and the prevention of many life-threatening and debilitating human conditions. Expanded globally, this vision of increased knowledge and power can move humankind closer to a state of living that, to date, has been science fiction—billions of people who were previously deprived will have adequate food, water, shelter, health care, and opportunity.

Glen Tullman, CEO of Allscripts and a New Health Age Change Vision author, writes, "The question in health care is not whether the information exists, but rather providing access to the right information at the right time. And the right time is at the point of care when the physician is in the decision-making process."

Companies such as Allscripts will market and implement HIT solutions that form and create new virtual health care communities, using electronic health and medical records (EMR) systems as the platform. These virtually connected communities will be created because patients' EMRs will be integrated and available to all health care providers—hospitals, physicians, diagnostic centers, nursing homes, ambulances, emergency rooms, and therapists.

Perhaps most critically, expanded amounts of health information will be available to the patient. Patients will be connected to their own electronic health records, some of the most personal and important information in a person's life.

Connectivity will simply be part one of the story. Part two means that people will be able to interact with their health information to improve their lives. Through secure and confidential patient portals, patients will gain increased access to their own personal health information and connect with powerful online educational sources that users can tailor to their individual health risks and conditions. Those at risk for cancer or heart disease can utilize technology to take measures to reduce their chances of getting these diseases. People already suffering from illnesses will have access to personalized drug cocktails that respond better to their illness thanks to national HIT registries that track thousands of treatment modalities to uncover better options. Change Vision author David Steinman's "Market of One" realized.

This new virtual technology will have no physical boundaries, so health information can travel across county, state, and national borders. Health information will be connected and accessible when health care providers need it the most, during the clinical decision-making process.

Health information will be freed and accessible and will change medicine, health care, and humankind, as we know it today.

Patient Health Information Must Be Protected

Without question, valuable patient health information must be protected and remain confidential from those who have no legal reason to use it. This necessity for confidentiality was the impetus for enacting numerous state and federal patient privacy laws that protect patient health information.

President Clinton signed the federal Health Information Portability and Accountability Act (HIPAA) of 1996 into law many years ago. This law has since become the national standard for protecting private health information. States have their own privacy laws, many of which are even stricter than HIPAA. HIPAA's Privacy and Security Rules dictate stringent confidentiality and security requirements for people or institutions that possess and utilize protected health information. Much like the financial services industry was required to do decades ago when financial information went digital, the health care sector will be required to abide by these confidentiality laws in The New Health Age.

Confidentiality will be the law of the land. Any violators will face severe penalties.

Patient Health Information Must Be Accessible in Useful Form for Patients and Health Care Providers

Digital health information must be useful in order to offer the greatest benefit. Otherwise, digital health information simply replaces the physical filing cabinet, nothing more. In The New Health Age, health information will be active and utilized to reduce medical errors and to treat, cure, and prevent illness and disease.

Studies have established that effective EMR implementation and networking could reduce health care costs by more than $81 billion annually simply by improving health care efficiency and safety.[9] HIT prevention and management tools aimed at reducing chronic disease could eventually double those savings, while increasing health and other social benefits.[10]

The patient safety benefits from EMR systems will be substantial. Special patient condition alerts, computer automated reminders, and drug interaction alerts, to name a few, will reduce medical errors committed by health care providers, such as physicians, nurses, and technicians.[11] Studies estimate that reducing medication errors and adverse drug events in hospitals and ambulatory care settings combined could eliminate over 2,000,000 adverse drug events in those settings annually, resulting in an annual savings of $4.5 billion.[12]

EMR systems will utilize evidence-based recommendations for preventative services, including screening exams, to help identify patients needing specific services. Automated reminders or "ticklers" will alert doctors and nurses that a patient is due for a cervical cancer screening, for example. The health benefit from screening for cervical cancer alone is projected to add 13,000 life-years annually to humankind, at a small relative cost for the screening.[13] EMR systems will be instrumental during the chronic disease management process by reminding caregivers to offer needed tests during patient visits. Developers will tailor systems so that physicians will be able to input patient data on customized tablet templates, leading to personalized treatment recommendations connected to national disease registries. EMR systems will produce low-cost e-mail reminders to patients regarding appointments and prescription refills.

For high-risk patients, effective case management is critically important. HIT will help to coordinate workflows when numerous health care providers are involved with a patient, including enhanced communication among multiple specialists, primary care doctors, nurses, and the high-risk patient.

Studies show that patients, on average, comply with medication regimens about half the time.[14] Patients comply with their physician's lifestyle recommendations, such as diet and exercise, only about 10 percent of the time.[15] If EMR systems simply improve these percentages by a few points through patient reminder tools, more communication instruments, and easier access to education, the net savings are well into the tens of billions of dollars.[16] Imagine the day when you receive an automated e-mail from your doctor or health plan reminding you to take a pill or administer insulin.

The advances are virtually endless.

Can Health Care Stakeholders Afford Not to Implement EMR?
According to various studies and published estimates, the cost of widespread implementation of EMR systems in the United States is estimated to be $28 billion per year during a 10-year deployment and an estimated $16 billion per year thereafter; however, as stated earlier, the net health care savings following widespread implementation could be upward of $81 billion per year for the foreseeable future.[17] That is not a bad return on investment.

This return on investment prompted Congress and President Obama, pursuant to the American Recovery and Reinvestment Act, to provide HITECH federal stimulus dollars, starting in 2011, to health care providers who implement EMR systems in the coming years. Physicians who follow the stimulus requirements by 2012 can realize the highest dollar amount, at $44,000 per physician.[18] One stated goal of HITECH is to stimulate investment in the short-term to save money long-term.

4. Each Active Flow Comes to Light and Life

Many of the flows discussed in Chapters 10, 11, and 12 relate to getting active and leaving passive behavior and negative thinking behind as historical relics. It is fitting then that we end Part II of this book by summarizing all the active flows that The New Health Age will bring about.

In The New Health Age…

- Our thinking changes from sickness to wellness, as we recognize that our lifestyle choices can bring about healthier and happier lives.

- We gain awareness and understanding about health and better health care thanks to access to new and connected health information and incentives that promote education about how to make healthy lifestyle choices.

- Stakeholders in America take action and come into alignment with incentives and measurements that reward wellness, prevention, and quality care at reduced costs. The result will be a new and greater economic prosperity for America, which is a fundamental prerequisite to sustaining our democracy, which we have spent more than 235 years fighting to preserve and expand.

- Stakeholders become proactive and will view their own health and health care delivery wholistically, to better prevent and cure diseases.

We end these four chapters with each of the dynamic flows coming together in an integrated and interconnected way, just like much of health care delivery will do in the coming years. All of the dynamic flows will act and function in a united, integrated way, for the betterment of America's health. America will be a healthier nation, with a happier and more productive workforce. America will be more globally competitive as these flows combine to improve health and health care, thus lowering our national health care costs.

There will be those in America who resist change, kicking and screaming all the way. Graveyards are full of businesses and individuals who failed to adapt, despite stark warnings and advice. They refused to recognize fundamental shifts and did not embrace new ideas, methods, and technologies. Unfortunately, there will be such victims again as we transition into The New Health Age.

It is our hope, as two proud Americans, that neither you nor the organizations that you affiliate with will become victims to the inevitable changes that are coming. We believe—we know—that our vision of the future in this book embodies the changing face of health care in America.

Acknowledge, accept, and welcome The New Health Age. An age when the health of many Americans improves and the world reveres the U.S. health care delivery system as the most efficient, high quality, and technologically advanced in the world. Bob Dylan stated decades ago "Those not busy being born are busy dying."

KEY POINTS

The three dynamic flows of the ECONOMICS of health care are

Procedures → Performance

Isolation → Integration

Nonefficient (Passive) → Efficient (Active)

1. Health care delivery systems and payers will implement pay for performance-based economic models. They are evolutionary, not revolutionary.

2. In response to new economic incentives and rewards for wellness and prevention, payers', patients', physicians', hospitals', and other health care providers' views, behaviors, and actions will change in The New Health Age.

3. Other businesses with separate delivery and service lines have figured out how to integrate their services, including the airlines, so it is time for health care providers to do the same.

4. Health care providers will integrate into dynamic, diverse, yet organized, delivery systems.

5. Patient health information will be accessible, yet protected, across America's entire health care system at a time when health care providers need the information the most, and it will be in a form that is most useful and helpful to all applicable Stakeholders.

◄ CHANGE VISION ▶

Andy Slavitt is Chief Executive Officer of OptumInsight, one of the world's leading health information, technology, services, and consulting companies. OptumInsight supports this vision with expertise in health intelligence, connectivity, and work-flow, helping turn information into insights that, delivered at the right time and place, can enable better-informed decisions throughout health communities.

With more than 14,000 team members in 40 countries worldwide, OptumInsight delivers business solutions to clients in four markets: health care providers (physicians and hospitals), government agencies, commercial payers, and life sciences (pharmaceutical, biotech, and medical device) companies.

Andy was named Chief Executive Officer of OptumInsight in 2006. Prior to joining OptumInsight in 2005 as Chief Operating Officer, he served as Chief Executive Officer of the consumer solutions business of UnitedHealth Group. He was responsible for leading consumer-driven health care, consumer portal development, and other initiatives to serve consumers and the uninsured.

Previously, Andy was founder and Chief Executive Officer of HealthAllies, one of the first consumer health care benefits companies focusing on the un- and underinsured, which was acquired by UnitedHealth Group in 2003. He also worked as a strategy consultant with McKinsey & Company and as an investment banker with Goldman Sachs.

Why Health Care Doesn't Really Need an iPad: The Call for Productive Innovation

By Andy Slavitt

Let's put innovation into a very practical context for our industry. In health care, our cost problem, our quality problem, and our uninsured problem are really the result of our failure to innovate.

Nobel Prize–winning economist Paul Krugman noted that a country's ability to improve its standard of living over time depends almost entirely on its ability to increase productivity. Any way that you look at it, the call for productive innovation is a national imperative.

How can we do it? We will succeed by leveraging the ingenuity of our entrepreneurs along with the capital and infrastructure investments that we have made in this country— advancements which already enable us to fit ever more data onto a microchip, deploy smart grids to bring solar power to small businesses, and access information from "the cloud."

In health care, we know that improving productivity— devoting more and better resources to treating people who need it most, and making care delivery more efficient for everyone—would allow us to provide health care services to 20 percent more people, without spending a dime more than we do today. Adding to the productive capacity of the health care system is the simple way to achieve more with the same, or even fewer, resources.

These are problems that will not be solved without new ideas. As we face new demands to take better care of a growing population of seniors and the chronically ill, amid a shortage of primary care physicians and without new money coming into the system, we need to employ the same type of innovative thinking that shrunk the microchip. We need a relentless supply of new ideas to address our massive gap in productivity.

It is important to distinguish productive innovation from two other types of innovation we think about more often: product innovation (e.g., the iPad) or business model innovation (e.g., Facebook). These types of innovation are noteworthy and important, but we need the intelligent information exchange that helps surgeons use patient data to guide their care decisions more than we need another MRI machine or new health savings account model.

Why It Doesn't Happen: Innovation Needs a Customer
The CEO of a Silicon Valley firm who is famous for innovation once told me that, when he reviewed which innovations his senior management team believed would be most successful, they were wrong 9 times out of 10. Today, he says he doesn't even ask. Instead, his customers vote and he uses their input to shape new offerings—a now common practice in Silicon Valley and other places that know how to innovate.

The health care delivery system faces a different challenge. Here, the people who build technology, which is supposed to spur productivity, do not generally focus on the customers who will use their innovations: they focus on who pays. Hospital-based EMRs are a good example. Follow the chain. Let's agree that EMRs need to be used by doctors to help treat patients; except that they are bought by hospitals, that are incented by government reimbursements, which require compliance with regulations created in Washington on behalf of a payer—typically the Centers for Medicare and Medicaid Services (CMS).

Whether the rules that benefit CMS are right or wrong is not at issue. What is important is that system design is far removed from the needs of the doctor and the patient. As a result, many EMRs, like investments made to implement ICD-10, are treated as compliance programs. There's little wonder why we don't see productivity improvements from many past health IT projects.

To achieve needed productivity gains, we need *customer-driven innovation* in health care. There is an epic amount of overtreatment for expensive and potentially harmful imaging. CT scans are an example. We in the health care industry attempt to use technology—like hospital-based medical records—to reduce unnecessary tests. But what happens in the real world? Any doctor will tell you that he or she can write "CT scan" on a pad a lot faster than they can log into a desktop with a password that changes every 48 hours. If he or she and their colleagues were involved in the product design, this would be solved.

Technology is invisible in good design. When you use an iPad, you don't think of it as using technology any more than think about how routers and switchers work to get on Netflix. Accessing EMRs and health information exchanges (HIEs) that connect different EMR systems should be as seamless to end-users.

So, What Does Innovation Look Like and Where Will It Come From?

Innovations usually come from the same source—other innovations, successes, or failures that came before them. In health care, new regulations and rules often spark those first innovations. Although these initial concepts are sometimes lacking, they lead to good innovation, which in turn inspires even better innovation.

When the rules change, innovators appear. A good example is Medicare Part D legislation, which created the "donut hole" that inspired $4 generics and convenience clinics. Health Savings Account legislation spawned health banks, which led to more rapid adoption of electronic payments. In each of these cases, by the third generation of innovation, productive innovation was occurring.

Now, the Patient Protection and Affordable Care Act (PPACA) and specifically its provisions for Accountable Care

Organizations (ACOs) are unleashing the same thing. Think what you will about the legislation, but at the end of the day, its success will be judged to be effective if it unleashes productive innovation.

Let's see how this might happen. ACOs are creating the opportunity to systemically realign payments with increases in care quality and patient satisfaction, and to motivate providers for more prudent use of resources, instead of for the volume of tests and procedures they conduct. This creates an opportunity for productive innovation by turning the user into the paying customer.

Love it or hate it, PPACA is also pushing payers and providers to reduce administrative costs because they won't get reimbursed for them. But where incentives stop, innovation has the opportunity to begin. At OptumInsight, we see our clients beginning to unlock new waves of innovation sparked by this new set of rules. For example,

- We have a payer client who is keeping behavioral health patients from getting readmitted to the hospital by linking them into social networks of similar patients.
- We have hospital clients deploying smart connectivity to make physicians aware of where their patients are and to predict who is most at risk of a hospital admission.
- We have an integrated delivery network client who has reduced imaging utilization by 50 percent by using data so physicians can share best practices and change workflows.
- We have clients who are using the power of design to wrap care around the needs of patients—delivering care at home, on mobile devices, in pharmacies, at summer camps, and barbershops.

It Begins and Ends With the Customer

Productive innovations like these aren't optional and must serve as a catalyst to bigger, better innovations. Customer-focused innovation has to be more than just an idea; we need to take action and remove barriers to enhance the health care experience. It all begins and ends with the customer—what they need, what they want, and how we deliver. When we begin to drive toward making things simpler, more consistent, and more effective for our customers—as they would judge it—that is when our innovations will begin to make a positive difference in the delivery of care and the health of populations.

PART III

The Landscape of The New Health Age

13

Transitions Are Difficult

"There is nothing so difficult to plan, more uncertain of success, nor dangerous to manage than the creation of a new order of things. For the initiator has the enmity of all those who would profit by the preservation of the old institutions and merely lukewarm defenders in those who would gain by the new ones."

—Machiavelli

In Part I of this book, we looked back at the history of medicine and health care. We mapped this history along the timelines of the Ages of Modern Man. We looked at the new century, the new age, and the new decade that we have entered. We looked to the incredible breakthroughs in medicine that lie immediately ahead. We showed how the world outside of health care delivery has profoundly changed and how these changes are now, inevitably, coursing through health care.

In Part II of this book, we presented the nine dynamic flows that have, are, and will reshape health care and the practice of medicine in the United States. These flows will completely alter the health care landscape for all health care Stakeholders in this country. Understanding these flows is essential to grasping the magnitude of the change and why what is occurring is fundamentally historically inevitable.

In Part III of this book, we present what the landscape of The New Health Age will look like and what all Stakeholders must know. We present what we think will be the new structures, the new ways of creating and implementing policy, and the social changes that will result. We will finally look ahead 5, 10, and 15 years and suggest a futuristic view of The New Health Age landscape in America.

First, we must look at where we are, which is a health care system beginning a transition. Not just any transition, but one that is of huge significance as it ushers in The New Health Age. Future historians will look at this time of transition as one of the most fundamentally important transitions in the entire history of medicine and health care. We are entering a transformational period.

Transitions are difficult. Be they of great human significance or just personal or cultural ones, transitions create upset, tension, resistance, excitement, and discouragement, and oftentimes a great deal of pain. Childbirth is a valid metaphor. Birthing a new age has similar aspects to the birthing of a child. There is a great amount of excitement, anxiety, and nervousness, an acceptance that one's life will change forever. Something lost but something much deeper and more beautiful to come. There is discomfort, attitude adjustment, new expenditures, and pain, a lot of pain.

Machiavelli did not experience the pain of childbirth, but he was correct that a new order of things is difficult to achieve. It is perhaps one of the hardest things humankind ever does when done on a grand scale. But achieve it we must. Our nation needs to become healthier and more globally competitive. Our health care costs must start to decline soon, our health as citizens must improve, or we will desecrate and squander the gift our enlightened Founding Fathers provided us.

In the short term, fear will increase, tempers will be lost, false prophecies will be made, false hopes will be raised. Most assuredly, costs will, in the short term, increase. The economics of transition are such that costs must go up as the existing order of things continues while the new order seeks its footing. There will be duplication, trial and error, and unforeseen problems that will arise, big and small. This short-term increase in overall costs will give fodder to those who resist the change—they will use increasing costs as evidence of the fallacy of the change. Others will see it correctly, as an inevitable part of the natural process of transition, an investment in the future. Think of the pain in transforming a company, of changing the dynamics of a family when a child leaves home, or when there is a death and a corresponding birth. All incur unforeseen costs. Think of the pain when a democracy is created.

At every step, it is easy to find evidence of failure and misdirection if that is what one is looking for. There is also the faith too soon. There will be evidence to support almost any view when a society undertakes a major transition. Some will think we have arrived before we actually have. Vigilance to see it through is essential. Major transitions always seem more painful during the process than after they have occurred. We must live through the pain to get to the place where the pain is harder to remember. A woman's pain during childbirth is practically unbearable, but that pain rapidly recedes when the newborn is held.

If we were to estimate the length of America's transition to The New Health Age, we suggest that it will be about 10 years, from 2010 to 2020. This will be the tough part, the major part, the part when all just mentioned will occur.

Many aspects of The New Health Age will come about prior to 2020. Some Stakeholders will see the exit from the transition sooner than 2020. Other Stakeholders will feel and think that the transition is still going after 2020. Both ultimately will be right.

Some will see the direction as it becomes clear, embrace it, and live it. Others will want to wait until there are historical data that confirm it. Both positions are valid. The transition though has a strong sense of historical inevitability about it. It is, therefore, much more dangerous to be one who waits to see what occurs. Those who face it, embrace it, and adapt to it will be like early movers or adapters in any market; they will have an advantage of being ahead of the curve. The inevitable curve that forges the landscape of The New Health Age is on the upslope.

We now spend the rest of this book looking at the landscape of The New Health Age in America. We hope that having a clear vision of this new landscape will help to lessen the pain of the transition that we have entered as a country.

KEY POINTS

1. America's health care system is beginning a transition of huge significance as it ushers in The New Health Age.

2. Transitions are difficult.

3. In the short term, fear will increase, tempers will be lost, false prophecies will be made, and false hopes will be raised.

4. In the short term, costs will increase. The economics of transition are such that costs must go up as the existing order of things continues while the new order seeks its footing.

5. We estimate the length of America's transition to The New Health Age will be about 10 years, from 2010 to 2020.

14

The New Structures
of Health Care

*"A mind once stretched by a new idea never
regains its original dimensions."*

—Oliver Wendell Holmes

History shows us that new centuries and new ages bring about
the birth of new institutions and the reorganization of existing ones. What was the norm in one century or age is replaced
by a new norm. The New Health Age will be no different.

The existing structures of the health care delivery system in
the United States were largely established in the Industrial Age
during the twentieth century. Some of these structures and institutions will survive in The New Health Age, but in altered form.
Others will cease to exist. Entirely new structures will arise that
will reshape, reorder, and reorient the American health care delivery system, resulting in lower health care costs. This chapter looks
at what some of the new structures will be and explains why they
will work and how they will interact.

We will focus on five new fundamental health care structures that will profoundly reshape and dominate the health care landscape throughout The New Health Age:

1. Integrated delivery systems (IDS)
2. Accountable care organizations (ACOs)
3. Employer Accountable Care Organizations (EACOs)
4. Medical homes
5. Health insurance exchanges

Additional new structures will arise going forward, but these five will exist at the core of The New Health Age. We will start by defining each one.

An *integrated delivery system* (IDS) is defined best by looking at illustrious examples already in existence today, such as the Cleveland Clinic, the Mayo Clinic, the Geisinger Health System, Kaiser Permanente, the University of Pittsburgh Medical Center, and HealthCare Partners. These leaders in the health care delivery marketplace will serve as models going forward and help to define where integrated health care can and will be in The New Health Age. Stated simply, the Cleveland Clinic defines itself as a "multispecialty academic medical center that integrates clinical and hospital care with research and education."[1]

Accountable care organizations (ACOs) have recently emerged as an integral part of health care reform laws and appear in Section 3022 of PPACA under the title "Shared Savings Program." PPACA defines ACOs as a structure of health care providers established for achieving quality thresholds and as an instrument to share in the related cost savings to the Medicare program. ACOs must be accountable for the overall care of their Medicare beneficiaries, have adequate participation of primary care physicians, define processes to promote evidence-based medicine, report on quality and costs, and coordinate care.[2]

An ACO was also recently defined in a *Health Affairs* article titled "A National Strategy to Put Accountable Care into Practice" as follows:

> ACOs consist of providers who are jointly held accountable for achieving measured... per capita improvements in quality and cost.... ACOs should have ... accountability for achieving these improvements while caring for a defined population of patients.
>
> ACOs may involve a variety of provider configurations, ranging from integrated delivery systems and primary care medical groups to hospital-based systems and virtual networks of physicians such as independent practice associations.[3]

As futurists, we have branded Employer Accountable Care Organizations, or EACOs. We think that EACOs will be one of the most significant and influential structures in The New Health Age. Large employers, or aggregations of smaller sized employers, will create their own EACOs, replicating the ACO model but designing them exclusively for their own employees. This way the payers—both employees and employers—create entirely contained EACOs that operate the same way that a Medicare ACO would, benefiting from all of the integrated thinking described and defined later in this chapter.

Kaiser Permanente's CEO, George Halvorson, whom we have cited numerous times throughout this book because of his forward thinking work related to health care, defines *medical homes* as organizations "where designated caregivers can coordinate and support all of the care needs of a given patient ... contrasted to uncoordinated, unlinked, unconnected, incident-based patterns of care."[4]

PPACA defines *health insurance exchanges* as state-regulated and standardized health care plans from which individuals and small businesses may purchase health insurance, with government subsidies in limited cases.[5]

We have presented the concise definitions, but what does it all mean and how will these new structures function during The New Health Age?

1. The new structures of health care will bring about great integration of health care providers.

Many integrated delivery systems (IDSs) will arise in The New Health Age and become clinically and fiscally accountable for patient outcomes and coordination of health care services. Some IDSs will be extremely cohesive, meaning that all physical assets are ultimately owned by the same affiliated companies and operated by a common group of leaders and caregivers, whereas other IDSs will be less cohesive and will unite through joint ventures, co-management arrangements, and partnerships. IDSs will take form in numerous shapes and sizes and to varying degrees and scope.

Full integration will operate and be characterized as follows:

1. IDSs will function with principles that embrace a one-team philosophy, bringing best practices together across an entire IDS to provide superior patient care and experience for the highest economic value.

2. IDSs will view their marketplace regionally versus locally, because isolated thinking falls away in The New Health Age.

3. IDSs will fully integrate or collaborate with community health centers that focus on underserved populations, such as the indigent and uninsured.

4. IDSs will organize largely integrated, multispecialty physician groups where physicians are valued and actively participate in IDS leadership.

5. IDSs will manage fully equipped community and/or tertiary hospitals.

6. IDSs will run "Clinical Centers of Excellence" across the enterprise, focusing on specific medical specialty areas, such as cardiology, orthopedics, neurology, and so on.

7. IDSs will incorporate various other service divisions, including diagnostic centers, surgery centers, therapy centers, behavioral health and social services centers, post-acute and long-term care providers, home health, hospice, and others.

8. IDSs will operate and control ACOs and EACOs and private health insurance plans and will sell these products in the marketplace, bringing payers, providers, and patients to the same negotiating table.

9. IDSs will direct and offer strong wellness and disease prevention centers for the community at large, employers, and government health plans.

10. IDSs will drive advanced research and development programs and operate or affiliate with academic medical teaching institutions.

11. IDSs will activate strong health information technology platforms, including integrated electronic medical records, online patient portals, and health data analytical software tools, so that health information can be effectively used, analyzed, and manipulated throughout the IDS as well as to health care providers and to health care insurance plans outside the IDS.

12. IDSs will adopt best clinical practice guidelines, protocols, and standards that incorporate evidence-based medicine into service lines to reduce medical errors, improve outcomes, and reduce costs.

This is what full integration will look like in The New Health Age, to its fullest extent. The model institutions cited earlier and these 12 attributes define and describe *totally integrated* health care delivery providers. Not all health care systems, however, will integrate to such a large scale, but some integration is inevitable and will be required to compete effectively in The New Health Age. The new dynamic flows coming to American health care will require that institutions collaborate, coordinate, and integrate, whether through joint ownership, partnerships, affiliations, or some combination. Health care providers that remain narrowly focused, isolated, and independent in their thinking will stand alone in the future, and it will be a lonely world.

IDSs will carry out two primary objectives. First, IDSs will improve health and health care quality at reduced costs. Second, IDSs will be responsive to patients, generating community and national benefits. Let's examine both briefly.

IDSs Will Improve Health and Health Care Quality and Reduce Costs

Integration eliminates redundancy in operations, fosters implementation and sharing of best practices, and enables economies of scale to emerge. At the hospital level, for instance, varying degrees of organizational consolidation lead to improved utilization of resources, both capital and operating.

Integration can enable the IDS, through coordinated activities, to meet the same level of demand with less capacity than that required by nonintegrated facilities. A larger scale of operations cultivates increased productivity, lowers staffing requirements, and reduces unit costs through joint activities. Reducing inappropriate and unnecessary resource use becomes a core principle of an IDS. Redundancy is lessened or eliminated. IDSs use capital and technology efficiently. All of these efforts combined reduce IDSs' administrative and overhead costs.

IDSs will foster the motivation and ability to share economic risk more effectively. By taking on and sharing more risk, IDSs will invest more capital and resources into new services, technologies, research, people, facilities, and ideas to promote and improve health and health care delivery within regions and communities. The economic advantage of IDSs is their ability to acquire capital more easily and at reduced cost. IDSs own a larger asset base and receive stronger revenue and income from which borrowed capital can be repaid.

In a nonintegrated health care environment, competing health care providers strive to shift costs to other providers. When health care providers come together to achieve profits at the integrated level, cost shifting is reduced, or even eliminated, because everyone strives to function as one, driving down costs.

IDSs will focus on producing good outcomes and achieving high quality across all services lines. Health care providers finger point less because an IDS performs as a cohesive enterprise. When patients receive treatment from HealthCare Partners, UPMC, the Mayo Clinic, the Cleveland Clinic, or Kaiser Permanente, they experience a united group of diverse health care providers that have integrated to function more like a team. The goal of an IDS is for the "them" mentality to become an "us" mentality to deliver better health care. IDSs believe in and seek to implement consumer responsiveness so that patients receive a seamless continuum of care.

Fully integrated IDSs in The New Health Age will exist within wealthy and poor areas of communities so that health care delivery systems address and promote the overall health of every citizen. Shifting and diverting patients "across town" because of their inability to pay for health care services will diminish because an IDS focuses on community care and health—not the pockets of patients. It will be in an IDS's economic interest to focus on community care because the system becomes ultimately responsible for the community's health care costs under risk-sharing models, including ACO and EACO structures, discussed in the following sections. IDSs will address the prevention of social issues that affect community health and embrace a much larger societal perspective when designing and delivering health care services.

IDSs Will Be Responsive to Patients, Generating Community and National Benefits

IDSs will strive to create unified organizations that become responsible for providing all health services, including delivery of care, collecting payment, and managing economic risk. The aim of an IDS is for patients to be able to experience a seamless continuum of services through a consistent point of access to all services. Their care will be better coordinated and managed.

Most patients today have primary health care relationships with individuals. "Dr. Jones is my doctor." While the doctor-patient relationship is and will remain sacred in The New Health Age, patients tomorrow will also form deep relationships with IDSs as institutions because people will find themselves moving throughout the IDS and they will receive care from a vast variety of IDS professionals. People will say, "Dr. Jones with HealthCare Partners is my doctor." Patients will perceive and feel that the entire health system is one united caregiver.

For physicians and other clinicians, IDSs deliver a broader range of services and programs with different levels of care and access to specialized personnel and equipment, giving them more tools and options for care delivery. Physician specialists within the IDS promote and allow for consultation and expanded patient referral networks, creating an internal marketplace for patients within the IDS. A strong and more clinically integrated organization will result in improved quality of care throughout the IDS. IDSs will share best practices among physicians, and a team mentality will become the culture at successful IDSs.

IDSs embrace a community health focus and accountability models and are dedicated to improving the health status of an entire community. Healthy communities lead to healthy states, and ultimately to a healthy country.

2. Accountable care organizations (ACOs) arrive during The New Health Age.

ACOs are perhaps the most talked about new health care structures in decades. ACOs will be a game changer, so it is imperative that health care delivery systems understand how they will function, grow, and develop as The New Health Age evolves.

Although birthed out of PPACA and originally designed to target the Medicare population, health care providers need to view ACOs more broadly, because they will function as such.[6] Accountable care models will be more expansive and inclusive structures in the future and will ultimately serve all Americans in some form and fashion—Medicare, Medicaid, and private insurance patients.

ACOs will trigger more integration in the coming decade than any other new structure in health care. Organizations that understand and prepare for ACOs will have a jump on the competition and will likely succeed. Health care providers who do not may very well fail or, at best, fall behind.

We resist comparing ACOs to other historical health care models because stereotyping can limit our thinking and our ability to be creative, which will be required to develop fresh and innovative ACOs throughout The New Health Age. If developers at Apple had designed the iPhone or the iPad by modeling these devices after those in existence at the time, the resulting products would have been constrained by the constructs of yesterday versus building Apple devices toward the visions and possibilities of tomorrow.

We often fear new structures because they represent the unknown, but Stakeholders should strive to understand and accept ACOs because these entities and the health care models that ACOs develop will become dominate in the years to come. We have seen in the dynamic flow chapters how health care payment systems will move away from episodic-, volume-, and treatment-based paradigms to wholistic-, preventative-, and wellness-based ones. In an environment where health care providers will receive less income as sickness decreases and procedure volumes decline, those who capitalize on ACOs will be able to replace their lost revenue with new revenue possible through ACOs. The payment models will be different, thus understanding them is critical for success.

ACOs will essentially pay providers for doing less, or better said, doing what is appropriate. ACO partners who produce healthier patient populations requiring less care will be paid more from shared savings and resulting profits. That is the true definition of accountable care payment models, and this model will become the new norm going forward. Don't be fooled—less care in an ACO world does not equate to worse care. Successful ACOs will implement practices and programs that reach out to patients to foster positive behavioral change, so that ACO patients make better lifestyle choices oriented toward improving health. We discuss more about that topic below.

Specifically, ACOs will

1. Integrate providers to deliver comprehensive, patient-centered, coordinated, and collaborative health care services, either through an IDS, as described earlier; a medical home; or other structure that brings independent provider groups together purely for the purpose of offering accountable care to health plans, both public or private.

2. Manage the financial side of health care delivery by assuming degrees of economic risk through episodic payment systems (i.e., $40,000 for a hip replacement), pay-for-performance (i.e., bonuses for reducing chronic diseases and following clinical practice guidelines), and shared savings models (i.e., share in surgery department profits through efficiencies and cost savings) that we explored in Chapter 12.

3. Coordinate effective case management so that patients receive interactive and proactive care to prevent disease, promote wellness, and achieve faster recoveries from health events, such as surgeries.

4. Analyze patient health data, including family history, genetic information, and other risk data, so that health benefit plans can be tailored and designed to the health needs of the targeted population.

5. Connect health information and data utilizing technology so that this information becomes usable, active, and dynamic, as discussed in Chapter 12.

6. Select and participate with quality clinical health care providers to achieve the best outcomes possible.

7. Contract with government benefit plans, including Medicare and Medicaid, private insurance, and employer health plans, to provide the services described.

As ACOs develop and emerge, some question whether these new structures may violate federal antitrust laws which, in sum, prohibit price fixing and the creation of monopolies that possess too much market power. We believe that the goals of the antitrust laws and ACOs are congruent—to improve quality and reduce costs. Policy makers designed the antitrust laws to protect against the opposite result—reduced quality at higher costs. That said, federal regulatory bodies have and will continue to issue guidance over the coming decade regulating ACOs to ensure compliance with applicable laws. Recall, however, that it is now the federal government that is promoting ACOs, so we should expect that the same body charged with enforcing antitrust laws would certainly find means and methods to ensure that ACOs operate and function appropriately under federal law.

States and local governments may also need to adjust antitrust and other laws, rules, and regulations that may be in conflict with ACOs. During The New Health Age, the marketplace will demand accountable care models to bring down health care costs, increase health, and improve health care quality. State laws will also adapt accordingly to further these new structures.

In fact, more procompetitive behavior will exist in the health care marketplace moving forward, not less. To achieve the ACO goals and objectives, ACO organizers and operators will strive to collaborate with health care providers that produce the best outcomes, products, and services for the least cost. That will be the name of the game.

For instance, few ACOs will partner with an orthopedic surgeon with high post-surgery infection rates. ACOs will seek out surgeons with the lowest infection rates, because these surgeons will practice medicine for less cost and produce higher quality outcomes. By assuming financial risk for care (i.e., a $40,000 capitated rate for a hip replacement), ACOs will not be able to afford health care providers who do not produce high-quality results. ACOs will be resistant to contracting with hospitals with low patient satisfaction rates as well.

ACOs will assume economic risk for managing care for defined population groups, such as Medicare or Medicaid populations and employee groups, discussed below. To be profitable, ACOs will be required to make these populations healthier. ACOs will aim to contract with physician-driven medical homes, also discussed in the following, that have developed the best models and programs for reducing and preventing chronic diseases. These examples of new structures, behaviors, and incentives demonstrate that competition will increase in the future, promoting a more vibrant and strong health care marketplace.

Health care will function similar to many other markets in America. Take the American automotive industry. The "Big Three" of yesterday—General Motors, Chrysler, and Ford—were ultimately forced to compete on a global stage with new competitors. The car manufacturers who built the best cars for the greatest value excelled. Those that did not failed. Capitalism and more competition are simply now coming to health care.

We predict that properly structured ACOs will not run afoul of antitrust laws. ACOs are here to stay. It is, therefore, imperative that health care providers acknowledge and accept how critical participation within ACOs will be in the future. Those who reserve and maintain a seat at the "ACO table" today will prosper. Those who are left behind will not. Hospitals, physicians, pharmacies, home health agencies, long-term care organizations, rehabilitation providers, hospices, behavioral health groups, and others should be instigating dialog and communication with each other to prepare for ACOs. They are coming—they are here.

3. Employer Accountable Care Organizations (EACOs) will drive accountable care development and models.

While government-promoted Medicare and Medicaid ACOs will evolve slowly, privately driven EACOs will form and expand quickly. When will this begin to occur? Yesterday! As we discussed in Chapter 12, we predict that employers will be the initial driving force behind accountable care models by creating EACOs.

EACOs will incorporate all the traditional ACO services described above and more, including enhanced health benefit design tools that promote medical and disease management, employee assistance programs, behavioral health programs, smoking cessation plans, pharmacy advocacy, diabetes care management, nutritional programs, and weight management and fitness education. How will EACOs be different from ACOs? EACOs target employees, primarily employees of companies with self-funded health insurance plans.

By offering the right incentives to employees and health care providers to drive wellness and accountability across the spectrum of these Stakeholders, employers will save on health insurance costs, resulting in higher corporate profitability. Equally important, by cultivating healthier employees through EACOs, employers will reduce employee absenteeism and enhance productivity.

The direct and indirect economic benefits resulting from reducing the number of days that employees miss work and from increasing employee productivity are tremendous. Let us repeat because this is so important: The direct and indirect economic benefits resulting from reducing the number of days that employees miss work and from increasing employee productivity while at work are tremendous. Unscheduled employee absences can cost a company an estimated $750 or more per employee annually.[7] Reduce absenteeism, increase employee productivity, and the results go straight to the bottom line. Health insurance costs go down. Workers compensation insurance rates decrease. Employee morale increases. Productivity goes up. The benefits derived from effectively run EACOs cannot be overlooked by American businesses.

We encourage readers to investigate Virgin HealthMiles as an international model of what EACOs will look like.[8] As part of the Sir Richard Branson family of companies, Virgin Health-Miles provides employee health programs that pay people to get active and healthy so they can make measurable changes to their health. Numerous employers, government entities, insurers, and other network partners already work with Virgin HealthMiles. In fact, Branson's company represents more than 500,000 employees across the United States. On Virgin's homepage, companies can model the amount of dollar savings that EACOs can produce. According to Virgin HealthMiles, a company with 5,000 employees, earning an average wage of $50,000 each, will save over $7 million over three years with simply 50 percent employee participation. That number tops $10 million at 70 percent employee participation.[9] As we have stated throughout the book, EACOs can foster and produce tremendous increases in corporate profitability.

Corporate America will not wait for government ACOs to take shape; it can't afford to. American businesses will, in fact, drive EACOs, and the government will end up following their example. ACO and EACO development will be a great instance of American capitalism functioning at its best—the government launches an idea, but the private sector subsequently drives and implements it, resulting in a more competitive America.

Think of NASA. President John F. Kennedy proclaimed that an American astronaut should be the first to the moon. Through public and private partnerships, President Kennedy's vision became reality. The long-term and widely reaching economic benefits resulting from President Kennedy's space agenda were enormous. Think of the many electronics that exist today and how many of these devices can trace their invention back to NASA. Great monetary benefits will result from ACOs and EACOs too; it is time to get to work on creating these new structures for a healthier America.

4. Patient-centered medical homes will create symbiotic and proactive doctor-patient care models in communities.

Medical homes, led by primary care physicians, will create a symbiotic and balanced relationship among the patient care team, the patient, and his or her family. Medical homes will function at the center of health care and be the catalyst for community-based collaborative care networks, expanding access to primary care and general health care services.

Let us stress that medical homes will be *led by physicians*. For those physicians who fear that coming changes will somehow cut them out of health care, fear not! For those physicians who fear that coming changes will somehow take away their ability to earn a good income, fear not! Physicians who learn, adapt, and acknowledge the future changes will continue to succeed. Physicians who expect for health care to remain status quo are in trouble. The choice of which approach to take is yours.

Yes, the global thinking about health care will move to prevention and wellness, but physicians will remain at the core of health care and the new models emerging, including medical homes. In fact, physicians who embrace The New Health Age will be called to *lead* the care team.

In addition to physicians, the medical home team will include many other caregivers: physician assistants, nurse practitioners, dieticians, nutritionists, fitness trainers, and behavioral health counselors. Primary care physicians will refer their medical home patients to leading specialty physicians in the network when specific medical conditions require more focused skills. Physicians will continue to remain in charge, just in new and different ways.

Indeed, medical home payment models will be different, but twenty-first century thinking physicians will still be able to capitalize and profit from the new structures. Today, physicians are paid on a per-patient, per-service basis—the old episodic payment method. Tomorrow, wholistic payment models will become more prevalent.

Group health payment systems will be commonplace in medical homes, enabling physicians to be paid based on patient volume. The more patient relationships that a physician can foster in the future, the more influential and economically prosperous a physician will be. Picture a leading wellness physician speaking before a group of medical home patients about how to prevent heart disease and being paid for each patient who attends. Today, a physician might earn $100 per patient visit after expenses and squeeze four visits into one hour. That is $400 an hour. Tomorrow, physicians can charge $20 per patient and speak to 100 patients in one hour, leading to $2,000 an hour.

Medical home physicians will receive payments for making their patients healthier. Reduce the number of obese employees in a company by 10 percent and physicians will receive a bonus payment from the EACO.

Today, and certainly more so in the future, physicians can enter risk-based insurance, Medicare, and Medicaid contracts and agree to provide care to patients in exchange for receiving pay-for-performance and capitated payments, on a per-member, per-month basis. During numerous interviews of doctors while we were writing this book, future-minded physicians shared with us that their incomes have increased substantially as a result of accepting risk-based patients, but with a major caveat. All of these physicians embraced the medical home philosophy. These physicians had implemented powerful disease management tools, case management, became proactive and engaged with their patients, focused on wellness, reduced hospital admissions, and actively drove and inspired patient accountability; and the payers rewarded them for doing so! The physicians warned that it took several years to receive meaningful economic returns in the medical home model because instilling a well-minded lifestyle culture with patients and implementing disease management is a longer term venture. The result for the doctors that we interviewed, however, was that they reported having happier and healthier patients, combined with enjoying higher incomes than in years past.

Other fresh payment models are coming, too. Indeed, the payment systems in the new structures will be different, but they will be full of profitable opportunities.

By interacting with patients in a positive, communicative, and proactive manner, medical home physicians and other caregivers will motivate and educate patients to change their lifestyles— "lifestyle medicine." Medical home case managers directed and led by physicians, will inspire patients to comply better with their treatment plans and monitor medication and therapy compliance, diet, and so forth. Physicians and other caregivers working in medical home environments will concentrate on and identify patient health trends so that the care delivery team can address early on any material variation in a patient's health.

Medical homes, as a key provider under EACO plans, will develop in close physical proximity to employment centers and contract with employer health plans to foster strong employee health. Medical homes will construct centralized employee clinics with nutrition centers, educational programs, exercise rooms, exam rooms, and case managers.

A company called GenerationsHP is doing exactly that—developing medical-home-driven EACOs in communities across America.[10] Company founder, Bob Goodman, won the 2009 Benny Award for Innovation and Management for his health benefit design and leadership.[11] Goodman stated the following during a research interview for this book,

> The future for the United States is to be able to compete in the global economy. Employers can no longer afford to think that they are able to control health care costs by shifting the costs to employees through premium and deductible price increases. Medical benefit costs, today and tomorrow, will only be controlled through effective medical benefit plan design that promotes positive lifestyle behavioral change rather than payment for poor lifestyle behavioral choices. Employers' number one goal must be to build a "fit" workforce and a healthy community. American business must change how they design their health benefit plans. Every member of a family must be individually held accountable for their lifestyle choices.

Community health centers, focused on underserved populations, will promote medical home models and wellness in deprived American neighborhoods. Medical homes in underserved communities have already emerged and serve as innovative examples for others. ConnectFamilias is a nonprofit community partnership serving Miami-Dade, Florida. This organization has pioneered a care team model that connects and coordinates families with a wide range of social and health services.[12] Connect-Familias partners with nearly 50 local organizations to provide a link for families in need of formal services and informal social support. A member of the Care Coordination team goes out into the community and helps build bridges between needy families and medical homes, so that people have access to community health centers. They make home visits, place phone calls, and accompany underserved family members to doctor appointments. The Care Coordinators provide assistance related to preventative health services to reduce the number of emergency clinic or hospital visits.

Manatee County Rural Health Services (MCRHS) in Tampa Bay, Florida, serves as another beacon for community health centers in America.[13] This organization serves three counties in the Tampa Bay area and has reduced chronic disease rates in the underserved population through an advanced medical home model. MCRHS also collaborates with local hospital emergency room departments and identifies patients who the hospital can redirect to MCRHS's outpatient clinics versus utilizing expensive emergency room resources unnecessarily. During an interview with us, MCRHS reported that it saved local hospitals more than $18 million over a 3-year period because of its emergency room diversion program.

The Tampa Bay, Florida, region also hosts other innovative health care models coming in The New Health Age. The New Medicine Community is a newly developing, global patient-centered destination connecting consumers, physicians, and payers (self-insured groups, insurance companies, and government-funded programs) to the power and possibilities of real health solutions and lifestyle medicine. The physicians of The New Medicine Community will lead the way from the current high cost care model of a "pill for every ill" and "disease oriented care" into the twenty-first century, where physicians will treat real root causes and imbalances, not symptoms, empowering patients to become active participants in reversing and preventing disease with their new prescription for health: good food, exercise, stress reduction, and the appropriate amount of sleep. These are some of the foundational components of lifestyle medicine that will reduce epidemic chronic health conditions. Greater education, information, and supporting programs for lifestyle change are a few of the missing links in today's current health experience.

The new models of care will provide inspiring evidence-based programs and a lifestyle team of experts including nutritionists, chefs, fitness, and mind-body professionals to support patients and physicians as partners in healing. Physicians of the future will embrace the importance of treating the whole person, mind-body-spirit, and serve as role models and motivators of healthy living for their patients. Physicians will create medical homes that bring together experts and leading edge programs, local and global, that promote self-care with the most effective and least invasive innovative solutions, reducing the use of prescription medications, expensive diagnostics, and needless surgeries. This will be the cost saving sustainable way of The New Health Age.

Medical home models such as these demonstrate new caregiver methods where physicians and other health care providers step beyond the role of simply treating sickness and disease. Health care providers build proactive relationships with people in communities using contemporary techniques designed to prevent disease and illness and to promote patient responsibility, so that people will make better lifestyle choices to promote wellness.

5. Health insurance exchanges will increase access to health care services.

During the time that we were writing this book, the notion of state-based health insurance exchanges was one of PPACA's most debated agendas. At the core of the debate were the following key issues: disagreement over the amount of federal and state subsidies targeted at certain Americans who cannot otherwise afford health insurance, the formation of exchanges to promote greater access to affordable insurance, and proposed taxes to help fund the subsidies.[14]

This book is about the future of health care and people can debate how certain elements of such a future should be constructed. This book is about what will come to be regardless of the outcome of the societal and legal attacks against PPACA and the exchanges. Whether society names them "insurance exchanges" or something else, The New Health Age will bring about increased access to health care through new and creative insurance programs. Why will this occur? As we have seen throughout this book, increasing access to preventative health care and teaching personal responsibility for one's own health are prerequisites to controlling health care costs and improving the health of Americans, and policy makers and modern health insurance products will help drive this goal. This movement began prior to PPACA and will continue into The New Health Age.

Blue Cross Blue Shield (BCBS) of Florida, for example, started building retail-oriented stores across Florida in 2007. A BCBS store may now be located next to a Starbucks. The goal behind this contemporary concept is to personalize health insurance by bringing health plans into communities in a physical way. When customers walk into a BCBS retail store, they gain an enhanced awareness of wellness and prevention by completing an online health risk assessment and immediately reviewing printed reports related to their overall health. By creating a "retail store experience," BCBS can increase its services and access to health insurance and empower customers with new products that will bring down health insurance costs.[15]

Insurance exchanges will function at the state and local levels and serve as a clearinghouse, enrolling agent, and massive purchaser of health insurance, all of which will drive down insurance premiums by increasing access to the *right type* of health care, as discussed below. Through web portals, Americans will be able to make side-by-side comparisons of insurance products in the marketplace, empowering consumers and fostering increased competition. Exchanges will accept enrollment into health plans and function as an organized purchaser of health insurance on behalf of the masses.

Think of Expedia, Travelocity, or Cheap Tickets. Today, people can use their smartphones to purchase the cheapest airline tickets in a manner of minutes. The power and ability to purchase health insurance in such a manner will occur eventually through health insurance exchanges. Increased and easier access to insurance products will empower and enable more Americans to access lifestyle-medicine based health plans, enhance competition among insurance companies, and ultimately drive down premium costs.

Unfortunately, many health insurance agents will go the way of the travel agent in The New Heath Age, but forward thinking and adaptable individuals in the health insurance profession can prepare themselves for the significant changes ahead and adjust accordingly. New entrepreneurial opportunities will present themselves to those who accept that change is occurring and who adapt quickly in advance of the shift. Review David Steinman's Change Vision in this book for starters. He shares various contemporary products taking shape within the health insurance marketplace.

Insurance advisors who become more than an "insurance salesman" for their clients can continue to thrive going forward if they develop innovative personal responsibility, wellness, and disease prevention plans that complement traditional health plan policies. Insurance firms that leverage online technology to increase their clients' ability to educate themselves about good health and to make decisions that are more informed when purchasing health insurance will enjoy an advantage.

Why will exchanges survive and evolve amidst all the current debate and controversy? Because Americans will ultimately see through the cloud of debate and focus on the following fact: Without increased access to health care resources and lifestyle medicine, too many Americans will continue to suffer from the chronic diseases that are consuming too much of our health care dollars.[16]

Corporations, governments, and taxpayers have reached a tipping point and simply cannot afford the current system. As the data have demonstrated in other chapters of this book, if we prevent, treat, manage, and reduce chronic disease, America's overall health care expenditures will go down while our health, happiness, taxes, and corporate profits will go up.

America was built on ingenuity and capitalism. Our ideals are no different today—in fact, ingenuity and capitalism are more alive today than ever. To promote capitalism and a strong economy, new ideas and structures like health insurance exchanges will continue to emerge and take hold. More Americans need greater and more affordable access to health care. Indeed, some of the current establishment will resist and oppose exchanges. But, ultimately, opponents will not be able to stall the progression of exchanges because the benefits that exchanges will bring to states and citizens will become abundantly clear. People will get healthier through progressive health insurance plans and medical home models. Costs will eventually go down. Most states see the potential benefits however many policy makers remain doubtful and suspicious. When PPACA became law, 48 states applied for federal grants to commence forming exchanges.[17] Only Alaska and Minnesota elected to stand on the sideline and not participate.[18] State insurance exchanges will occur, yet for many it is hard to believe in the benefits that exchanges can produce.

Remember, once people actually believed that the world was flat! The likes of Aristotle, Christopher Columbus, and Galileo dispelled those beliefs, but many rebuffed these men at the time. Today their views are reality. Oliver Wendell Holmes' quote at the beginning of this chapter is worth restating: "A mind once stretched by a new idea never regains its original dimensions." America won't go back. Exchanges will be a new structure during The New Health Age.

Exchanges will serve as an alternative for Americans who do not have employer-sponsored health insurance options or who do not qualify for a traditional government benefit plan, such as

Medicare or Medicaid. Exchanges are intended to offer people with moderate incomes, but who are otherwise ineligible for public programs, the opportunity to select among a number of private health insurance plans, with limited federal premium subsidies that are scaled to household incomes.

Exchanges will provide an option for small businesses and independent workers in America who do not otherwise have access to affordable health care insurance. We are not talking about the homeless population or illegal aliens—that is a different discussion which needs to occur but is outside of the scope of this book. Exchanges will target and help working Americans and small business, including waiters, waitresses, farmers, migrant workers, landscaping crews, construction workers, mechanics, and fishermen, to name a few. The United States will not turn its back on these Americans, because they serve as the backbone to our society in countless ways. These hardworking people represent dedicated Americans trying to live the American dream. No, they do not work for large businesses with employee benefit plans and they do not qualify for government support under current programs, but they still require and deserve access to affordable health care insurance.

Take your mind out of the health care debate for a moment. After World War II, under the leadership of President Dwight D. Eisenhower and the U.S. Congress, America decided to construct a national interstate highway system, at a cost estimated at $114 billion (adjusted for inflation).[19] Why? American leaders saw a vision of the future for this great nation. They realized that we needed to better connect the communities across this country, from coast to coast, to enhance the flow of commerce and to grow our economy. Commerce and people needed to be able to move from place to place faster and safer after World War II. This nation decided to make a massive investment in a transportation infrastructure never seen before, so that we could receive an economic return on that investment for decades, centuries, or even millennia to come.

Many Americans do not use our nation's interstate system on a daily basis, but when citizens need it, the highway is now there for us. We accept without much debate that our country should continue to invest in a national roadway transportation infrastructure for the betterment of our society.

In The New Health Age, Americans will come to view health care in the same way. Ensuring access to health care for all Americans will not be viewed as an *entitlement*, but will be regarded as an investment in our economic prosperity. Without a nation of healthy people, we become a weaker nation—politically, economically, and morally.

Americans have never accepted anything that weakens us as a country. Will we change that admirable characteristic as we move ahead? America will continue to make choices and implement systems and structures that make our nation strong. We always have. Ensuring access to health care is simply a component of maintaining and growing a great nation. As that old chestnut of wisdom makes clear, "If you don't have your health, you don't have anything."

When absolutely necessary, subsidy-supported health insurance will be an investment in people's health and well-being, not a handout to maintain the status quo. In fact, in order to receive subsidies, enrollees should be required to participate in lifestyle medicine, wellness, and disease prevention plans, which ultimately drive down the costs for health care and the resulting cost of insurance.

Recall from earlier chapters that incentives drive changes to our behavior. Exchanges should offer health plans that operate with incentives at the core, in the same way that large employer health plans will function. If an overweight person qualifies for a subsidy to purchase insurance through an exchange, reducing his or her obesity should be a key goal in the plan going forward. If the individual refuses to participate in wellness and prevention programs that are aimed at reducing his or her weight, the subsidy should be lost. Freedom of choice, a fundamental American belief, will continue. Choose to lose weight, and your health care expenditures will go down. Choose not to lose weight, and your health care expenditures will go up. Your choice! Americans will have to play by the rules, and most will ultimately want to do so to receive affordable benefits and coverage in The New Health Age.

America will ultimately view exchanges no differently than the investment that America made—and continues to make—in its interstate highway system. Healthy people lead to a productive workforce and a stronger economy. Why not invest in that result?

Let's be clear about an important fact. Insuring more lives will not, however, by itself reduce premiums and health care costs in a meaningful way. If we simply add more unhealthy lives to insurance pools, costs do not change. In fact, they will increase. The goal is to get America healthier through exchanges, medical homes, ACOs, EACOs, and elsewhere. Healthy citizens, not more citizens in insurance pools, drive down health insurance premiums and health care costs.

The economics of health insurance is actually fairly straightforward. Although administrative costs can be reduced through exchanges by having greater economies of scale and higher efficiencies, easier access to insurance products, and lower sales commissions, 85 to 90 percent of health insurance premiums relate to *health care services*, not administrative costs.[20] Exchanges will not reduce health insurance costs simply by increasing the numbers of lives in a risk pool. Premium dollars can only decrease in a meaningful way by making insured people healthier.

So exchanges will become a new payment structure during The New Health Age because Americans are smart, driven, and patriotic people who want to preserve the strongest and greatest nation on earth. Americans are coming to the realization that our state of health, as explored throughout this book, is slipping. Every individual Stakeholder needs access to the right health care— health care that is focused on lifestyle medicine, wellness, and prevention to avoid sickness and disease.

Each of the new structures discussed in this chapter will reshape, reorder, reorient, and lower costs in the American health care delivery system. More models will evolve and progress in The New Health Age.

Even the new structures discussed in this chapter will eventually change, but one constant will remain—America wants to remain the greatest nation on Earth. In order to achieve this sustained goal, we need new structures and systems that promote healthier Americans.

KEY POINTS

1. New integrated health care systems (IDSs) will bring about great integration of health care providers, leading to increased quality in health care and cost reduction, both of which foster a greater nation.

2. Accountable care models and organizations (ACOs and EACOs) will create new integrated structures within health care delivery systems during The New Health Age.

3. Patient-centered medical homes will create symbiotic and proactive care models in communities across America. Medical homes will foster and promote lifestyle medicine that will motivate Americans to assume greater personal responsibility for their own health.

4. Health insurance exchanges will increase access to health care services, eventually lowering costs, leading to a more competitive America.

‹ CHANGE VISION ›

Stuart Levine, MD, *serves as the Corporate Medical Director and Regional Medical Director of HealthCare Partners Medical Group of California. In this role, he oversees the company's clinical initiatives, including care management and other programs for frail and senior patients, and a variety of growth initiatives and innovations. Dr. Levine completed fellowships through University of California, San Francisco, and Stanford University, sponsored by the California Health Care Foundation in both Health Care Leadership and Policy and Medical Biodesign and Innovation. He also serves as an Assistant Clinical Professor of Internal Medicine and Psychiatry at the David Geffen School of Medicine at UCLA and as the Director of Behavioral Health Education at St. Mary's Medical Center Internal Medicine Residency program in Long Beach, California. Prior to joining HealthCare Partners, Dr. Levine served as Medical Director for SCAN Health Plan. A psychiatrist, Dr. Levine graduated from the University of Illinois College of Medicine at Chicago. He is also the Director for Behavioral and Health Services Education for the Primary Care Internal Medicine Residency at St. Mary's Medical Center/UCLA, and holds a master's degree in Healthcare Administration from George Washington University in Washington, D.C. He is the author or coauthor of over 60 scientific papers and the recipient of numerous grants and other awards, including a Mead Johnson Fellowship from the American Psychiatric Association and a Burroughs Wellcome Fellowship in community medicine from the American Medical Association.*

The Evolution of Managed Care as the Foundation for Health Reform: ACOs as Care Integrators and Coordinators for All Patients

By Stuart Levine, MD

Background, Vision, and Mission

HealthCare Partners Medical Group provides care to 685,000 patients in California, Nevada, and Florida, including 173,000 Medicare Advantage patients, 511,000 commercially insured individuals, and 25,000 dual eligibles (i.e., those eligible for both Medicare and Medicaid). Just under half (45 percent) of HealthCare Partners' physicians are employees, while 55 percent are under contract in a wraparound independent practice association (IPA).

One of the first accountable care organizations (ACOs) in the nation, HealthCare Partners takes full capitated risk, with both staff and IPA physicians, organized into pods with financial incentives to reduce emergency room visits and admissions. The savings generated allows the group to pay physicians roughly 140 percent of Medicare fees and also fund the infrastructure and financial incentives needed to provide high-quality, low-cost care on a consistent basis.

HealthCare Partners vision is to "be the role model for integrated and coordinated care, leading the transformation of the national health care delivery system to assure quality, access, and affordable care for all." To that end, its daily mission is to "partner with patients to live life to the fullest by providing outstanding health care and supporting physicians to excel in the healing arts." HealthCare Partners views any hospitalization as a failure of the health care system. (Roughly 40 percent of all deaths occur in the hospital. By contrast, at HealthCare Partners less than 20 percent of patient deaths occur in the hospital, and the organization's goal is to bring this figure down below 10 percent.)

Living up to the Mission

Living up to this ambitious vision and mission requires great execution, with sophisticated IT and other systems to ensure that hand-offs go smoothly and that patients do not fall through the cracks. But success requires more than IT. Rather, it requires a true connection with the patient. To that end, the organization strives to let patients know that they have a voice and that their doctors have not lost the art of caring or of being advocates. The goal is to make services and care so good that fee-for-service (FFS) patients and other patients used to having a choice of provider no longer want that choice.

Success also requires good care processes, which cost money. While virtually all organizations are investing in electronic medical records (EMRs) and other IT systems, many end up computerizing bad care processes. At Health-Care Partners, however, care processes are being continually studied and redesigned, as necessary, to ensure the right processes are in place that center on the patient. While maintaining the sanctity of the physician-patient relationship, HealthCare Partners has invested in new payment systems and infrastructure that allow doctors to get out of the "see something, do something, get paid" mind-set of FFS medicine. The medical group pays an upfront per-member/per-month (PMPM) fee to cover infrastructure, plus generous FFS payments that allow doctors to spend time with patients. For example, HealthCare Partners pays physicians to provide advance care planning every year to patients and their families. HealthCare Partners has also invested in patient-centered IT systems that allow use of technology in patients' homes and enable a portal that puts patients' relevant medical data at physicians' fingertips, even if those physicians don't have access to the EMRs.

HealthCare Partners accepts "all willing" primary care providers (PCPs), as long as they meet National Committee for Quality Assurance (NCQA) and Institute for Medical Quality (IMQ) quality standards, in order to not disenfranchise patients from their PCP. To make the system work, the organization has built systems to support physicians in identifying and proactively managing at-risk patients, with different programs available (e.g., primary care, complex care/disease management, comprehensive care and post-discharge clinics, home care, end-stage renal disease medical home, and palliative care), depending on level of risk. This risk stratification process is outlined in the chart on the next page.

Although not yet functioning at maximum capability, HealthCare Partners' risk-stratification process has helped to reduce hospital admissions by 85 percent in high-risk patients. This success has been the result of multiple programs aimed at getting at-risk patients the care they need to keep them out of the hospital and providing lower risk patients with the support they need to self-manage and stay healthy. Examples of various programs include the following:

- **Team-based home care.** Teams of physicians, nurse practitioners, care managers, and social workers provide care to the riskiest patients (top 2 to 3 percent) in their homes. Each team takes responsibility for 200 frail patients in need of patient- and family-centered home care, providing them with a comprehensive assessment (e.g., of living conditions, social and financial needs, medications, and medical and behavioral health), advance care planning, and palliative care. The substantial

HealthCare Partners Offers Four Levels of Care Management

Stratifying Patients into the Appropriate Program
Using Evidence-Based Medicine

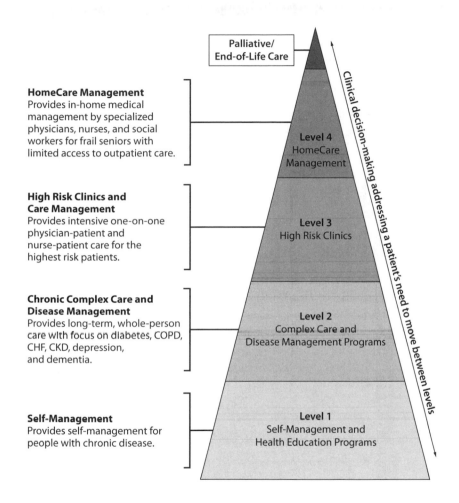

HomeCare Management
Provides in-home medical management by specialized physicians, nurses, and social workers for frail seniors with limited access to outpatient care.

High Risk Clinics and Care Management
Provides intensive one-on-one physician-patient and nurse-patient care for the highest risk patients.

Chronic Complex Care and Disease Management
Provides long-term, whole-person care with focus on diabetes, COPD, CHF, CKD, depression, and dementia.

Self-Management
Provides self-management for people with chronic disease.

Palliative/ End-of-Life Care

Level 4
HomeCare Management

Level 3
High Risk Clinics

Level 2
Complex Care and Disease Management Programs

Level 1
Self-Management and Health Education Programs

Clinical decision-making addressing a patient's need to move between levels upfront cost for this program more than pays for itself by reducing admissions and improving quality. In fact, the program has significantly reduced both inpatient admissions and emergency room visits for the 967 patients enrolled.

- **Comprehensive care centers.** This program—originally designed for seniors but now being transitioned to the commercial population—provides services to stabilize patients, facilitate smooth care transitions, and supply ongoing chronic care management, including medication reconciliation, disease/care plan education, behavioral health assessments, post-hospitalization care, and advance care planning. The commercial version will incorporate a greater focus on mental/behavioral health. This program has led to dramatic (90 percent or more) reductions in emergency room visits and inpatient admissions for the 426 patients served.

- **End-stage renal disease (ESRD) medical home.** Health-Care Partners sends a nurse practitioner to the dialysis center to provide primary care services, including mental health evaluations. Most ESRD patients spend so much time at the dialysis center each week that they do not want to make a separate visit for primary care. This program allows them to avoid the need for such visits, while also providing them with critical support and human interaction during what might otherwise be stressful and lonely dialysis sessions. It has led to significant reductions in emergency room visits and inpatient admissions.

- **Integrated collaborative care, behavioral health.** Patients do not like "carve-outs" for mental health, but instead want to receive mental health services in the primary care setting. HealthCare Partners co-locates social workers in primary care clinics (including IPAs). These behavioral health specialists focus on patients with depression, anxiety, dementia, and chemical dependencies. Most primary care clinics would not have the resources to invest in a social worker on their own.

- **Advance care planning and palliative care.** This program focuses on improving health care providers' competency in end-of-life management and on helping patients develop an end-of-life care plan based on their values, a realistic assessment of treatment options, and their clinical condition (e.g., prognosis, quality of life).

Through these and other programs, HealthCare Partners has worked to educate its patients that hospitalization should no longer be viewed as a "benefit" to be demanded. Rather, by aligning patients, families, and physicians, all stakeholders now strive to avoid hospitalizations. To achieve this transition and put these programs into place, HealthCare Partners has reengineered medical management infrastructure and care processes through a formal innovation process. Innovation teams engaging in this process include representation from corporate and regional operations and local clinical and care management staff. The overall process encourages a culture of innovation built on experimentation and failures, which ultimately leads to success.

The process relies on a set of patient-centered medical home principles for high-risk patients, as outlined below:

- Recognize that the whole is greater than the sum of the parts.
- Design programs for the most frail, chronically ill patients with the highest admission rates, and then adapt them for use with other patients.

- Design programs for IPA patients first, and then adapt them for group-/staff-model patients, because it is more complex to manage high-risk patients with contracted physicians whose behavior you do not directly control. If successful in an IPA clinical innovation, the application of this innovation to an HealthCare Partners group site where we control staff and processes will be guaranteed to be even more successful.
- Use statistical/clinical risk stratification to identify patients and match them with needed programs.
- Measure clinical results and return on investment from programs over time.
- Use continual process testing and improvement of programs and constant reengineering.
- Conduct regional experiments, using one region as a "research and development shop" for the entire organization.
- Use cross-regional fertilization and sharing of best practices to achieve optimal results.

The culture of innovation has been created through leadership that emphasizes the strict adherence to the following:

- Respect and credibility for innovation leaders. These leaders represent "jacks-of-all-trades" who have some expertise and are passionate, individualistic, motivated, and creative. These problem solvers also bring "out-of-the-box" views of the world to their work.
- Do not accept the status quo.
- Motivate and reward change, energy, and passion.

- Use nonhierarchical decision making throughout the organization, giving everyone the responsibility to innovate and the right and authority to be wrong.
- Value collaboration from all levels.
- Reward and learn from failure, which fosters creativity, tension, and collective memory.
- Stage chaotic change and thrive in uncertainty.
- Celebrate the human spirit.
- Mind the organization so that the "right hand" knows and trusts the "left hand" without supervision.

These principles and the culture of innovation have allowed the organization to reduce inpatient days per 1,000 among Medicare Advantage beneficiaries to 600, well below the California average for Medicare Advantage (982) and Medicare FFS (1,660), and less than one-third of the nationwide Medicare FFS average of 1,900 days per 1,000 (with some states averaging over 2,500 days).

Key Features for Success
Key features that drive HealthCare Partners' success include the following:

- Allow for physician "ownership" of the patient.
- Use team-based care and teamwork to support the physician and patient to enhance outcomes.
- Motivate and incentivize physicians and the health care team.
- Provide the right care at the right time in the right place, every time.

- Remember that the best quality care is the most cost-effective care.

- Educate patients on their disease, care plan, and how, where, and when to access care.

- Provide quick access to care.

- Use risk stratification to identify at-risk patients prior to catastrophic need.

- Recognize that technology and clinical intervention is needed to improve care.

- Provide life planning and quality care planning, with documented decisions.

- Provide a comprehensive clinical and social assessment, along with medication reconciliation.

- Make sure that IT makes all relevant care information available.

- Invest in infrastructure to care for the highest risk patients (top 20 to 30 percent of patients in the highest intensity high-risk programs).

- Constantly communicate, because there can never be too much communication.

- Commit to the patient and his or her quality of life.

- Integrate best practices from around the country.

How ACOs Complete the Picture

ACOs help to complete the picture of what organizations need to do by ending the traditional "vendor" relationship between hospitals and physicians through creation of a risk arrangement that affects all parties, including patients and employers. ACOs highlight the need for hospitals, providers throughout the care continuum, and patients to work collaboratively to ensure appropriate, high quality, efficient, and cost-effective care. Large medical groups, especially those that participate in managed care, will be in a good position to lead ACOs that focus on improving population health and preventive care so as to reduce inpatient utilization over the long term.

To be successful, providers need to revisit investment decisions and ensure that such investments strengthen medical management infrastructure, connectivity, and data sharing/communication along the continuum of care to truly coordinate all care, regardless of payer source. Success also requires consideration of investment in outpatient/outreach and access points (e.g., home care, high-risk clinics, hospitalists, physician incentives, hospital partnerships, satellite clinics, electronic visits, alternatives to the emergency room) to accommodate the increased demand for access to care. Physicians, particularly primary care doctors, must prepare themselves for an increase in newly insured patients who will seek care from a coordinated care team. Finally, patients must be actively engaged to take responsibility for their health, while physicians and hospitals must adopt a population health perspective.

HealthCare Partners' leadership believes that ACOs can be a vehicle to achieve this type of success. The organization has been selected as one of five national sites for a Dartmouth-Brookings ACO pilot program with Anthem Blue Cross. The organization is also engaged in several ACO pilot programs with other organizations in the local community.

15

What Health Care Institutions and Practitioners Need to Know and Do in The New Health Age

"Believe you can and you're halfway there."

—Theodore Roosevelt

You have now seen the huge and fundamental tsunami of change that is beginning to completely redefine medicine and health care delivery in America. This transformation and shift are unprecedented in our nation's history. During such times of dramatic and reorganizational change, there will be winners and losers. Winners will be those who acknowledge and understand the change, its historical imperative, the social and economic need for it, and who act accordingly. Losers will be those who think they can continue to function as they have before or who doubt that the change will be permanent.

In our conversations with the thought leaders in medicine and health care today for the writing of this book, many of whom have already been cited in or contributed to this book, there was a loose consensus regarding this ability to embrace the change now beginning. The consensus was the prediction that 60 percent of those in the existing health care delivery system will survive, and in fact thrive because of their ability to adapt and embrace the change. The remaining 40 percent will resist the transformation or, ostrich-like, plunge their heads into the sand, fail, and go away.

This chapter is both for those 60 percent who need, want, and accept necessary guidance and those 40 percent who might need some help to unlock their thinking. Hopefully, this book can save some in the 40 percent class from failure and extinction.

We divide this chapter into two sections. The first focuses on what health care providers need to know. The second makes recommendations regarding what health care providers should do next.

1. What do health care institutions and practitioners need to know?

We trust, after reading the prior chapters of this book, that the answer to the above question is much clearer and more self-evident than when you started on page one. To clarify what readers should know going forward, we will boil everything down for clarity and efficiency:

- Modern Man has been on this planet for approximately 150,000 years. It is only in the last 4,500 years that there has been any real history of medicine. It is only in the last 150 years that the scientific foundations of current medicine have occurred. Expected health and wellness and an ever-extending natural lifespan are very recent developments.

- The speed of medical innovation and discovery is on an accelerating growth curve. Health care delivery is starting to experience rapid change as we enter the twenty-first century. Both of these dynamics are moving toward the ushering in of The New Health Age.

- Amazing change has occurred in the last 30 years through increased connectivity and technology. The three-decades-old Information Age initiated a historically unprecedented amount of social, economic, and cultural change. The health care sector of the American economy did not keep up with the electronic and connectivity revolution that occurred almost everywhere else.

- Health care spending approximates 20 percent of GDP. GDP spending in other areas approximates 80 percent. The 80 percent non-health-care world has embraced and utilizes technology and connectivity much more than the 20 percent world of health care. The 80 percent world is coming to the 20 percent world, and fast!

- Humanity has entered a new age, the Shift Age. The three forces of the Shift Age are Accelerating Electronic Connectedness, the Flow to Global, and the Flow to the Individual.

- The forces of the Shift Age have radically transformed and reshaped humanity and many of its institutions. The Shift Age has now ushered us into The New Health Age.

- We are now fully in the twenty-first century, and 2010–2020 is the Transformation Decade. The definition of transformation is "a change in form, nature, and appearance or character."

- The Transformation Decade starts The New Health Age with medical breakthroughs and health care delivery restructuring that will transform humanity, health, society, health care costs, and even our definitions of life itself. It is essential for America to acknowledge, embrace, and prepare for it, for it will be grand!

- Change is needed and change is coming because America's state of health, the economic models driving health care choices and costs, and America's health care delivery systems do not adequately foster the right incentives for American Stakeholders to (1) increase the quality of their health, (2) improve health care service to everyone, or (3) control health care costs. This reality is contributing to the rapid decline of America's pride, financial strength, and competitive advantage in a global marketplace. It is, therefore, essential for America to acknowledge, embrace, and foster The New Health Age.

- The New Health Age will be defined by fundamental dynamic flows that move from the history of medicine and health care to its coming future. The flow dynamics of The New Health Age are

  How we THINK about health care:
  ○ Sickness → Wellness
  ○ Ignorance → Awareness/Understanding
  ○ Opposition → Alignment

  How we DELIVER health care:
  ○ Treatment → Prevention
  ○ Reactive → Proactive
  ○ Episodic → Wholistic

  The ECONOMICS of health care:
  ○ Procedures → Performance
  ○ Isolation → Integration
  ○ Nonefficient (Passive) → Efficient (Active)

- The task is at hand and the work to do are massive, but it will be done.

- The transition will be very difficult, contentious, and certainly disruptive. Change most often triggers fear, uncertainty, and resistance in people. Yet if we can see the future and understand that the long-term benefits will be substantial, that the economic savings will be huge, and that it is something essential for America to remain great, then we can hopefully come together to move through the near-term transition.

- The new structures of health care will bring about great integration of health care providers and an environment of collaboration among providers, payers, and patients.

- ACOs and EACOs will create new care delivery models within integrated health care delivery systems that are focused on cost control, patient responsibility, and improved health care provider performance. American businesses through EACOs will focus on health plan benefit design and create incentives to motivate employees to live out healthier lives and to take on more responsibility for their own health. On the public side, governments will increasingly implement policy changes, including excise taxes, to discourage unhealthy habits, such as smoking and consuming a poor diet.

- Patient-centered medical homes will create symbiotic and proactive care models in communities across America, centering on wellness and prevention of disease. Physicians will practice lifestyle medicine within medical homes and foster a culture and dedication among their patients to live out healthier lives, taking into account, environment, genetics, and personal choices.

- Existing models will expand and new models and structures will grow to support end-of-life care. America will engage in more societal discussions about how families should handle a terminal event for a loved one, but health care providers will not initiate the end-of-life.

- Health insurance exchanges will increase the availability of affordable health insurance focusing on wellness and prevention, thus increasing access to health care services for small businesses and others, and thereby improving health and reducing costs.

There you have it. We have built a significant foundational base of knowledge to now build upon and take action.

2. What do health care institutions and practitioners need to do?

We Must Change Our Perspectives and Open Our Minds to New Ideas

We are all creatures of habit. We all live in self-defined accepted realities. These habits and these accepted realities often keep us from seeing something new or choosing to consider a different way. We seldom take the time to view and observe the things that surround us with new perspectives. Relationships, habits, careers, procedures, systems, and things become so assimilated into our existence that we often take them for granted and fail to stop and ask one basic question: How can I view the world and function in it *differently* to make our earthly experience better?

We become creatures of habit who operate and think in the same manner day after day. Society resists the exercise of challenging whether our customs, practices, and traditions should change. We continue on until there is a catalyst for change or until something provokes us to have an "aha!" moment.

One of the key goals and purposes of this book is to be that catalyst for changing thinking that is based on habit, self-accepted reality, and the confines of the current context. Should the customs, practices, and traditions in health care and maintaining America's health be regarded differently in response to the transformations that have occurred around us? We say yes!

This discussion will be of much greater value if you unlock your mind to be able to view new perspectives. Release and enable your thinking to examine health and health care delivery very differently. Your view of something may well change not because the thing you are viewing has changed but because you have changed. You see a new point of view. You have a new way of thinking.

Create Strong and Effective Leaders, Management, and Employees

Medical education fails to teach "Business 101" to most health care professionals. This places too many health care providers at an extreme disadvantage throughout their careers. Many physicians admit that they have a difficult time managing and administering all the business aspects of medicine because that is not what they were trained to do and often do not want to do in their medical practices. Many traditional hospitals struggle to find strong management talent who possess the full range of skills required to lead a hospital into an integrated delivery environment with numerous and diverse component parts. In The New Health Age, ACOs and EACOs will form strong partnerships with hospital systems, requiring that hospital management understand risk-based and pay-for-performance reimbursement models that rely upon effective disease and case management.

Now, perhaps more than any other time in the history of health care delivery, it is vitally important for health care providers of all types to bring strong leaders and managers into their organizations to help guide them through the challenging transition ahead. It is time to engage the "A team" at every level of human resource planning. Health care leaders and managers must possess instinctive, keen, and up-to-date knowledge regarding how to lead effectively a health care organization into a totally new and changing environment.

Simply possessing a bachelor's or master's degree in business administration or public health will not be enough. Health care providers need to add dynamic, honest, intelligent, skilled, and confident leaders to their operational team.

Every good orchestra has a strong conductor. Winning Super Bowl teams have great coaches. To win the World Series requires an excellent manager. To achieve great profitability requires a first-class CEO.

Health care organizations will need to build highly skilled and effective employees beyond senior management as well. "Talent management" will become increasingly important in the years ahead as health care becomes more competitive and dynamic. Employers need systems and measurements for assessing effective employee placement, based on personality, skill sets, and experience. Even top talent will require ongoing training and education in The New Health Age to stay abreast of new developments in health care. We are living in an economy that demands a "lifetime of learning," so strong employers need to promote and facilitate opportunities for employee advancement. Much of the content of this talent management will be delivered online, always available as needed for the never-ending need for knowledge.

To thrive and prosper during The New Health Age, health care organizations must have a best in class work force, without question.

Develop a Health Information Technology Plan and Execute That Plan

Throughout the book, we have referenced how health information technology (HIT) will transform health care delivery and improve health in countless ways. Whether because of electronic medical or health records systems (EMRs), patient health records, health care administration systems, telecommunications, cutting-edge medical equipment, software analytics, or otherwise, health care providers have every reason to adopt HIT into every aspect of their profession in The New Health Age. Health care providers will rely upon HIT to succeed, perhaps even survive, going forward.

HIT will become one of the most important tools and instruments in health care. Providers will need HIT to communicate with each other; access patient health information; interface with cutting-edge, evidence-based medicine guidelines; manage disease; demonstrate outcomes under pay-for-performance payment systems; and interact with EACOs and ACOs. The use of HIT will be constrained simply by the degree of ingenuity that the health care sector places on itself; otherwise, HIT uses and benefits are virtually limitless.

For those health care providers who have already developed HIT strategic plans and commenced with implementation of such plans, execution and follow through will be critical. Health care providers in the midst of creating an HIT strategic plan should focus on developing open networks that will promote integration and connectivity at all levels. Health care providers waiting to begin HIT strategic planning are already significantly behind in the race and cannot afford to delay any longer.

An HIT strategic plan should focus on the following key elements:

1. Assessing needs, both internal and external, to the organization. A formal appraisal should review the organization's IT structure, functions, resources, strengths, and limitations.

2. Creating a compelling vision to accelerate the adoption of HIT, including getting electronic medical records and personal health records systems installed and fully utilized, and implementing telehealth and e-prescribing.

3. Communicating the HIT plan to others, both internally and externally to the organization.

4. Collaborating with all interested parties applicable to the HIT plan.

5. Fostering relationships with local, state, or national health information exchanges (HIEs). HIEs will be independent organizations and will hold the hardware and software necessary for separate and unique EMR systems to interface and communicate with each other. HIEs will be responsible for moving and translating electronic health information to and from end users.

6. Ensuring that broadband infrastructure is in place to transmit telehealth data, whether such information is in the form of voice, data, or images.

7. Developing an HIT workforce that can prepare, install, support, and maintain the provider's HIT system.

8. Ensuring financial viability and sustainability of the HIT plan. The HIT component of the American Recovery and Reinvestment Act (ARRA) that went into effect February 17, 2009,[1] provides economic incentives to health care providers to implement EMR systems. Over a 5-year period, physicians and certain health care providers can each receive up to $44,000 if they demonstrate "meaningful use" of EMR technology.[2] By 2015, health care providers will be penalized for failing to implement EMRs.[3] Such stimulus funds will help promote the financing of EMR costs, but such funding will certainly not cover all expenses. Budgets should, therefore, take HIT spending into account.

9. In order to plan, implement, and maintain each element of the HIT strategic plan, health care providers should strive to build a strong team of advisors to take them through the coming years of explosive growth in the HIT space.

Recall the 80/20 chapter. The 80 percent of IT in the rest of the economy is coming to the 20 percent.

Health Care Providers Will Integrate to Survive and Function Effectively in The New Health Age

Health care providers need to develop strategic integration plans for their future and execute them. The following are several action items to consider.

Uniqueness

Each organization and every health care community is unique in terms of its market conditions, finances, employees, professionals, patients, payers, competitors, and other characteristics. No "one size fits all" approach exists when developing a strategic integration plan because of the differences that exist across health care providers. Health care providers should acknowledge this reality and tailor strategic plans to their specific community, circumstances, and characteristics.

Power and Control
Organizations must address how much power and control they are willing to surrender during the process of integration. When organizations integrate, through acquisition, merger, or contract, one side or another agrees to give up some degree of power and control. The acquired succumbs to the acquirer. The employee yields to the employer. The minority partner has less control than does the majority owner. Some organizations and individuals can accept yielding more power than others. Organizations must address this issue as part of any integration plan. The key question to answer is what will ultimately yield the most-efficient, cost-saving, and quality integration. By addressing this issue, organizations can better assess the degree to which they are comfortable integrating. Health care providers that are comfortable yielding control to others will likely be comfortable integrating to the fullest degree. Those who wish to maintain some control should integrate with caution and to a lesser degree.

Full integration includes physicians selling their medical practices to hospitals and becoming employees. Providers who want to retain more autonomy may integrate in other ways. Joint ventures and co-management agreements are examples of less integration and can result in more balance of power. In a co-management arrangement, a hospital and medical practice execute agreements whereby the medical group manages a department or service line for the hospital. This brings hospital departments and physicians closer together to achieve and meet quality and cost alignment goals without completely integrating.

Culture
Health care providers contemplating integration should analyze the cultures of different entities frankly and openly during any integration process to confirm that the integrated organizations will be capable of "playing well together in the sandbox." A for-profit

hospital located in the affluent suburbs has a very different culture than an academic hospital institution. Merging these two hospitals into one cohesive IDS may pose cultural challenges. Obstacles can be overcome, but culture is a key point for consideration and organizations must address it.

Governance, Management, and Authority

Determining the right governance and management structure for an IDS and establishing authority levels is central to success. The cultures of the joining organizations and their respective needs for power and control should drive and influence the resulting governance and management structure. An IDS will be doomed to failure if it acquires powerful and independent-minded physicians and refuses to give them participation in the IDS's governance or management structure. If an IDS comes together through the merger of two hospitals and three skilled nursing facilities, the organization should include representatives from each of these operating divisions into the IDS's governance and management structure. The more that departments and service lines are represented in the governance and management structure the better, because collaboration and team-spirit results.

Financial Strength

All parties contemplating integration should assess accurately and truthfully their respective financial strength. Two strong economic players coming together and uniting in the marketplace will likely produce an even stronger enterprise following the integration. Two weak organizations may make a bad economic situation even worse. Determining the financial condition of all the interested parties is essential so that participants can perform proper planning.

Markets

Completing a market analysis is imperative. Organizations should strive to understand the markets in which they participate so that critical planning can take place to optimize the integrated systems.

In the case of two hospitals merging within the same community because of overlapping markets, perhaps one facility should be converted into an outpatient clinic or medical office building to reduce unnecessary resources. In other cases, hospitals might unite from different regions with no market overlap. In the second example, perhaps the hospitals form separate centers of excellence at each location and develop referral programs between the two facilities. One hospital might form a woman's center and the other an orthopedic program. Each hospital would cross-refer patients within the region to the appropriate center of excellence, be able to invest more capital and resources into developing superior programs, thereby avoiding cost duplication while striving for better quality.

Service Lines

As demonstrated in the example above, IDSs should assess the service lines that result when previously separate providers integrate and come together. In many cases, IDSs will restructure previously duplicated clinical care lines into logical divisions that function more as cohesive units. Specialty areas, such as cardiology, orthopedics, neurology, urology, and so forth, should reorganize and deliver care in a unified and coordinated manner following integration. IDSs can achieve this objective by forming one single multispecialty physician group to provide services to the various IDS hospitals in a coordinated manner. Prior to integrating, the physicians likely functioned through separate medical practices and moved from hospital to hospital. Post-integration, integrated medical groups owned by the IDS can schedule and relocate physicians and dedicate them to one hospital, creating greater focus and efficiencies, as opposed to physicians covering multiple hospitals and moving from one to another, often in the same day.

Competitive Forces

Parties must assess competitive market dynamics as part of an integration strategy. Integration should create competitive advantages, whether by creating increased market power, service and quality excellence, or economic supremacy. In instances where a hospital system is already known for providing outstanding woman's care, perhaps the system should integrate with more obstetrics and gynecology medical practices to solidify its market share. If two competing hospitals are both building an IDS, independent physician medical groups are likely to be courted by both systems, often simultaneously. If a particular medical specialty practice relies on another group for its patient referrals, these two groups should likely collaborate and join the same hospital so that they can continue to refer patients as part of the IDS. These examples demonstrate how competitive realities must contribute to integration strategies.

Reputation for Quality Care

The reputations that organizations hold within communities are typically well known within health care circles. "This hospital is excellent." "This hospital is a dump." Parties must carefully consider the respective reputations of those interested in becoming part of an integration plan. A medical group that prides itself on achieving best outcomes for its patients cannot afford to integrate with a hospital system that does not share these goals. The same holds true for separate physician medical groups seeking to merge to achieve economies of scale and enhanced collaboration. If one group's clinical standards and dedication to patient service are higher or lower than the other, the two groups will not likely mesh well after integration.

Workforce

Organizational workforces in place should be taken into account as part of any integration strategy. Any merger or corporate restructuring forces management to examine job positions, skills, productivity, and other factors with the aim of improving workforce utilization and controlling salaries and benefit costs, which are often one of the highest line items of any enterprise's budget. Duplication of workers or excess workers should be identified.

The strong workers should be leveraged and the weaker workers retrained or eliminated. Workforce reductions frequently save costs and achieve greater economies of scale. That said, integration can benefit workers in cases where employee benefits are improved. Added career ladders exist within larger organizations, so employees often relocate and change job positions as part of integration. Developing an integration strategy will, in and of itself, produce useful workforce data that can be utilized to ensure that the proper workforce is in place and that compensation and benefits are competitive. As mentioned earlier, "talent management" is an integral part of any IDS strategy.

Infrastructure and Capital Assets

To create larger, fully integrated IDSs requires significant capital and infrastructure to support the resulting organization. Integration strategies should analyze and assess the assets and infrastructures in place and identify items that need to be repaired, replaced, or added. When multiple health care systems integrate, there may be overlap in these areas, creating an opportunity to sell or liquidate items that the IDS no longer requires. Parties should assess the useful life of assets and infrastructures and determine which items might require replacement so that IDSs can budget accordingly. Facility planning is an element of infrastructure analysis. IDS should be proactive to ensure efficient use of facilities. IDS should not operate their administrative services in high-rent clinical space. Clinical departments should relocate and align so that synergies and collaboration occur. HIT is another infrastructure item that IDS must assess and take into account.

Marketing and Community Awareness

Health care organizations need to develop marketing and public relations strategies as part of any integration strategy. Forming an IDS will create branding and community awareness opportunities that organizations should seize as they come together.

Compensation

IDSs must develop employee compensation plans that create the right incentives. If third-party payers are going to pay based on performance, compensation models should follow suit. As stated earlier in the book, "follow the money" and ensure that compensation rewards the behavior and outcomes that an IDS seeks to achieve. In most cases, the days of physician guaranteed salary models are over. Compensation plans should reward productivity, quality outcomes, high patient satisfaction, appropriateness of care, cost containment, and ingenuity, to name a few.

Stay Educated and Informed Because The New Health Age Brings About Dynamic and Fluid Changes on a Daily Basis

If you had to change careers tomorrow, what would you need to do first? Get re-educated. When people move into different jobs or careers, retraining is a prerequisite for success. New jobs require new skills, thinking, and knowledge.

The New Health Age will bring about dynamic and comprehensive changes to health and how America delivers health care. The economies, systems, participants, and perspectives will all be different in one year, five years, ten years, and beyond. Health care providers will require constant re-education, training, and access to the latest information to keep pace with all the coming developments.

It will take a "lifetime of learning" to survive and prosper in the world ahead. The world is changing too fast to rest or rely on the false notion that we already "know it all." What we think and know today as being true may not be true tomorrow. Health care providers will come to this realization, if they haven't already, and stay intensely devoted to keeping themselves and their organizations educated regarding every dynamic aspect of The New Health Age. They need to know what is occurring in the moment and the next day, too.

Knowledge equals power, a power that no one can take away. Health care providers should seek as much power from knowledge as they can access to prepare for The New Health Age. Knowledge alone may be what gives some organizations a competitive advantage over others, especially during the early transformational times of the coming era. "The early bird gets the worm."

All Stakeholders functioning within health care today find themselves, like it or not, in a fiercely competitive race to figure out The New Health Age, what it means and what it will bring. If you stay ahead of the pack, the others may never catch up. Reading, but more importantly, comprehending this book will already place you out front in this race. Congratulations!

Maintain Flexibility and the Ability to Adapt Quickly to an Ever-Changing Environment

Previous chapter discussions have mentioned how fast the environment around medicine and health care delivery is changing. Whether because of medical advances, regulatory mandates, or changes in payment models for health care services, major changes can have dramatic effects in the industry.

A team of researchers from the National Cancer Institute's Centers of Cancer Nanotechnology Excellence have teamed up to develop a "cocktail" of different nanometer-sized particles, all laboring together within the bloodstream to locate, adhere to, and kill cancerous tumors.[4] This form of treatment will likely one day reduce or even eliminate the need for more harmful treatments to the body, such as radiation therapy and chemotherapy. If advances in nanotechnology, for example, reach a point where they cause the demand for chemotherapy or radiation oncology to decrease substantially, cancer centers across the country that have failed to prepare or adapt to this newly emerging technology will be unprepared and will go out of business very quickly.

Remember your old local video store where you would walk down an isle and select a VCR tape movie for the weekend? The likes of cable television's video on demand, Netflix, and iTunes drove most of these establishments into bankruptcy and extinction. This story simply highlights how changes in a market can impact the underlying economics at a rapid pace.

One benefit to integration in health care is that providers can diversify and spread risk across the IDS. Competitive forces can change quickly, requiring alterations to integration strategies. One large physician group in a community may perceive that it dominates the market but discover that a competing IDS has acquired a smaller group as part of an aggressive expansion plan. One transaction in a community can change the face of competition quickly and require immediate response or action. Such immediacy requires that organizations be open to change and remain flexible enough to change.

Avoid Taking Quick, Reactionary Actions That Are Not Well Thought Out

Change creates fear and fear often results in organizations making decisions too quickly. Today, many health care providers are simply reacting out of fear in the market place, similar to the panic sell orders that occur in numerous other markets, such as Wall Street.

Let's examine recent changes in the physician market place as an example. Physicians who have practiced independent medicine for decades are deciding in today's changing environment to sell their medical practices to local hospitals for low values on the assumption that fully integrated IDSs will function better and that hospitals will offer more stability, security, and expanded resources. In 2005, more than two-thirds of medical practices were physician-owned.[5] This rate had held steady for many years, according to a recent article published in the *New York Times*.[6] However within the last three years, the percent of physician-owned practices has dropped below 50 percent, and analysts say that the slide will continue.[7] This exemplifies how fast the marketplace is changing.

Fully integrated physician employment models may prove to be the best method of achieving the goals of an IDS. Or they may not; therefore, health care providers should avoid taking quick, reactionary actions that are not well thought out. Quick decisions often result in bad decisions or decisions followed by regret, that is, "What the heck have I done?" kinds of decisions. In addition, selling during panic conditions rarely results in the seller receiving higher values.

Health care providers should make steady, educated, methodical, and well-reasoned decisions as we enter The New Health Age. The stakes are too high to ask for second chances following failure.

We have already stated that integration of many forms will and should occur. Indeed, the pace of change is quick, but balance the want and desire to be proactive against caution and wisdom.

Choose Between Positive or Negative Thinking

Is the glass half-full or half-empty? American Stakeholders can choose to view our entrance into The New Health Age as the most challenging and depressing era of all time. Alternatively, Stakeholders can view the massive change to The New Health Age as creating new opportunities for success, within a different system and a different approach to health care.

There is certainly plenty of negativity, fear-based, and reactionary thinking to go around.

- "Will American medicine become socialized?"
- "Will I get to see my own doctor again?"
- "Will I have to wait for months to receive my surgery?"
- "Higher taxes may put me out of business."
- "Changes to payment systems may put my health care business under."

Alternatively, American Stakeholders can choose to avoid coming to quick conclusions, gather and analyze the facts surrounding all of the debate over health care, avoid fearing the future simply because it is unknown, and begin to shape their views, perspectives, and conclusions on actual data as The New Health Age unfolds in the years to come. Certain data revealed in this book bring to light potentially marvelous elements and business opportunities that The New Health Age will provide for America.

- "Modern medicine is nearing cures or better treatments for horrible diseases, such as cancer."
- "If my heart fails, I can grow a new one!"
- "America can become the healthiest nation on Earth."
- "Access to care will be expanded enabling more Americans to receive incentives for wellness, leading to healthier lives and reduced expense."
- "EACOs will lead wellness in the workplace, which will bring down the cost of employee health insurance, create more productive workers, and produce more profitable companies in America."
- "Integration and technology will make the delivery of health care more efficient and effective, resulting in better quality."

Friedrich Schiller once said, "Mankind is made great or little by its own will." The choice is ours to make.

KEY POINTS

1. A huge and historically inevitable tsunami of change is coming to health care in America.
2. We must change our perspectives and open our minds to new ideas.
3. Health care providers must develop a health information technology plan and execute that plan.
4. Organizations in health care will require and demand strong and effective leadership and management, and will implement talent management programs.

5. Health care providers and institutions must continually remain educated and informed, because The New Health Age will bring about dynamic and fluid changes on a frequent basis.

6. Health care providers must integrate to survive and function effectively in The New Health Age.

7. Health care organizations must maintain flexibility and the ability to adapt quickly to an ever-changing environment.

8. Avoid taking quick, reactionary actions that are not well thought out.

9. Choose positive thinking and succeed to become part of the 60 percent that will survive and thrive.

◀ CHANGE VISION ▶

Paul Duck currently serves as the Chief Executive Officer for Coastal Orthopedics and Pain Management in Bradenton, Florida. Previously, Mr. Duck served as the Chief Executive Officer for an outpatient diagnostic imaging services company with five locations in the greater Orlando market, Florida Radiology Imaging (FRI), where he led the construction of three new centers within the first calendar year. The company experienced unprecedented growth in 2007 and 2008 under his leadership in addition to recognition and notoriety for the customer service initiatives that he brought to revolutionizing the culture of the company. In September 2008, Mr. Duck received an award by Inc. Magazine for leading FRI as one of America's fastest growing companies.

Culture and Efficiency in The New Health Age

Culture and Efficiency Matter: How to Streamline, Out Maneuver, and Differentiate Your Company in the New Era of Health Care

By Paul Duck

In the health care industry—or, more commonly, as I like to refer to it, the health change industry—we constantly have to embrace change, deal with change, expect the unexpected, and function with many rules of engagement that are not present in other industries. Any health care executive has two choices today: You can react to change or you can be the driver and leader of change. I have, am, and will be a leader of change. It is the only way to ensure success in the years ahead.

In every company I have led, every associate has had a mind-set of using customer service acuity, instilled into the company culture and corporate DNA, as a secret weapon. One characteristic many highly successful corporations in non-health-care industries have focused on is the qualities of efficiency and collaborative culture and how those serve as a catalyst for differentiating their respective brands from competition—and ultimately leading to profitability. When we think of great examples of cultural greatness that has lead to a company and brand success and/or dominance in an industry, we think of names such as Ritz Carlton, Apple, Nordstrom, Southwest Airlines, and Starbucks. In each of these great brands are embedded great people, great systems, and great training. Each company has made recruiting and retention of great people a very high priority. In health care, the industry has traditionally focused on the technical skill of each person. In our organization, we place an upfront emphasis on the nontechnical cultural fit before even considering the person's technical job skill.

Because the health care industry is highly regulated, there are fewer ways for health care companies to differentiate themselves. Unlike the automobile industry, health care cannot offer deals or discounts on services; in other words, there is really no way to compete on price. Some will claim they can compete on quality alone, but have a very difficult time convincing the patient/consumer that there really is a difference in quality. However, one clear factor in patient retention is customer satisfaction. As Walt Disney once said, "You want them to tell their friends and family." When Coastal Orthopedics' patients tell their friends and family about their great experience with our company, we have created evangelists—they want to tell others about this great experience.

In Ken Blanchard's book, *Raving Fans*, he talks through three metaphorical stories about how satisfied customers aren't good enough; your customers need to walk away shocked and surprised at how well they were greeted and treated. The other very important point is to identify all of your constituent customers. In health care, our customers include patients, vendors, hospital administrators, insurance companies, and, of course, fellow associates within our company.

That positive, proactive culture not only creates the kind of work environment where each person is more productive and happy doing what they do, it also has tangible financial benefits. In measuring financial results before and then one year later with several companies I have led, the average financial impact, as a result of installing this cultural change is an 8 percent increase in net income and an 8.5 percent increase in EBITDA (adjusted earnings). The associate retention measurements have gone from a revolving door to less than 4 percent turnover rate, and most of those associates left because they had a spouse move out of the area.

Coastal Orthopedics has quickly become the health care employer of choice in South Tampa Bay-Bradenton, Florida. This cultural impact has a significant impact in today's health care marketplace, but it is even more critical in the health care industry that Coastal is now entering!

At Coastal, we know there is a strong correlation between customer experience and brand loyalty. Companies that deliver superior customer service also build strong brand loyalty. The brand image and perception are largely determined at the customer touch. Brand loyalty is determined at each and every point of customer contact.

This is undoubtedly the most difficult thing to control. There are so many associates within our organization that have contact with the patient, and each one of them can make or break the experience. It's very difficult to control all of these contacts. But it is imperative that we create a culture, an environment, where there is consistent attention and a strong emphasis on positive customer service.

Yes, technology, convenience, services, and a host of other things are important, but in a consumer-directed economy, customer service is at the top. The customer experience will determine how our brand is viewed and if there is any brand loyalty.

In this New Health Age, the creation of a highly energized, customer-centric culture will move from a competitive edge to an absolute necessity. In this New Health Age, the culture of the enterprise will be measured by accrediting bodies and will have payment amounts determined partly on customer/patient satisfaction. The norms in this new paradigm will be marked with

- Very short wait times
- Easy access to medical record information online in a highly secure way
- Easy access to payment information in an easy-to-understand way
- A very high-quality experience at every touch point
- A standard expectation for friendly and efficient treatment
- Interior design and environmental factors playing a significant role in expectations
- Highly transparent benchmarking of clinical quality and patient satisfaction
- Quality experience driving reimbursement for services
- Concierge health care services more as the standard expectation, rather than being sold at a premium
- Associates within the health care enterprise that possess a "how can I serve you" mentality

One other key to The New Health Age is ensuring that human resources management is leveraged completely differently than it has traditionally been in health care. At Coastal, the person who heads up human resources is titled the Chief People Officer. Why? We are in a people business. Investing in training and organizational development is a key success factor. Although the CEO is still the visionary and the driver for this type of organizational change and commitment, the new era of health care requires that a key executive be part of senior management, to be the co-collaborator with the CEO and responsible for executing on key aspects of the shift. A Chief People Officer who is responsible for these deliverables demonstrates both the organizational commitment as well as the seriousness to which this shift must occur in The New Health Age.

In addition, any CEO or any other C-level executive in health care must be the driver(s) to the shift in culture and to ensure that the culture of customer service is strategic. At Coastal, we hold one annual company meeting to be certain that everyone, in every position, understands the importance and the expectation for culture in the company. Gone are the days where a budget and operating plan are the drivers to measure success. We complete a budget and develop an operational strategy, but we also develop a well-defined cultural strategy for the coming year. Without it, we simply will not have the commitment or the know-how to invoke the kind of change necessary to create a winning health care enterprise and, ultimately, building a brand strongly associated with shocking and surprising—raving fan—customer service!

In addition to culture, we have made a rigorous commitment to efficiency. We have looked at every way we can improve our business and our brand through increased efficiencies. In the last 12 to 18 months, we have

- Reduced patient wait times for appointment scheduling from over 3 minutes to under 30 seconds (for those who have to hold on the phone)

- Reduced the abandoned phone calls into Coastal from almost 5 percent to virtually zero

- Gone from having patients leaving over 200 voicemail messages per day (with only 20 percent of those being returned) to zero

- Increased patient satisfaction (on a 4 point scale) from 1.4 to 3.65

It's very important to note that all of this was done without increasing personnel cost. We found that the effort was all about understanding how we were going to put the patient first, studying our workflow, and perfecting what we expected as an outcome. Then we measured several key metrics to ensure that our new systems were working and expectations were being met. This sounds very simple to most, but it is critical to realize that you must first have the people who desire to serve the customer (in our case, the patient customer), then to do whatever it takes to deliver the experience that would support our commitment. This starts with an unwavering commitment from the CEO and others in the senior management team.

In The New Health Age that we have entered, efficiency and a customer-focused culture will be every bit as important to success as it has been in most other businesses in this country. Embrace both and you will thrive. Lastly, to those leaders in health care organizations or those organizations that support and serve the health care industry, make sure that your company's culture and efficiency is part of the very DNA of your organization and, as the leader, that you are passionate about instilling these into everything you do!

16

What Policy Makers and Educators Need to Do

"If you don't have your health you don't have anything."

—Anonymous

In The New Health Age that we have entered, legislation and education will be more important to the health and well-being of America than it has ever been. Enlightened and knowledgeable policy makers and educators will lead, design, construct, and teach the new path down which we have started our journey. We hope that this chapter will provide some guidance and suggestions as to how best to succeed in this critically important undertaking.

As we enter the global stage of human evolution in the twenty-first century, two of our nation's greatest responsibilities are to promote well-educated and healthy citizens. Most American citizens think that this nation is the greatest country in the world.

If we tie greatness to health then we can become the healthiest country in the world.

Many Americans worry that the country is losing its competitive greatness and wonder if our time of greatness might have passed. Creating a healthier nation is a big next step to putting these fears aside.

Policy makers and educators possess great power and influence in the United States. Policy makers mean governments and educators include teaching and academic institutions of every type. This power is supreme, because it includes the ability to make laws and policies and set agendas that Americans follow. In addition, this power influences how Americans perceive and react to the agendas that policy makers and educators establish.

When policy makers and educators use their influence to provoke disagreement, Americans take sides and typically choose to support one view or another. Some disagreement and debate during policy making is often healthy, because it can foster the process of deliberation and enable people to eventually reach compromise and consensus around a controversial issue.

Parties can often reach compromise by taking various extreme positions and breaking them down into component parts that people with opposing views can work through to accept on a limited basis. The extreme positions are put aside in this process while parties who were originally in complete opposition embrace the ideas that eventually become mutually acceptable.

Disagreement and debate, however, can at some stage in the policy-making process become destructive and create hindrances to achieving greatness because policy makers accomplish nothing, except for the disagreeing and debating. When disputes drag on, for whatever reason, whether because the parties get stuck on arguing about old issues, are stuck in legacy thinking from the past, get too emotionally charged and lose sight of the facts, or the process becomes overly political, then the disagreeing parties need to hit the "reset button," or in the PC world, CTRL-ALT-DELETE.

When disagreements reach resistance to compromise, hitting CTRL-ALT-DELETE forces the debating parties to temporarily put their disagreements aside and can help to reshape the discussion toward points on which they can reach consensus. The primary purpose of this chapter is to find common ground and acceptable vision statements that policy makers and educators can agree upon. Once parties obtain commonality of ideas, these notions take shape and great plans, policies, and agendas will emerge. Reaching accord, however, is critical.

President Obama's and the 111th Congress' health care reform agenda, known as the Patient Protection and Affordable Care Act (PPACA), is now law. The PPACA laws are the current topic of significant debate and intense controversy in America today. This book, however, is not about convincing readers whether PPACA is "good or bad" for the future of this country. In fact, a great majority of The New Health Age will occur regardless of whether PPACA is ultimately challenged before the U.S. Supreme Court and found to be unconstitutional and void.

This book is about hitting the reset button and delineating points of discussion that every American should and can agree upon, not necessarily because the points are "right or wrong" but because they "will be." We must, therefore, work together to discover and better understand the consensus points.

Many people are frustrated over the PPACA. This dissatisfaction has resulted in continued fighting and bickering among local, state, and federal policy makers. Rest assured America, this state of disturbance is a natural and expected part of the transformative process that we are in. Times will get better and, as authors, we take it as our role to move this progression forward:

The Dark Age came before the Age of Enlightenment.

War precedes peace.

It is darkest before dawn.

The New Health Age has arrived, but most policy makers and educators simply can't see it yet. The sooner they do, the sooner the disruption and chaos surrounding the disagreements over health care will end.

1. Policy makers and educators need to develop positions related to health care reform that everyone can agree upon, so that new, productive agendas will emerge.

Let's begin by putting aside the issues prompting disagreement and focus on points that every American Stakeholder will ultimately agree upon. Once we reach agreement on these core principles, policy makers and educators can begin to effectuate agendas that will bring about positive action focused on accomplishing the established goals.

We set forth the following 10 positions that we believe every American Stakeholder will adopt moving forward:

1. America must promote medical advancement and innovation because new advances have the capability of furthering greater health, longevity, and well-being in the future, thus lowering costs.

2. Americans must reward health care providers and educators for improving health and health care delivery while controlling costs.

3. We are a caring nation, with a majority of the population in support of giving people a "hand up" more so than a "handout."

4. Americans want to prevent chronic diseases that accelerate death and expend too many economic resources.

5. Many Americans must get healthier. Personal choice and accountability for one's actions is key to moving America toward a culture of good health.

6. America must reduce the spending on unnecessary health care costs.

7. Federal, state, and local government must reduce their budget deficits and debts.

8. American companies need a healthier workforce and must control health insurance costs to compete in a global marketplace.

9. America must utilize technology to improve health and health care.

10. The United States remains the greatest nation on Earth. Americans will not be held back or refuse to address these issues and ideals going forward, because our nation always rejects defeat.

If policy makers and educators can embrace these 10 positions and legislate and educate around each one, the backbiting, wrangling, disputing, and debating occurring today will evolve into progressive ideas that will lead to legislative agendas and laws that will make America's health and health care delivery the best in the world.

2. What should policy makers and educators do?

Perhaps as authors we can initiate progress toward The New Health Age by helping to answer this overarching yet critical question of the times. What follows is a breakdown of the 10 positions listed and related ideas and suggestions for policy makers and educators. The ideas below are simply a start, but every journey toward a new age must have a beginning.

1. America should promote medical advancement and innovation because new advances have the capability of furthering greater health, longevity, and well-being in the future, thus lowering costs.

   Policy makers should

   - Think carefully before unduly taxing entities that cultivate innovation, because innovation ultimately improves health in this nation, thus reducing the costs attributable to injury, illness, and disease.

   - Create economic incentives and adopt stimulus programs that increase health care innovation, such as research, development, and invention that is targeted toward wellness and preventing disease and illness.

- Create agendas that will reduce administrative burdens within health care delivery, because unnecessary inconveniences do not better health nor reduce costs. Simply put, reduce the red tape.

Educators should

- Foster creativity in curricula at every level of education so that professors, teachers, researchers, and students will be inspired to develop innovations in medicine. Education reformer John Dewey once stated, "Every great advance in science has issued from a new audacity of imagination." Educators must foster such imagination in America.

- Seek out partnerships with private enterprise—offering private companies some ownership in newly developed intellectual property, when necessary—as education budgets come under pressure in response to federal and state budget deficits. Joint ventures will ensure that research, development, and innovation continue.

- Form global alliances with international universities and other education institutions so that the world connects ideas, resources, and agendas that promote increased medical innovation.

2. Americans needs to reward health care providers and educators for improving health and health care delivery in America while controlling costs.

Policy makers should

- Further health care reimbursement systems that pay providers for achieving good results for their patients, such as achieving wellness, preventing disease, and producing good outcomes, while controlling costs.

- Transition new pay-for-performance and accountable care reimbursement models into The New Health Age, recognizing that organizations have been built around the historical models of yesterday. Too much change too quickly can have catastrophic economic results, because organizations need time to educate, plan, and adjust. For example, do not cut traditional Medicare or Medicaid reimbursements by 20 percent in one budgetary cycle.

Educators should

- Fund and establish teaching and administrative positions at every level of education focused on healthy lifestyles programs, including those targeted at diet, nutrition, and fitness.

- Design compensation plans that reward educators for improving student health and their own health.

- Establish rewards programs for students who achieve greater health.

3. We are a caring nation, with a majority of the population in support of giving people a "hand up" more so than a "handout."

Policy makers should

- Recognize that improving access to health care will ultimately lead Americans to healthier lives and reduce our health care costs, provided that such access links Americans to wellness and disease prevention programs.

- Accept that sometimes costs must go up before they can come down. America had to spend money building interstate highways before we were able to drive on the roads.

- Have the courage to invest money now to get Americans healthier tomorrow, so that we can save money for generations. Our nation's children need us now more than ever. They are the ones who must carry our heritage forward. The youth in this nation need education and social support systems to teach them how to live out healthier lives—physically, emotionally, and spiritually.

- Embrace the statement by author William Gibson, "The future is already here—it's just not evenly distributed."[1]

- Apply Gibson's concept to health care in America; the United States possesses the best health care system in the world, it is just not evenly distributed. Once it is evenly distributed, the costs will go down.

- Embrace health insurance exchanges or similar programs discussed in Chapter 14 because access to health care, wellness, and prevention programs will bring down costs if affordable health insurance and wellness programs are available to small businesses and middle-class Americans.

Educators should

- Partner with local community health centers and health departments so that new lifestyle educational curricula, including healthy diet, nutrition, and exercise programs, can be implemented across American communities, at every age level and socioeconomic class.

- Further these partnerships and open up after-hours public physical education facilities, including gyms, workout rooms, and athletic fields, to establish community fitness programs.

- Establish community garden programs aimed at teaching students about the differences between organic and processed foods, while also producing free organic food to serve low-income households in communities. Schoolyard gardening projects will teach children about agriculture and how to have healthier perspectives about their food.

4. Americans want to prevent chronic diseases that accelerate death and expend too many economic resources.

Policy makers should

- Fund, encourage, and promote policies aimed at achieving wellness and prevention of disease across the nation.

- Continue to fund and support research and development programs aimed at treating, curing, and preventing chronic diseases in America.

Educators should

- Recognize that school systems are frequently among the largest employers in every community and educators should set the standard for wellness and chronic disease prevention programs within their own enterprises.

- Partner with local medical homes to implement school system EACO programs.

- Focus on researching, developing, and teaching best guidelines for treating, curing, and preventing chronic diseases in America.

5. Many Americans need to get healthier.

Policy makers should

- Establish a bold and inspirational national health agenda, similar in size and scope to the NASA space program, which began in the 1960s. Let's name it the "Race to a Healthy America." We will discuss the Race in more detail below.

- Support wellness and disease prevention programs discussed throughout this book.

- Provide better funding to the nation's medical education systems to be used toward training more lifestyle medicine oriented, family medicine, and primary care physicians.

- Support health education programs and nutritional meal programs that center on wellness and disease prevention. If we teach and educate wellness early in life, good habits are hard to break.

- Promote city and state building codes that promote the design and construction of "healthy communities," including space for bike paths, sidewalks, parks, and community gardens.

Educators should

- Adopt new lifestyle medicine curricula at every level of education, focusing on healthy diet, nutrition, and exercise.

- Design meal programs that promote healthy eating in school system cafeterias.

- Enhance and invest in physical education facilities, including gyms, pools, workout rooms, and outdoor facilities, to support student fitness classes and community programs.

- Establish healthy community garden programs, as discussed earlier.

- Redesign aspects of medical education to promote wellness and disease prevention, such as training doctors to think about health care wholistically versus in isolation.

- Focus on training twenty-first century doctors and other professionals how to practice lifestyle medicine.

- Start training and educating more primary care physicians and other caregivers, such as nurses, physician assistants, technicians, and others.

6. America needs to reduce the spending on unnecessary health care costs.

Policy makers should

- Continue to implement initiatives that will eliminate fraud and abuse in the health care system.

- Enact national tort reform to reduce costs attributable to the defensive practice of medicine and frivolous lawsuits.

- Continue to fund stimulus money to promote the adoption of health information and administrative technology aimed at cutting out unnecessary costs attributable to health care administration, such as billing and collecting from payers.

Educators should

- Expand business classes throughout medical education curricula so that physicians and other health care providers possess greater business skills that will enable them to focus on business-oriented efficiencies, economies, service, and quality.

- Immediately form EACOs to provide better health care to educators more efficiently and at reduced cost.

7. Federal, state, and local governments must reduce their budget deficits and debts.

Policy makers should

- Accept and understand that government entitlement spending in the areas of Medicare, Medicaid, and elsewhere will not go down until Americans get healthier and we reduce or prevent chronic diseases, because 70 percent of health care spending is attributable to chronic diseases.

- Adopt a national agenda around promoting appropriate and valued end-of-life care, which consumes nearly 40 percent of Medicare dollars in the last month of life, recognizing that this agenda will compel Americans to confront the dying process and oblige them to contemplate when medical intervention becomes futile during the course of death.

Educators should

- Establish EACO programs, which will enable institutions to shift the related insurance cost savings to health and wellness curricula and programs.

- Establish new revenue streams by opening public school systems' fitness facilities to private employers so that corporate America will have greater and less expensive access to fitness facilities for their employees. We can't have too many gyms, pools, and fields in America when the Race to a Healthy America kicks into high gear.

8. American companies need a healthy workforce and must control their health insurance costs to compete in a global marketplace.

Policy makers should

- Encourage through tax incentives American corporations to embrace EACO employee wellness programs. Healthier employees lead to more profitable companies, which stimulates economic growth that results in the increased tax revenues that are necessary to ultimately balance government budgets. The return on investment is obvious.

Educators should

- Develop curricula across America focused on teaching future business leaders and health care providers how to develop EACOs and employee wellness programs. Every business school and medical school graduate should understand EACOs.

- Use teachers to partner with corporate EACOs and medical homes to teach America's workforce how to make good lifestyle choices related to health and wellness.

9. Technology must be used to improve health and health care.

Policy makers should

- Continue to provide stimulus funding for the adoption of health information technology (HIT), including electronic medical records (EMR) and health information exchange (HIE) systems so that health information can flow and connect easily and efficiently throughout America's health care delivery systems, making the data transfer process more efficient and fully connected, thereby reducing administrative expenses and improving access to health information.

- Support research, development, and innovation in the area of health information technology so that new technologies will be invented aimed at reducing administrative costs and improving health using technology.

Educators should

- Acknowledge that America is moving from the Information Age into the Shift Age, which will require more educated, skilled, and creative Americans to develop new technologies in a more competitive global marketplace. Education systems should design academic programs that foster creative learning for this new age.

- Develop education programs for the coming decade to teach the American workforce how to invent, deliver, implement, and utilize HIT throughout the health care marketplace.

10. America remains the greatest nation on earth. Americans will not be held back or refuse to address these issues and ideals going forward, because our nation always rejects defeat.

Policy makers should

- Embrace these common and united ideals and take action to solve these issues.

- Demonstrate courage and leadership, which will require bringing all policy makers to the same table in cooperation to promote well-educated and healthy citizens.

- Surrender the local, state, and national battles around health care reform and replace these battles with a united war against an unhealthy America.

- Accept that America will ultimately demand that we solve the challenges addressed in this book to avoid societal and economic destruction in the United States.

- Adopt the Race to a Healthy America initiative and roll it out over five years. Here are a few ideas to get started:
  - The president should call a special meeting of all state governors to announce that the Race "is on."
  - The Department of Health and Human Services (DHHS) should be the lead federal agency responsibility for the Race to ensure national accountability and responsibility.

○ DHHS should work with all 50 states, and each state should create or assign a mirror local agency to coordinate the Race.

○ Businesses and school systems should be offered incentives to establish their own or shared EACOs within the first two years of the Race. This will begin the process of creating employee wellness programs that bring down employee health insurance costs, reduce absenteeism, and increase productivity. The initial incentives should be paid back from the employers' savings over a 10-year period.

○ DHHS, in collaboration with the Centers for Disease Control (CDC), should develop a targeted plan and schedule for reducing the top chronic diseases in America.

○ DHHS and CDC should develop a public awareness campaign utilizing all media—television, radio, Internet, print, and others.

○ Federal and state governments should adopt onetime tax credits for media in exchange for advertising and promoting the Race.

○ DHHS and its state counterparts should affiliate with national sports idols and teams to promote and encourage participating in the Race.

○ Encourage Medicare-eligible Baby Boomers to join the Race by enhancing Medicare benefits in exchange for participating in wellness programs.

○ State Medicaid beneficiaries should be offered incentives for participating in wellness programs.

○ Create a special tax for unhealthy foods, such as foods with trans-fats and sugary drinks, similar to cigarette taxes, to fund a new food credit program for low-income Americans. The food credit must be applied toward purchasing healthy food items. This program would create the right incentives for good nutrition.

- ○ Create an annual national holiday to promote Race activities, such as walks, marathons, exercise classes, and sports tournaments, to encourage participation and to help change America's culture toward healthier living.
- ○ Partner with national restaurant chains and offer every American one free meal in exchange for reading a short guide on to how to live a healthy lifestyle, such as *Eat Right for Life* by Ann G. Kulze, MD, and published by the Wellness Council of America. This short and easy-to-read book is one of the best commonsense guides to living well and eating right that we have discovered during our research for this book. It is a must read!
- ○ Promote certain PPACA grants and funding for educating more primary care physicians who will be needed for new medical homes and the Race.

Educators should

- Inspire their teachers and administrators to lead and educate the youth in America so that they can join in and continue the Race for decades and generations to come. Our national pride and security depend on it.

- Create scholarships for students who participate in wellness programs. Additional scholarships should be available for students who achieve high health grades. High health grades should become as important as class grades.

- Adopt the Race by implementing many of the ideas previously mentioned in this chapter and create new ideas, too.

Mr. President, Congress, Governors, University Trustees, Chancellors, School Boards, Superintendents, Principals, Professors, and Teachers, as critically important Stakeholders, adopt and declare that The Race to a Healthy America is on! Declare it loudly and declare it quickly! Time is not on our side. Make it yours.

Make it a success. America's future health and economic prosperity depends on it. We are depending on you.

KEY POINTS

1. Our disagreements surrounding health care in America will soon transition into consensus around points that most Americans will agree on and The New Health Age will arise.

2. Policy makers and educators will find common ground and create visions and agendas for a healthier America.

3. The common agenda that policy makers and educators will rally behind is that two of our nation's greatest responsibilities are to promote well-educated and healthy citizens.

4. This agenda will be named the Race to a Healthy America, and it will be promoted within school systems, communities, corporations, and throughout America.

5. Americans will win the Race to a Healthy America because we refuse to accept defeat as a nation!

17

What Medicine and the Health Care System Will Look Like in 2015, 2020, and 2025

"We should try to be the parents of our future, rather than the offspring of our past."

—Miguel de Unamuno

The New Health Age has begun. In the next 10 to 20 years it will fully bloom, ushering in a new age in the practice of medicine and the delivery of health care.

Where are we going? What will it look like? How will it be? What will be the impact on America? What will it be like to be a patient, a doctor, a nurse, an employee, or an employer? How will all of America's Stakeholders in our national health care system think about, feel, and benefit from the changes that we have identified, defined, and forecasted in this book? In this final chapter we offer, in 5-year increments, a look at the country's future health care landscape.

1. 2015

Many of America's Stakeholders will have familiarity with the new structures of The New Health Age. ACOs, medical homes, EACOs, and IDSs will be a reality for a growing number of Americans in some shape or form. We will all be thinking about health care more through the filter of the dynamic flows than we do today. We will be learning the benefits of prevention both for the country and ourselves as well. We will be beginning to see that, indeed, The New Health Age can be a time when health care costs can be lowered.

The fears and incendiary political rhetoric so prevalent at the time this book was written will have died down, as the health, social, and economic benefits of The New Health Age will now begin to be apparent. As a country, we will have found consensus around the 10 points of common agreement in the last chapter.

Yes, there will still be those who cling to wanting it back to the way it was before 2010. Yes, there will still be only a small amount of data showing that the dynamic flows are in fact creating a new healthy health care landscape. The developing sentiment in the country will be one of newness, excitement, and commitment to health and a new way to think about health care.

If the Race to a Healthy America has taken root, then we will have begun a national quest for health, longevity, and lower medical costs. We will be feeling stronger as a nation, as we have once again risen to a critical challenge. America will be on the move to a fitter, healthier, and happier state. The notion of holding Americans accountable for their lifestyle choices will be migrating through the American culture. Many states and possibly the federal government will enact excise taxes on unhealthy foods and beverages. This vision will serve to bring us together as we work to help ourselves and each other get healthier. We will feel better about ourselves and about our country. Our doubts about our country's future will have lessened as we are all taking action every day toward a better, healthier future.

Physicians who feared for their very livelihoods will be settling into their reconfigured practices and will be fulfilled to see healthier patients and be excited to actually be paid for keeping people healthy. That said, there will still be many people who are sick, who do not have easy access to the new health care structures, because the journey that we have begun is both enormous and long.

Some of the medical breakthroughs that we have predicted earlier in the book will have come to be. Organ replacements, technological innovations, and other breakthroughs will be well publicized. Genetic knowledge will have begun to enhance all forms of medical practice. Former paraplegics and quadriplegics will be walking with exoskeletons. The treatment of aging as a disease will start to have some very preliminary success. The incidence of chronic diseases, so costly and deadly, will have early indications of starting to decline. Americans will have opened the discussions surrounding how to deliver end-of-life care humanely, and more families will be taking proactive steps toward ensuring that loved ones don't spend their final days in hospital intensive care units, with minimal quality of life and at extraordinary costs.

Many of us will clearly see, feel, and experience the dawning of The New Health Age.

2. 2020

It will now be clear that The New Health Age is a real, truly new age of health, medical practice, and integrated, intelligent health care delivery. The health care system will have finally caught up to most of the rest of the economy and society in terms of electronic connectivity and information integration. This connectivity will bring new cost savings and efficiencies to the health care industry that will make us look back on 2010 with amazement that we lived for so long with such antiquated silos, practices, and systems.

Americans will be able to search and compare how well health care organizations and individuals are performing in their role of creating health, lowering costs, and providing care that produces positive results. Stakeholders will be able to find quickly what they need to know about all their personal health records and information. Stakeholders will know who is good at providing procedures and who is not. Stakeholders will feel the empowerment that comes from knowledge and will no longer have to tolerate anything that is not transparent.

By 2020, there will be enough data that the move to prevention will be having a dramatic effect on our country's health. We will be able to document and see that chronic disease and poor health have declined, resulting in noticeable cost reductions. We will be able to see and feel that we are living in a healthier country, and that as a nation America has once again risen to a great challenge. The Race to a Healthy America will have moved to the center of how we live our lives. Holding Americans accountable for their lifestyle choices will be a major component of the American culture. Governments at the state and federal levels will be taxing unhealthy foods and beverages to compensate for care that is required by those who continue to live unhealthy lives.

What will be truly different in 2020 will be the actual improvement in our lives because of the amazing medical breakthroughs that have moved into mainstream medicine and health care. The costs of complete genetic mapping will have dropped so low that everyone in America will be able to have it done. Hospitals will provide genetic profiles to the parents of a newborn when they leave the facility with their new child. This will mean that the move to prevention will be complete. If you, as a parent, know that your newborn has a genetic disposition to the early onset of Alzheimer's, you initiate, and the child, as he or she grows up, will take whatever actions current medical knowledge suggest might slow the onset of the disease. If a 21-year-old man finds out that he has a genetic propensity for heart disease, it will prompt him to exercise, eat right, and perhaps medicate accordingly.

This low-cost access to genetic knowledge will have accelerated the move to more personalized medicine. It will allow pharmaceutical companies to slice the DNA code ever thinner, so that everyone gets exactly the medicine that they need based on genetic analysis. Those current advertisements that have two pages of small-print disclaimers will largely go away, because the era of lowest denominator drugs will end. Why take a drug for high blood pressure that could result in serious side effects? Drugs will be completely personalized and tied to one's unique DNA. If we think generally about health, we can see that most afflictions, conditions, and diseases come from the environment, lifestyle, or genetics. This low-cost genetic mapping will address genetics. The dynamic flows of The New Health Age, along with the Race to a Healthy America, will have addressed the environment and lifestyles issues of health care that are so crippling as this book is being written.

The seemingly ancient times of 2010 to 2012, when paraplegics and quadriplegics were relegated to severely restricted lives, will seem almost barbaric in this time of universal mobility. This bionic revolution will enable those with failing eyesight or with total blindness to receive artificial eye implants that provide a lifetime of sight. The breakthroughs in nanotechnology and stem cell research will have transformative effects in the treatment of cancers and viruses and will promote new forms of cellular regeneration. Tissue regeneration will have reached the stage when waiting for an organ will be a matter of weeks, not a remote possibility that might end in one's death due to the unavailability of an organ.

All of these medical breakthroughs and the close to universal availability of them to all Stakeholders will usher in a new expansion in life expectancy. Someone born in 2020 in America will, for the first time, have a life expectancy of 100 years. This, combined with the benefits that Americans are receiving from the Race to a Healthy America, will result in an ever-escalating retirement age, increasing the lifetime productivity of all Americans. Living healthier lifestyles will be commonplace. Many unhealthy foods and beverages will be extremely costly because of excise taxes. This, in turn, will recast the entire social entitlement landscape, which is currently so daunting and scary.

Those who resisted changing to face The New Health Age will have been squeezed out, eliminating the drag of legacy-thinking holding America back. The surge forward to a new health awareness, new point of view, and a bright future will be palpable!

3. 2025

Healthy living, ever-increasing life expectancy, and dramatically lower health care costs on a per capita basis will be the medical and health care reality in America. Young people will realize how fortunate they are to have been born in The New Health Age, as the possibilities of always being healthy, of living to an age never imagined even a century ago, of always having options and choices not available to their parents and grandparents (those reading this book), will be something both precious and expected.

Medical breakthroughs, practically unimaginable, will rapidly move into mainstream health care. Significant moral questions of human cloning, living for 125 years and longer, and altering DNA for the creation of superior—in all senses of the word—humans will be center stage in social and philosophical debates. We will marvel over the powers that we will have to adjust, alter, improve, and extend human lives.

The view of the state of medicine and health care as it was in 2011, from the view of 2025, will be similar to the view that we have today of what health care was like 100 years ago, before antibiotics, vaccines, scanning diagnostics, and the discovery of DNA.

When seen through the filter of this 2025 view, can we afford not to embrace The New Health Age?

4. Final Thoughts

We are confident that much of what we have forecast will become the new reality. We are also confident, even with our deep immersion in the subject, that our developed abilities to forecast successfully will prove to be woefully inadequate. Breakthroughs will accelerate and surprise us all. Transformations take on their own dynamics, creating whole new forces and alterations that cannot always be foreseen. There will be much that will occur between now and 2025 that is not in this book. We do stand confidently in the position that much of what you have read in this book will in fact prove accurate and will come to be.

We hope that our book will have lessened the pain of transition for many of you. We urge everyone to be open to act in a way where your self-interest aligns with national interest and our society's collective interests. Understand that we are rapidly leaving the past behind.

We know and fervently believe that all now alive, particularly those who are younger, will have a definition of a healthy life that millennia, centuries, and decades ago would have been unthinkable. The long history of humanity and the shorter history of the United States have now come to this—The New Health Age. Welcome to it! Good health to us all!

Glossary of Abbreviations

AALL—American Association for Labor Legislation
ACO—Accountable Care Organization
ALK—Anaplastic Lymphoma Receptor Tyrosine Kinase
AMA—American Medical Association
AMU—After Meaningful Use
ATM—Automated Teller Machine
BCBS—Blue Cross Blue Shield
BMU—Before Meaningful Use
CBC—Complete Blood Count
CD—Compact Disc
CDC—Centers for Disease Control and Prevention
CMS—Centers for Medicare and Medicaid Services
COPD—Chronic Obstructive Pulmonary Disease
CPOE—Computerized Physician Order Entry
CT—Computed Tomography
DALE—Disability-Adjusted Life Expectancy
DHHS—U.S. Department of Health and Human Services
DNA—Deoxyribonucleic Acid
DRA—Deficit Reduction Act
DRG—Diagnostic Related Group
EACO—Employer Accountable Care Organization

EBITDA—Earnings Before Interest, Taxes, Depreciation, and Amortization

EGFR—Epidermal Growth Factor Receptor

EHR—Electronic Health Records

EMR—Electronic Medical Record

ESAW—Economic Spending According to Wealth

ESRD—End Stage Renal Disease

FDA—Food and Drug Association

FFS—Fee for Service

GAO—General Accounting Office

GDP—Gross Domestic Product

GE—General Electric

GPS—Global Positioning System

HCP—Healthcare Partners

HEDIS—Healthcare Effectiveness Data and Information Set

HITECH—Health Information Technology for Economic and Clinical Health

HIE—Health Information Exchange

HIPAA—Health Information Portability and Accountability Act

HIT—Health Information Technology

HIV/AIDS—Human Immunodeficiency Virus/Acquired Immune Deficiency Syndrome

HMO—Health Maintenance Organization

HRA—Health Risk Assessments

ICD—International Classification of Diseases

ICU—Intensive Care Unit

IMQ—Institute for Medical Quality

IMR—Infant Mortality Rate

IPA—Independent Practice Association

IT—Information Technology

JAMA—*Journal of the American Medical Association*

K-RAS—A protein in humans

MBA—Master of Business Administration

MCRHS—Manatee County Rural Health Services

METI—Medical Education Technologies, Inc.

MGI—McKinsey Global Institute
MRI—Magnetic Resonance Imaging
NASA—National Aeronautics and Space Administration
NCQA—National Committee for Quality Assurance
NEJM—*New England Journal of Medicine*
NIH—National Institutes of Health
OECD—Organisation for Economic Co-operation and
     Development
PC—Personal Computer
PCP—Primary Care Provider
PDA—Personal Digital Assistant
PMPM—Per Member/Per Month
PPACA—Patient Protection and Affordable Care Act
UCC—Urgent Care Center
VA—U.S. Department of Veterans Affairs
WHO—World Health Organization

Endnotes

INTRODUCTION

1. Houle, D. (2007). *The shift age*. Chicago: David Houle and Associates.

CHAPTER 2: A QUICK LOOK BACK AT THE HISTORY OF MEDICINE AND PAYMENT SYSTEMS

1. Garrison, F. H. (1917). *An introduction to the history of medicine*. Philadelphia: W. B. Saunders Company.
2. Koenig, H. G., McCullough, M. E., & Larson, D. B. (2001). *Handbook of religion and health*. New York: Oxford University Press.
3. Koenig, H. G., McCullough, M. E., & Larson, D. B. (2001). *Handbook of religion and health*. New York: Oxford University Press.
4. Leguit, P. (2004). Hospital as a temple. *Patient Education and Counseling, 53*, 27–30.
5. Leguit, P. (2004). Hospital as a temple. *Patient Education and Counseling, 53*, 27–30.
6. Leguit, P. (2004). Hospital as a temple. *Patient Education and Counseling, 53*, 27–30.
7. Leguit, P. (2004). Hospital as a temple. *Patient Education and Counseling, 53*, 27–30.
8. Subbarayappa, B. V. (2001). The roots of ancient medicine: An historical outline. *Journal of Biosciences, 26*(2), 135–143.
9. Subbarayappa, B. V. (2001). The roots of ancient medicine: An historical outline. *Journal of Biosciences, 26*(2), 135–143.
10. Wujastyk, D. (2003). *The roots of Ayurveda: Selections from Sanskrit medical writings*. London, England: Penguin Books.

11. Subbarayappa, B. V. (2001). The roots of ancient medicine: An historical outline. *Journal of Biosciences, 26*(2), 135–143.

12. Tung, M. P. M. (1994). Symbolic meanings of the body in Chinese culture and "somatization." *Culture, Medicine, and Psychiatry, 18*(4), 483–494.

13. Réquéna, Y. (1997). *Chi kung: The Chinese art of mastering energy.* Rochester, VT: Healing Arts Press.

14. Meiner, S., & Giesler Lueckenotte, A. (2006). *Gerontologic nursing.* St. Louis, MO: Mosby Elsevier.

15. Meiner, S., & Giesler Lueckenotte, A. (2006). *Gerontologic nursing.* St. Louis, MO: Mosby Elsevier.

16. Millman, B. S. (1997). Acupuncture: Context and critique. *Annual Review of Medicine, 28*, 223–234.

17. Millman, B. S. (1997). Acupuncture: Context and critique. *Annual Review of Medicine, 28*, 223–234.

18. Ackerknecht, E. H. (1982). *A short history of medicine.* Baltimore: The Johns Hopkins University Press.

19. Cheng, T. O. (2001). Hippocrates, cardiology, Confucius, and the Yellow Emperor. *International Journal of Cardiology, 81*(2), 219–233.

20. Yount, L. (2001). *The history of medicine.* San Diego, CA: Lucent Books.

21. Bhattacharya, K., & Cathrine, N. (2006). Da Vinci's code for surgeons. *Indian Journal of Surgery, 68*(5), 283–285.

22. Milanchi, S., & Allins, A. D. (2007). Amyand's hernia: History, imaging, and management. *Hernia, 12*(3), 321–322.

23. Garrison, F. H. (1917). *An introduction to the history of medicine.* Philadelphia: W. B. Saunders Company.

24. Filler, A. G. (2009). *The history, development, and impact of computed imaging in neurological diagnosis and neurosurgery: CT, MRI, and DTI.* Santa Monica, CA: Institute for Nerve Medicine.

25. Bayer. (n.d.) Bayer: Science for a better life. (2010, July 13). Retrieved from http://www.bayer.com/en/felix-hoffmann.aspx.

26. Hurst, J. W. (1991). Paul Dudley White: The father of American cardiology. *Clinical Cardiology, 14*(7), 622–626.

27. Levy, J. (2002). *Really useful: The origins of everyday things.* Buffalo, NY: Firefly Books.

28. Fowler, M. J. (2008). Diabetes treatment, part 3: Insulin and incretins. *Clinical Diabetes, 26*(1), 35–39.

29. Plotkin, S., Orenstein, W., & Offit, P. (2004). *Vaccines.* Philadelphia: Saunders Elsevier.

30. Hessenbruch, A. (2000). *Reader's guide to the history of science.* London: Fitzroy Dearborn.

31. Waksman, S. A., Reilly, H. C., & Harris, D. A. (1948). Streptomyces griseous. *Journal of Bacteriology, 56*(3), 259–269.

32. Compans, R., & Orenstein, W. (2009). *Vaccines for pandemic influenza.* New York: Springer.

33. Wilfred, G. Bigelow: Chance favors the prepared mind. (2001). *Edge Magazine, 2*(1). Retrieved from http://www.research.utoronto.ca/edge/spring2001/greatDiscoverers.html.

34. Salk Institute for Biological Studies. (n.d.) Discovery timeline. Retrieved from http://www.salk.edu/about/discovery_timeline.html.

35. PBS. A science odyssey: People and discoveries: Watson and Crick describe structure of DNA. Retrieved from http://www.pbs.org/wgbh/aso/databank/entries/do53dn.html.

36. Harrison, I. (2006). *Where were you when? 180 unforgettable moments in living history.* Pleasantville, NY: Reader's Digest.

37. Centers for Disease Control. (2006, October 16). Vaccines: Vaccine timeline. Retrieved from http://www.cdc.gov/vaccines/pubs/vacc-timeline.htm.

38. Scripps-Howard News Service. (1985, December 8). Chicken pox vaccine on way. *Chicago Tribune.*

39. Sherry, C. (2006). *Opportunities in medical imaging careers.* New York: McGraw-Hill.

40. The first test-tube baby. (1978, July 31). *Time.* http://www.time.com/time/magazine/article/0,9171,946934,00.html.

41. PBS. (n.d.). A science odyssey: People and discoveries: World health organization declares smallpox eradicated. Retrieved from http://www.pbs.org/wgbh/aso/databank/entries/dm79sp.html.

42. Gallo, R. C., & Montagnier, L. (2003). The discovery of HIV as the cause of aids. *New England Journal of Medicine, 349,* 2283–2285.

43. BBC News. (1993, February 14). Dolly the sheep clone dies young. Retrieved from http://news.bbc.co.uk/2/hi/science/nature/2764039.stm.

44. U.S. Department of Energy Genome Program. (2011, February 3). Human genome project information. Retrieved from http://www.ornl.gov/sci/techresources/Human_Genome/home.shtml.

45. Naughton, S. (2010, November 2). Medical revolution. Retrieved from http://www.universityobserver.ie/2010/11/02/medical-revolution/.

46. Naughton, S. (2010, November 2). Medical revolution. Retrieved from http://www.universityobserver.ie/2010/11/02/medical-revolution/.

47. Berger, D. (1999). Diagnosing illness: From ancient times through the 19th century. *Medical Laboratory Observer.* Retrieved from http://www.mlo-online.com.

48. Porter, R. (1997). *The greatest benefit to mankind: A medical history of humanity.* New York: W. W. Norton.

49. Petty, T. L. (2002). John Hutchinson's mysterious machine revisited. *Chest, 121*(5), 2195–2235.

50. Espicom Business Intelligence. (2011). *The medical device market: USA.* Princeton, NJ: Author.

51. Espicom Business Intelligence. (2011). *The medical device market: USA.* Princeton, NJ: Author.

52. Acton, J., Adams, T., & Packer, M. (2006). *Origin of everyday things.* New York: Sterling Publishing.

53. Suchetka, D. (n.d.). Cleveland medical advancements. Retrieved from http://www.cleveland.va.gov/features/Cleveland_Medical_Advancements.asp.
54. Suchetka, D. (n.d.). Cleveland medical advancements. Retrieved from http://www.cleveland.va.gov/features/Cleveland_Medical_Advancements.asp.
55. Clements, I. P. (n.d.). Discovery health: How prosthetic limbs work. Retrieved from http://health.howstuffworks.com/medicine/modern/prosthetic-limb.htm/printable.
56. Hamarneh, S. (1962). Rise of professional pharmacy in Islam. *Medical History, 6*(1), 59–66.
57. Pfizer. (n.d.). A pioneering spirit on the frontiers of medicine. Retrieved from http://www.pfizer.com/about/history/timeline.jsp.
58. Eli Lilly. (n.d.). History. Retrieved from http://www.lilly.com/about/history/.
59. Pfizer. (n.d.). A pioneering spirit on the frontiers of medicine. Retrieved from http://www.pfizer.com/about/history/timeline.jsp.
60. Eli Lilly. (n.d.). History. Retrieved from http://www.lilly.com/about/history/.
61. Kaphingst, K. A., & DeJong, W. (2004). The educational potential of direct-to-consumer prescription drug advertising. *Health Affairs, 23*(4), 143–150.
62. Zacks Equity Research. (2010, November 9). Pharma and biotech industry outlook. Retrieved from http://www.zacks.com/stock/news/42996/Pharma+%26amp%3B+Biotech+Industry+Outlook+-+Nov.+2010.
63. Zacks Equity Research. (2010, November 9). Pharma and biotech industry outlook. Retrieved from http://www.zacks.com/stock/news/42996/Pharma+%26amp%3B+Biotech+Industry+Outlook+-+Nov.+2010.
64. Zacks Equity Research. (2010, November 9). Pharma and biotech industry outlook. Retrieved from http://www.zacks.com/stock/news/42996/Pharma+%26amp%3B+Biotech+Industry+Outlook+-+Nov.+2010.
65. Kimbuende, E., Ranji, U., Lundy, J., & Salganicoff, A. (2010). *U.S. health care costs: Background brief.* Retrieved from the Kaiser Family Foundation website: http://www.kaiseredu.org/Issue-Modules/US-Health-Care-Costs/Background-Brief.aspx.

CHAPTER 3: A QUICK HISTORY OF HEALTH CARE DELIVERY

1. Rannan-Eliya, R .P., & Nishan, M. (1997). *Resource mobilization in Sri Lanka's health sector* (Institute of Policy Studies/Harvard University Report).
2. Risse, G. (1999). *Mending bodies, saving souls: A history of hospitals.* New York: Oxford University Press.
3. Yount, L. (2001). *The history of medicine.* Farmington Hills, MI: Lucent Books.
4. Hamarneh, S. (1962). Rise of professional pharmacy in Islam. *Medical History, 6*, 59–66.
5. Sims, R. (n.d.). Library notes. Retrieved from http://www.galter.northwestern.edu/library_notes/40/salerno.cfm.

6. Rider, E. J., & Hartley, C. L. (2004). *Nursing in today's world: Trends, issues, and management*. Philadelphia: Lippencott Williams & Wilkens.

7. Slettedahl Macpherson, H. (Ed.). (2005). *Britain and the Americas: Culture, politics, and history*. Santa Barbara, CA: ABC-CLIO, 588.

8. Tulchinsky, T., & Varavikova, E. (2009). *The new public health*. Burlington, MA: Elsevier.

9. American Medical Society. (n.d.). 1847 to 1899. Retrieved from http://www.ama-assn.org/ama/pub/about-ama/our-history/timelines-ama-history/1847-1899.shtml.

10. Northern California Neurosurgery Medical Group. (2007). History of health insurance—United States—coverage. Retrieved from http://www.neurosurgical.com/medical_history_and_ethics/history/history_of_health_insurance.htm.

11. University of Pittsburgh. (2005, June 5). History of American health insurance. Retrieved from http://www.pitt.edu/~super1/lecture/lec20171/003.htm.

12. American Hospital Association. About the AHA. Retrieved from http://www.aha.org/aha/about/index.html.

13. University of Pittsburgh. (2005, June 5). History of American health insurance. Retrieved from http://www.pitt.edu/~super1/lecture/lec20171/003.htm.

14. Spielvogel, J. J. (2009). *Western civilization since 1500*. Boston, MA: Wadsworth.

15. Dutton, P. (2007). *A differential diagnoses: A comparative history of health care problems and solutions in the United States and France*. Ithaca, NY: ILR Press.

16. FDR Library. (n.d.). Franklin D. Roosevelt presidential library and museum—our documents. Retrieved from http://docs.fdrlibrary.marist.edu/odssa.html.

17. Physicians for a National Health Program. (n.d.). A brief history: Universal health care efforts in the U.S. Retrieved from http://www.pnhp.org/facts/a_brief_history_universal_health_care_efforts_in_the_us.php?page=all.

18. General Assembly of the United Nations. (1948). The Universal Declaration of Human Rights (G.A. res. 217A (III), U.N. Doc A/810 at 71).

19. PBS. (n.d.). The online newshour: Timeline—nursing homes in America. Retrieved from http://www.pbs.org/newshour/health/nursinghomes/timeline.html.

20. Centers for Medicaid and Medicare Services. (n.d.). Key milestones in Medicare and Medicaid history, selected years: 1965–2003. Retrieved from https://www.cms.gov/HealthCareFinancingReview/downloads/05-06Winpg1.pdf.

21. McNutt, B. (n.d.). Home health care delivery. Retrieved from http://ezinearticles.com/?Home-Health-Care-History&id=4264841.

22. Hospice Foundation of America. (n.d.). What is hospice (about hospice). Retrieved from http://www.hospicefoundation.org/pages/page.asp?page_id=47055.

23. Mor, V., Angelelli, J., Gifford, D., Intrator, O., Gozalo, P., & Laliberte, L. (2002). Access to post-acute nursing home care before and after the BBA. *Health Affairs, 21*(5), 254–264.

24. PBS. (n.d.). Online newshour: The healthcare debate between March 21, 1994 and the end of 1994. Retrieved from http://www.pbs.org/newshour/forum/may96/background/health_debate_page3.html.

25. California Department of Health Care Services. (n.d.). Medicare Part D. Retrieved from http://www.dhcs.ca.gov/services/medi-cal/Pages/MedicarePartD.aspx.
26. Obama signs health care overhaul bill, with a flourish. (2010, March 23) *New York Times*. Retrieved from http://www.nytimes.com/2010/03/24/health/policy/24health.html.
27. Mahavamsa.org. (n.d.). The Mahavamsa—great chronicle—history of Sri Lanka—mahavamsa. Retrieved from http://mahavamsa.org.
28. Woods, M., & Woods, M. (1999). *Ancient medicine: From sorcery to surgery*. Minneapolis, MN: Runestone Press.
29. Yount, L. (2001). *The history of medicine*. Farmington Hills, MI: Lucent Books.
30. Yount, L. (2001). *The history of medicine*. Farmington Hills, MI: Lucent Books.
31. Rider, E. J., & Hartley, C. L. (2004). *Nursing in today's world: Trends, issues, and management*. Philadelphia: Lippencott Williams & Wilkens.
32. Kaufman, W., & Slettedahl Macpherson, H. (2005). *Britain and the Americas: Culture, politics, and history, a multidisciplinary encyclopedia*. Santa Barbara, CA: ABC-CLIO.
33. American Hospital Association. (n.d.). Resource center: Fast facts on U.S. hospitals. Retrieved from http://www.aha.org/aha/resource-center/Statistics-and-Studies/fast-facts.html.
34. Buhler-Wilkerson, K. (2007). No place like home. *Home Healthcare Nurse, 25*(4), 253–259.
35. PBS. (n.d.). The online newshour: Timeline—nursing homes in America. Retrieved from http://www.pbs.org/newshour/health/nursinghomes/timeline.html.
36. Dowdal, T. (n.d.). Medicare commission. Retrieved from http://thomas.loc.gov/medicare/history.htm.
37. Mayes, R. (2007). 1969—The origins, development, and passage of Medicare's revolutionary prospective payment system. *Journal of the History of Medicine and Allied Sciences, 62*(1), 21–55.
38. Smith, W. (2005, July 19). Dame Cecily Saunders. Retrieved from http://www.weeklystandard.com/Content/Public/Articles/000/000/005/ 846ozowf.asp.
39. Hospice Foundation of America. What is hospice (about hospice). Retrieved from http://www.hospicefoundation.org/pages/page.asp?page_id=47055.
40. Starr, P. (1949). *The social transformation of American medicine*. New York: Basic Books.
41. Starr, P. (1949). *The social transformation of American medicine*. New York: Basic Books, 39.
42. Starr, P. (1949). *The social transformation of American medicine*. New York: Basic Books, 8.
43. American Medical Society. (n.d.). 1847 to 1899. Retrieved from http://www.ama-assn.org/ama/pub/about-ama/our-history/timelines-ama-history/1847-1899.shtml.
44. Light, D. (2004). Ironies of success: A new history of the American health care "system." *Journal of Health and Social Behavior, 45*(Suppl.), 1–24.
45. Light, D. (2004). Ironies of success: A new history of the American health care "system." *Journal of Health and Social Behavior, 45*(Suppl.), 1–24.

46. Burrow, J. (1977). *Organized medicine in the Progressive era*. Baltimore: Johns Hopkins University Press, 119.

47. Flexner, A., & The Carnegie Foundation for the Advancement of Teaching, (1910). *Medical education in the United States and Canada*. New York: Carnegie Foundation for the Advancement of Teaching.

48. Richmond, J., & Fein, R. (2005). *The health care mess: How we got into it and what it will take to get us out*. Cambridge, MA: Harvard University Press, 10.

49. De Miranda, M., Doggett, A., & Evans, J. (2005). *Medical technology contexts and content in science and technology*. Columbus, OH: Technology Education Program, College of Education and Human Ecology.

50. De Miranda, M., Doggett, A., & Evans, J. (2005). *Medical technology contexts and content in science and technology*. Columbus, OH: Technology Education Program, College of Education and Human Ecology.

51. U.S. Census Bureau. (2011). Physicians by sex and specialty: 1980 to 2008. Retrieved from http://www.census.gov/compendia/statab/2011/tables/11s0160.pdf.

52. U.S. Census Bureau. (2011). Physicians by sex and specialty: 1980 to 2008. Retrieved from http://www.census.gov/compendia/statab/2011/tables/11s0160.pdf.

53. America's Health Insurance Plans. (2010). Accountable care organizations and market power issues. Retrieved from http://www.americanhealthsolution.org/assets/Uploads/Blog/ACO-White-Paper.pdf.

54. Retief, F. P., & Cilliers, L. (2006). The evolution of hospitals from antiquity to the renaissance. *Acta Theologica, 26*(2), 213–232.

55. Library of Congress. (n.d.). Germany: Country studies (Library of Congress Call Number DD17.G475 1996). Retrieved from http://lcweb2.loc.gov/frd/cs/detoc.html.

56. Library of Congress. (n.d.). Germany: Country studies (Library of Congress Call Number DD17.G475 1996). Retrieved from http://lcweb2.loc.gov/frd/cs/detoc.html.

57. Library of Congress. (n.d.). Germany: Country studies (Library of Congress Call Number DD17.G475 1996). Retrieved from http://lcweb2.loc.gov/frd/cs/detoc.html.

58. Gilbert, B. B. (1965). The British National Insurance Act of 1911 and the commercial insurance lobby. *Journal of British Studies, 4*(2), 127–148.

59. Dutton, P. (2007). *A differential diagnoses: A comparative history of health care problems and solutions in the United States and France*. Ithaca, NY: ILR Press, 10.

60. Austin, D. A., & Hungerford, T. L. (2009). The market structure of the health insurance industry (Report 7-5700). Washington, DC: Congressional Research Service. Retrieved from http://www.fas.org/sgp/crs/misc/R40834.pdf.

61. Austin, D. A., & Hungerford, T. L. (2009). The market structure of the health insurance industry (Report 7-5700). Washington, DC: Congressional Research Service. Retrieved from http://www.fas.org/sgp/crs/misc/R40834.pdf.

62. Blue Cross Blue Shield. Healthcare coverage glossary. Retrieved from http://www.bcbs.com/coverage/glossary/.

63. Austin, D. A., & Hungerford, T. L. (2009). The market structure of the health insurance industry (Report 7-5700). Washington, DC: Congressional Research Service. Retrieved from http://www.fas.org/sgp/crs/misc/R40834.pdf.

64. Austin, D. A., & Hungerford, T. L. (2009). The market structure of the health insurance industry (Report 7-5700). Washington, DC: Congressional Research Service. Retrieved from http://www.fas.org/sgp/crs/misc/R40834.pdf.

65. Dutton, P. (2007). *A differential diagnoses: A comparative history of health care problems and solutions in the United States and France.* Ithaca, NY: ILR Press, 12.

66. Dutton, P. (2007). *A differential diagnoses: A comparative history of health care problems and solutions in the United States and France.* Ithaca, NY: ILR Press, 14.

67. Eisenstark, R., Weber, J. L., & Friedenthal, L. (2010). *Progressivism.* New York: Chelsea House.

68. Physicians for a National Health Program. (n.d.). A brief history: Universal health care efforts in the U.S. Retrieved from http://www.pnhp.org/facts/a_brief_history_universal_health_care_efforts_in_the_us.php?page=all.

69. Eisenstark, R., Weber, J. L., & Friedenthal, L. (2010). *Progressivism.* New York: Chelsea House.

70. Dutton, P. (2007). *A differential diagnoses: A comparative history of health care problems and solutions in the United States and France.* Ithaca, NY: ILR Press, 39.

71. Dutton, P. (2007). *A differential diagnoses: A comparative history of health care problems and solutions in the United States and France.* Ithaca, NY: ILR Press, 39.

72. Dutton, P. (2007). *A differential diagnoses: A comparative history of health care problems and solutions in the United States and France.* Ithaca, NY: ILR Press, 57.

73. Dutton, P. (2007). *A differential diagnoses: A comparative history of health care problems and solutions in the United States and France.* Ithaca, NY: ILR Press, 60.

74. Dutton, P. (2007). *A differential diagnoses: A comparative history of health care problems and solutions in the United States and France.* Ithaca, NY: ILR Press, 27.

75. Dutton, P. (2007). *A differential diagnoses: A comparative history of health care problems and solutions in the United States and France.* Ithaca, NY: ILR Press, 27.

76. Starr, P. (1949). *The social transformation of American medicine.* New York: Basic Books, 269.

77. Dutton, P. (2007). *A differential diagnoses: A comparative history of health care problems and solutions in the United States and France.* Ithaca, NY: ILR Press, 85.

78. Dutton, P. (2007). *A differential diagnoses: A comparative history of health care problems and solutions in the United States and France.* Ithaca, NY: ILR Press, 85.

79. Dutton, P. (2007). *A differential diagnoses: A comparative history of health care problems and solutions in the United States and France.* Ithaca, NY: ILR Press, 85.

80. The Wagner-Murray-Dingell bill. (1944). *American Journal of Nursing, 44*(4), 326–333.

81. The Wagner-Murray-Dingell bill. (1944). *American Journal of Nursing, 44*(4), 326–333.

82. PBS. (n.d.). PBS-healthcare crisis: Healthcare timeline. Retrieved from http://www.pbs.org/healthcarecrisis/history.htm.

83. Dutton, P. (2007). *A differential diagnoses: A comparative history of healthcare problems and solutions in the United States and France.* Ithaca, NY: ILR Press, 111.

84. Starr, P. (1949). *The social transformation of American medicine.* New York: Basic Books, 381.

85. Nixon, R. (1974, January 30). State of the Union address. Washington, DC.

86. Starr, P. (1982). *The social transformation of American medicine: The rise of a sovereign profession and the making of a vast industry.* New York: Basic Books, 404–405.

87. Ford, G. (1976, February 25). Special message to the Congress proposing health care reform. Washington, DC.

88. Watts, S. (1995). It's the institutions, stupid! Why comprehensive national health insurance always fails in America. *Journal of Health Politics, Policy and Law, 20*(2), 329–372.

89. Dukakis, M. S. (1992). The states and health care reform. *New England Journal of Medicine, 327,* 1090–1092.

90. Etheredge, L. (1983). Reagan, Congress, and health spending. *Health Affairs, 2*(1), 14–24.

91. Quadagno, J. (2004). Why the United States has no national health insurance: Stakeholder mobilization against the welfare state, 1945–1996. *Journal of Health and Social Behavior, 45,* 25–44.

92. Bledon, R. L., & Benson, J. M. (2001). Americans' views on health policy: A fifty-year historical perspective. *Health Affairs, 20,* 34–48.

93. Quadagno, J. (2004). Why the United States has no national health insurance: Stakeholder mobilization against the welfare state, 1945–1996. *Journal of Health and Social Behavior, 45,* 25–44.

94. Quadagno, J. (2004). Why the United States has no national health insurance: Stakeholder mobilization against the welfare state, 1945–1996. *Journal of Health and Social Behavior, 45,* 25–44.

95. Executive Order No. 13,335 69 C.F.R. 84(2004).

96. Medicare Prescription Drug, Improvement, and Modernization Act of 2003, Pub. L. No. 108-17, 94 Stat. 2647 (2003).

97. Health Policy Alternatives, Inc. (2003). *Prescription drug coverage for Medicare beneficiaries: A summary of the Medicare Prescription Drug, Improvement, and Modernization Act of 2003.* Menlo Park, CA: The Henry J. Kaiser Family Foundation.

98. Deficit Reduction Act of 2005, Pub. L. No.109-171, 120 Stat. 4 (2005).

99. Obama, B. (2009, September 9). Remarks by the president to a joint session of Congress on health care. Washington, DC.

100. HR 3590 (2010).

101. Norbert, G. (1993). The AMA faces down FDR and wins. *Physician Executive, 19*(1), 3–8.

102. Truman, H. (1945, November 19). Special message to the Congress recommending a comprehensive health program. Washington, DC.

103. Kennedy, J. (1965, July 30). Address at a New York rally in support of the president's program of medical care for the aged. New York, NY.
104. *Public Papers of the Presidents of the United States: Lyndon B. Johnson, 1965.* (1966). Volume II, entry 394, 811–815. Washington, DC: Government Printing Office.
105. Nixon, R. (1974, January 30). State of the Union address. Washington, DC.
106. Carter, J. (1977, April 25). Health care legislation message to Congress. Washington, DC.
107. Reagan, R. (1983, June 23). Remarks at the annual meeting of the American Medical Association house of delegates, Chicago, IL.
108. Clinton, W. (1993, September 22). Speech before joint session of Congress. Washington, DC.
109. Bush, G. (2000, October 11). The second presidential debate. Wake Forest University, Winston-Salem, NC.
110. Obama, B. (2008, October 4). Rally in support of Barack Obama's presidential run. Victory Landing Park, Newport News, VA.
111. Obama, B. (2010, March 23). An event after the signing ceremony. Washington, DC.

CHAPTER 4: THE PRESENT LANDSCAPE

1. Eran, D. (2006). 1990–1995: Planting software seeds. Retrieved from http://www.roughlydrafted.com/RD/Q4.06/2752F6C6-E2E2-48A8-A187-6F06E BEC2C94.html.
2. http://www.bestbuy.com/site/Laptop-Computers/Everyday-Laptops/pcmcat1 96200050013.c?id=pcmcat196200050013.
3. Flegal, K. M., Caroll, M. D., Ogden, C. L., & Curtin, L. R. (2010). Prevalence and trends in obesity among U.S. adults, 1999–2008. *Journal of the American Medical Association, 303*(3), 235–241.
4. U.S. Department of Health and Human Services, Centers for Disease Control and Prevention. (2009). Cigarette smoking among adults and trends in smoking cessation—United States, 2008. *Morbidity and Mortality Weekly Report, 58*(44), 1227–1232.
5. U.S. Department of Health and Human Services, Centers for Disease Control and Prevention. (2009). U.S. physical activity statistics: 2008 state summary data. Retrieved from http://apps.nccd.cdc.gov/PASurveillance/StateSum ResultV.asp.
6. U.S. Department of Health and Human Services, Centers for Disease Control and Prevention. (2009). Heavier drinking and drinking five or more drinks in a day among adults 18 years of age and over, by selected characteristics: United States, selected years 1997–2009, Table 65. Health, United States. Retrieved from http://www.cdc.gov/nchs/hus/healthrisk.htm#alcohol.

7. U.S. Department of Health and Human Services, Centers for Disease Control and Prevention. (2007). Ambulatory medical care utilization estimates for 2006, table 5. Retrieved from http://www.cdc.gov/nchs/fastats/mental.htm.

8. U.S. Department of Health and Human Services, Centers for Disease Control and Prevention. (2008). Prevalence of overweight, obesity and extreme obesity among adults: United States, trends 1976–1980 through 2005–2006. Retrieved from http://www.cdc.gov/nchs/data/hestat/overweight/overweight_adult.htm.

9. Finkelstein, E. A., Trogdon, J. G., Cohen, J. W., & Dietz, W. (2009). Annual medical spending attributable to obesity: Payer- and service-specific estimates. *Health Affairs, 28*(5), 822–831.

10. Murray, C. J., & Frenk, J. (2010). Ranking 37th—measuring the performance of the U.S. health care system. *New England Journal of Medicine.* Retrieved from http://healthpolicyandreform.nejm.org/?p=2610doi:10.1056/NEJMp09 10064.

11. U.S. Census Bureau. Retrieved from http://www.census.gov.

12. University of Miami School of Business Administration. (2011, January). Toward a better health care system. Retrieved from http://www.bus.miami.edu/faculty-and-research/conferences-and-seminars/gbf-2011/session-papers/sebelius.html.

13. University of Miami School of Business Administration. (2011, January). Toward a better health care system. Retrieved from http://www.bus.miami.edu/faculty-and-research/conferences-and-seminars/gbf-2011/session-papers/sebelius.html.

14. Alexander, S., Connor, T., & Slaughter, T. (2003). Overview of inpatient coding. *American Journal of Health-System Pharmacy, 60*(supplement), 11–14.

15. Zuvekas, S. H., & Cohen, J. W. (2010). Paying physicians by capitation: Is the past now prologue? *Health Affairs, 29*(9), 1661–1666. Retrieved from http://content.healthaffairs.org/content/29/9/1661.shortdoi:10.1377/hlthaff. 2009.0361.

16. Emanuel, E. J., & Fuchs, V. R. (2008). The perfect storm of overutilization. *Journal of the American Medical Association, 299*(23), 2789–2791. Retrieved from http://jama.ama-assn.org/content/299/23/2789.shortdoi:10.1001/jama.299.23.2789.

17. U.S. Department of Health and Human Services, Centers for Medicare and Medicaid Services. (2009, October 16). CMS announces Medicare premiums, deductibles for 2010. Retrieved from http://www.cms.gov/apps/media/press/factsheet.asp?Counter=3534.

18. Compdata. (2010, September). Benefits USA 2010/2011. Retrieved from http://www.worldatwork.org/waw/adimComment?&id=44136.

19. Compdata. (2010, September). Benefits USA 2010/2011. Retrieved from http://www.worldatwork.org/waw/adimComment?&id=44136.

20. Compdata. (2010, September). Benefits USA 2010/2011. Retrieved from http://www.worldatwork.org/waw/adimComment?&id=44136.

21. Mercer LLC. (2010, November 17). Health benefit cost growth accelerates to 6.9% in 2010. Retrieved from http://www.mercer.com/press-releases/1400235.

22. Halvorson, G. C. (2009). *Health care will not reform itself: A user's guide to re-focusing and reforming American health care.* New York: Productivity Press.
23. Halvorson, G. C. (2009). *Health care will not reform itself: A user's guide to re-focusing and reforming American health care.* New York: Productivity Press.
24. Halvorson, G. C. (2009). *Health care will not reform itself: A user's guide to re-focusing and reforming American health care.* New York: Productivity Press.
25. Halvorson, G. C. (2009). *Health care will not reform itself: A user's guide to re-focusing and reforming American health care.* New York: Productivity Press.
26. Angrisano, C., Farrell, D., Kocher, B., Laboissiere, M., & Parker, S. (2007). *Accounting for the cost of health care in the United States.* New York: McKinsey Global Institute. Retrieved from http://www.mckinsey.com/mgi/reports/.../ healthcare/MGI_US_HC_fullreport.pdf, 55.
27. Angrisano, C., Farrell, D., Kocher, B., Laboissiere, M., & Parker, S. (2007). *Accounting for the cost of health care in the United States.* New York: McKinsey Global Institute. Retrieved from http://www.mckinsey.com/mgi/reports/.../ healthcare/MGI_US_HC_fullreport.pdf, 37.
28. Zuvekas, S. H., & Cohen, J. W. (2010). Paying physicians by capitation: Is the past now prologue? *Health Affairs, 29*(9), 1661–1666. Retrieved from http://content. healthaffairs.org/content/29/9/1661.short doi: 10.1377/hlthaff.2009.0361.
29. U.S. Department of Health and Human Services, Centers for Medicare and Medicaid Services. (2011). National health expenditures 2009 highlights. Retrieved from https://www.cms.gov/NationalHealthExpendData/02_National HealthAccountsHistorical.asp#TopOfPage.
30. U.S. Department of Health and Human Services, Centers for Medicare and Medicaid Services. (2011). National health expenditures 2009 highlights. Retrieved from https://www.cms.gov/NationalHealthExpendData/02_National HealthAccountsHistorical.asp#TopOfPage.
31. Kaiser Family Foundation. (2007, January). *Health care spending in the United States and OECD countries.* Retrieved from http://www.kff.org/insurance/ snapshot/chcm010307oth.cfm.
32. Jensen, E. (2009). *Accounting for the cost of U.S. health care: A new look at why Americans spend more.* New York: McKinsey Global Institute. Retrieved from http://www.academyhealth.org/files/2009/monday/Jensene.pdf, 2.
33. Jensen, E. (2009). *Accounting for the cost of US health care: A new look at why Americans spend more.* New York: McKinsey Global Institute. Retrieved from http://www.academyhealth.org/files/2009/monday/Jensene.pdf, 2.
34. Jensen, E. (2009). *Accounting for the cost of US health care: A new look at why Americans spend more.* New York: McKinsey Global Institute. Retrieved from http://www.academyhealth.org/files/2009/monday/Jensene.pdf, 2.
35. Jensen, E. (2009). *Accounting for the cost of US health care: A new look at why Americans spend more.* New York: McKinsey Global Institute. Retrieved from http://www.academyhealth.org/files/2009/monday/Jensene.pdf, 2.
36. Jensen, E. (2009). *Accounting for the cost of US health care: A new look at why Americans spend more.* New York: McKinsey Global Institute. Retrieved from http://www.academyhealth.org/files/2009/monday/Jensene.pdf, 2.

37. Mitka, M. (2009). Growth in health care spending slows, but still outpaces rate of inflation. *Health Affairs, 301*(8), 815–816. Retrieved from http://jama.ama-assn.org/content/301/8/815.full doi: 10.1001/jama.2009.85.

38. U.S. Department of Health and Human Services. (2008, October 17). Medicaid spending projected to rise much faster than the economy [Press Release]. Retrieved from http://www.hhs.gov/news/press/2008pres/10/20081017a.html.

39. Office of Management and Budget. (2011). FY 2011 summary tables. Retrieved from http://www.whitehouse.gov/sites/default/files/omb/budget/fy2011/.../tables.pdf.

40. Rowland, D. (2009). Health care and Medicaid—weathering the recession. *New England Journal of Medicine, 360*(13), 1274. Retrieved from http://www.nejm.org/doi/full/10.1056/NEJMp0901072.

41. U.S. Census Bureau. (n.d.). Selected characteristics of baby boomers 42 to 60 years old in 2006. Age data of the United States: Selected age groups. Retrieved from http://www.census.gov/population/www/socdemo/age/general-age.html#bb.

42. Smith, C. H. (2011, January 18). Is fee-for-service what ails America's health care system? *Daily Finance.* Retrieved from http://www.dailyfinance.com/story/is-fee-for-service-what-ails-americas-health-care-system/19311085/.

43. Chua, K. P. (2009). *The case for universal health care.* Reston, VA: American Medical Student Association. Retrieved from http://www.amsa.org/AMSA/Libraries/Committee_Docs/CaseForUHC.sflb.ashx.

44. Kaiser Family Foundation and Health Research and Educational Trust. (2010). *Employer Health Benefits 2010 Annual Survey.* Menlo Park, CA: American Hospital Association, 75.

45. U.S. Department of Health and Human Services. (2010). *Insurance companies prosper, families suffer: Our broken health insurance system.* Washington, DC: Author. Retrieved from http://www.healthreform.gov/reports/insuranceprospers/index.html.

46. United Food and Commercial Workers. (n.d.). Hold the line facts for America's health care: Corporate greed vs. human need—the southern California supermarket strike/lockout. Retrieved from http://www.ufcw.org/your_industry/retail/strike_updates/southern_california/index.cfm.

47. U.S. Department of Health and Human Services, Centers for Disease Control and Prevention. (2010). NCHS health insurance data. Retrieved from http://www.cdc.gov/nchs/data/factsheets/factsheet_health_insurance.htm.

48. U.S. Department of Health and Human Services, Centers for Disease Control and Prevention. (2010). NCHS health insurance data. Retrieved from http://www.cdc.gov/nchs/data/factsheets/factsheet_health_insurance.htm.

49. U.S. Census Bureau. (2010). State and county quick facts: New York City. Retrieved from http://quickfacts.census.gov/qfd/states/36/3651000.html.

50. Meyer, J., & Smith, B. M. (2008, November 10). *Chronic disease management: Evidence of predictable savings.* Lansing, MI: Health Management Associates. Retrieved from http://www.healthmanagement.com/news_details.asp?newsarticleid=179.

51. Kaiser Family Foundation. (2010, February). *Prescription drug costs: Background brief.* Lansing, MI: Health Management Associates. Retrieved from http://www.kaiseredu.org/Issue-Modules/Prescription-Drug-Costs/Background-Brief.aspx.
52. Kaiser Family Foundation. (2010, February). *Prescription drug costs: Background brief.* Lansing, MI: Health Management Associates. Retrieved from http://www.kaiseredu.org/Issue-Modules/Prescription-Drug-Costs/Background-Brief.aspx.
53. Kaiser Family Foundation. (2010, February). *Prescription drug costs: Background brief.* Lansing, MI: Health Management Associates. Retrieved from http://www.kaiseredu.org/Issue-Modules/Prescription-Drug-Costs/Background-Brief.aspx.
54. Kaiser Family Foundation. (2010, February). *Prescription drug costs: Background brief.* Lansing, MI: Health Management Associates. Retrieved from http://www.kaiseredu.org/Issue-Modules/Prescription-Drug-Costs/Background-Brief.aspx.
55. Angrisano, C., Farrell, D., Kocher, B., Laboissiere, M., & Parker, S. (2007). *Accounting for the cost of health care in the United States.* New York: McKinsey Global Institute. Retrieved from http://www.mckinsey.com/mgi/reports/.../healthcare/MGI_US_HC_fullreport.pdf, 20.
56. Angrisano, C., Farrell, D., Kocher, B., Laboissiere, M., & Parker, S. (2007). *Accounting for the cost of health care in the United States.* New York: McKinsey Global Institute. Retrieved from http://www.mckinsey.com/mgi/reports/.../healthcare/MGI_US_HC_fullreport.pdf, 21.
57. Angrisano, C., Farrell, D., Kocher, B., Laboissiere, M., & Parker, S. (2007). *Accounting for the cost of health care in the United States.* New York: McKinsey Global Institute. Retrieved from http://www.mckinsey.com/mgi/reports/.../healthcare/MGI_US_HC_fullreport.pdf, 21.
58. Angrisano, C., Farrell, D., Kocher, B., Laboissiere, M., & Parker, S. (2007). *Accounting for the cost of health care in the United States.* New York: McKinsey Global Institute. Retrieved from http://www.mckinsey.com/mgi/reports/.../healthcare/MGI_US_HC_fullreport.pdf, 21.
59. Angrisano, C., Farrell, D., Kocher, B., Laboissiere, M., & Parker, S. (2007). *Accounting for the cost of health care in the United States.* New York: McKinsey Global Institute. Retrieved from http://www.mckinsey.com/mgi/reports/.../healthcare/MGI_US_HC_fullreport.pdf, 76.
60. Starfield, B. (2000). Is U.S. health really the best in the world? *Journal of the American Medical Association, 284*(4), 283–285.
61. Shreve, J., Van Den Bos, J., Gray, T., Halford, M., Rustagi, K., & Ziemkiewicz, E. (2010). *The economic measurement of medical errors.* Schaumberg, IL: Society of Actuaries, Health Section. Retrieved from http://www.soa.org/files/pdf/research-econ-measurement.pdf, 10.
62. Mello, M. M., Chandra, A., Gawande, A. A., & Studdert, D. M. (2010). National costs of the medical liability system. *Health Affairs, 29*(9), 1569–1577.
63. Hobson, K. (2009, August 9). Study puts cost of medical errors at $19.5 billion. *Wall Street Journal.* Retrieved from http://blogs.wsj.com/health/2010/08/09/study-puts-cost-of-medical-errors-at-195-billion.

64. Lowes, R. (2010, September 7). Malpractice litigation, defensive medicine cost less than thought. Retrieved from http://www.medscape.com/viewarticle/728128.

65. Mello, M. M., Chandra, A., Gawande, A. A., & Studdert, D. M. (2010). National costs of the medical liability system. *Health Affairs, 29*(9), 1569–1577.

66. Mello, M. M., Chandra, A., Gawande, A. A., & Studdert, D. M. (2010). National costs of the medical liability system. *Health Affairs, 29*(9), 1569–1577.

67. Halvorson, G. C. (2009). *Health care will not reform itself.* New York: CRC Press.

68. U.S. Department of Health and Human Services, Centers for Disease Control and Prevention. (2005, November). Chronic disease overview. Retrieved from http://www.cdc.gov/NCCdphp/overview.htm#2.

69. Halvorson, G. C. (2007). *Health care reform now! A prescription for change.* San Francisco: Jossey-Bass, 2.

70. Mensah, G. A., & Brown, D. W. (2007). An overview of cardiovascular disease burden in the United States. *Health Affairs, 26*(1), 38–48.

71. American Diabetes Association. (2005). Direct and indirect costs of diabetes in the United States. Retrieved from www.house.gov/degette/diabetes/docs/Costs.fs_Final.pdf.cost-of-diabetes-in-us.jsp.

72. U.S. Department of Health and Human Services, National Heart, Lung, and Blood Institute. (2004). *Morbidity and mortality: 2004 chart book on cardiovascular, lung, and blood diseases.* Bethesda, MD: National Institutes of Health.

73. Partnership for Solutions. (2004, May). *Depression: Common comorbidities.* Baltimore: Author. Retrieved from http://www.partnershipforsolutions.org/statistics/issue_briefs.html.

74. Charlson, M., Charlson, R. E., Briggs, W., & Hollenberg, J. (2007). Can disease management target patients most likely to generate high costs? The impact of comorbidity. *Journal of General Internal Medicine, 22*(4), 464–469.

75. Charlson, M., Charlson, R. E., Briggs, W., & Hollenberg, J. (2007). Can disease management target patients most likely to generate high costs? The impact of comorbidity. *Journal of General Internal Medicine, 22*(4), 464–469.

76. Charlson, M., Charlson, R. E., Briggs, W., & Hollenberg, J. (2007). Can disease management target patients most likely to generate high costs? The impact of comorbidity. *Journal of General Internal Medicine, 22*(4), 464–469.

77. Himmelstein, D. U., Thorne, D., Warren, E., & Woolhander, S. (2009). Medical bankruptcy in the United States, 2007: Results of a national study. *The American Journal of Medicine, 122*(8), 741–746.

78. World Health Organization. (2000). *Health systems: Improving performance.* Geneva: Author. Retrieved from http://www.who.int/whr/2000/en/.

79. World Health Organization. (2000). *Health systems: Improving performance.* Geneva: Author. Retrieved from http://www.who.int/whr/2000/en/.

80. World Health Organization. (2000). *Health systems: Improving performance.* Geneva: Author. Retrieved from http://www.who.int/whr/2000/en/.

81. World Health Organization. (2000, June 21). World health organization assesses the world's health systems [WHO Press Release], 44. Retrieved from http://www.who.int/inf-pr-2000/en/pr2000-44.html.

82 World Health Organization. (2000, June 21). World health organization assesses the world's health systems [WHO Press Release], 44. Retrieved from http://www.who.int/inf-pr-2000/en/pr2000-44.html.

83. Halvorson, G. C. (1993). *Strong medicine.* New York: Random House.

84. Wennberg, J. E., Fisher, E. S., Goodman, D. C., & Skinner, J. S. (Eds.). (2006). *The care of patients with severe chronic illness: An online report of the Medicare program by the Dartmouth Atlas Project. The Dartmouth Atlas of Health Care 2006.* Retrieved from http://www.dartmouthatlas.org/downloads/atlases/2006_Chronic_Care_Atlas.pdf.

85. Wennberg, J. E., Fisher, E. S., Goodman, D. C., & Skinner, J. S. (Eds.). (2006). *The care of patients with severe chronic illness: An online report of the Medicare program by the Dartmouth Atlas Project. The Dartmouth Atlas of Health Care 2006.* Retrieved from http://www.dartmouthatlas.org/downloads/atlases/2006_Chronic_Care_Atlas.pdf.

86. Wennberg, J. E., Fisher, E. S., Goodman, D. C., & Skinner, J. S. (Eds.). (2006). *The care of patients with severe chronic illness: An online report of the Medicare program by the Dartmouth Atlas Project. The Dartmouth Atlas of Health Care 2006.* Retrieved from http://www.dartmouthatlas.org/downloads/atlases/2006_Chronic_Care_Atlas.pdf.

87. Scarborough, N. (2008, February). *Medical misdiagnosis in America 2008: A persistent problem with a promising solution.* Franklin, TN: Premerus. Retrieved from http://www.medsolutions.com/images/Misdiagnosis_in_America.pdf.

88. Scarborough, N. (2008, February). *Medical misdiagnosis in America 2008: A persistent problem with a promising solution.* Franklin, TN: Premerus. Retrieved from http://www.medsolutions.com/images/Misdiagnosis_in_America.pdf.

89. Halvorson, G. C. (2009). *Health care will not reform itself: A user's guide to refocusing and reforming American health care.* New York: Productivity Press.

90. Halvorson, G. C. (2009). *Health care will not reform itself: A user's guide to refocusing and reforming American health care.* New York: Productivity Press.

91. Halvorson, G. C. (2009). *Health care will not reform itself: A user's guide to refocusing and reforming American health care.* New York: Productivity Press.

92. Halvorson, G. C. (2007). *Health care reform now! A prescription for change.* San Francisco: Jossey-Bass, 34.

93. Halvorson, G. C. (2007). *Health care reform now! A prescription for change.* San Francisco: Jossey-Bass, 34.

94. National Committee for Quality Assurance. (2010, October 26). NCQA health insurance plan rankings 2010–2011: Top 20 private health insurance plans. Retrieved from http://www.ncqa.org/tabid/1243/Default.aspx.

95. Halvorson, G. C. (2007). *Health care reform now! A prescription for change.* San Francisco: Jossey-Bass, 35–36.

96. Halvorson, G. C. (2007). *Health care reform now! A prescription for change.* San Francisco: Jossey-Bass, 36.

97. George, J. C., Allis, S., Dickerson, J. F., Booth, C., & McDowell, J. (1997, April 14). Backlash against HMOs. *Time.* Retrieved from http://www.time.com/time/magazine/article/0,9171,986182-2,00.html.

98. Press Ganey Associates, Inc. (2010). 2010 emergency department *Pulse Report.* Retrieved from http://www.pressganey.com/researchResources/hospitals/emegencyDepartment/emergencyPulsereport.aspx.

99. Jha, A. K., Orav, E. J., Zheng, J., & Epstein, A. M. (2008). Patients' perception of hospital care in the United States. *New England Journal of Medicine, 359,* 1921–1931.

100. Conference of Catholic Bishops. (1993). *A framework for comprehensive health care reform: Protecting human life, promoting human dignity, pursuing the common good.* Washington, DC: USCCB Publishing.

101. Patient Protection and Affordable Care Act. 42 U.S.C. 157.

102. U.S. Department of Health and Human Services, Centers for Disease Control and Prevention. (2005). Chronic disease overview. Retrieved from http://www.cdc.gov/nccdphp/overview.htm.

CHAPTER 5: AGES

1. Moore, G. (1965, April 19). Cramming more components onto integrated systems. *Electronics.* Retrieved from http://download.intel.com/museum/Moores_Law/Articles-Press_releases/Gordon_Moore_1965_Article.pdf.

CHAPTER 6: THE SHIFT AGE AND THE TWENTY-FIRST CENTURY

1. Leo, P. (2006, March 16). Cell phone statistics that may surprise you. *Pittsburgh Post-Gazette.* Retrieved from http://www.post-gazette.com/pg/06075/671034-294.stm.

2. Whitney, L. (2010, February 16). Cell phone subscriptions to hit 5 billion globally. Retrieved from http://reviews.cnet.com/8301-13970_7-10454065-78.html.

3. comScore. (2011). comScore releases January 2011 U.S. search engine rankings. Retrieved from http://www.comscore.com/Press_Events/Press_Releases/2011/2/comScore_Releases_January_2011_U.S._Search_Engine_Rankings.

4. Keckley, P. H., & Underwood, H. R. (2008) *Medical tourism: consumers in search of value.* New York: Deloitte Center for Health Solutions. Retrieved from www.deloitte.com/assets/../us_chs_MedicalTourismStudy(3).pdf.

5. Anand, G. (2009, November 25). The Henry Ford of heart surgery: In India a factory model for hospitals is cutting costs and yielding profits. *Wall Street Journal,* A16.

6. Anand, G. (2009, November 25). The Henry Ford of heart surgery: In India a factory model for hospitals is cutting costs and yielding profits. *Wall Street Journal*, A16.

CHAPTER 7: MEDICAL MIRACLES AROUND THE CORNER

1. Houle, David, www.evolutionshift.com.
2. Dictionary.com. (2011). Transformation. Retrieved from http://dictionary.reference.com/browse/transformation.
3. Kinsella, K., & Velkoff, V. A. (2001). *An aging world: 2001*. Washington, DC: U.S. Census Bureau. http://www.census.gov/prod/2001pubs/p95-01-1.pdf .
4. Kinsella, K., & Velkoff, V. A. (2001). *An aging world: 2001*. Washington, DC: U.S. Census Bureau. http://www.census.gov/prod/2001pubs/p95-01-1.pdf .
5. Kinsella, K., & Velkoff, V. A. (2001). *An aging world: 2001*. Washington, DC: U.S. Census Bureau. http://www.census.gov/prod/2001pubs/p95-01-1.pdf .
6. Cohen, M. N., & Armelagos, G. J. (1984). *Paleopathology at the origins of agriculture*. Orlando, FL: Academic Press, 51–73.
7. Oeppen, J., & Vaupel, J. W. (2002). Broken limits to life expectancy. *Science, 296*, 1029–1031.
8. Olshansky, S. J., Goldman, D. P., Zheng, Y., & Rowe, J. W. (2009). Aging in America in the twenty-first century: Demographic forecasts from the MacArthur Foundation research network on an aging society. *The Milbank Quarterly, 87*(4), 842–862.
9. Grossman, L. (2011, February 21). 2045: The year man becomes immortal. *Time*. Retrieved from http://www.time.com/time/health/article/0,8599,2048138,00.html.
10. National Human Genome Research Institute. (2010). The Human Genome Project completion: Frequently asked questions. Retrieved from http://www.genome.gov/11006943.
11. Davies, K. (2010). *The $1,000 genome: The revolution in DNA sequencing and the new era of personalized medicine*. New York: Free Press.
12. Lehmann-Haupt, R. (2010, March 4). Pacific bioscience has a $1000 genome test that could save your life—and the industry. BNET Healthcare. Retrieved from http://www.bnet.com/blog/healthcare/pacific-bioscience-has-a-1000-genome-test-that-could-save-your-life-and-the-industry/1824.
13. Craelius, W. (2002). The bionic man: Restoring mobility. *Science, 295*, 1018–1021.
14. Beijing 2008 paralympic games. (2008, September 9). Oscar Pistorius: Athlete, activist, fastest man on no legs. Retrieved from http://en.paralympic.beijing2008 . cn/news/special/features/n214592913.shtml.
15. IAAF.org. (2008, January 14). Oscar Pistorius—independent scientific study concludes that cheetah prosthetics offer clear mechanical advantages. Retrieved from http://www.iaaf.org/news/kind=101/newsid=42896.html.
16. Rustad, K. C., Sorkin, M., & Levi, B. (2010). Strategies for organ-level tissue engineering. *Organogenesis, 63*(3), 151–157.

17. Bengni, A., Morigi, M., & Remuzzi, G. (2010). Kidney regeneration. *The Lancet, 375,* 1310–1317.

18. Wake Forest Baptist Medical Center, Institute for Regenerative Medicine. (2011). Laboratory-grown urethras implanted in patients, scientists report. Retrieved from http://www.wakehealth.edu/News-Releases/2011/Laboratory-Grown_Urethras_Implanted_in_Patients,_Scientists_Report.htm.

19. Fiester, A. (2005). Ethical issues in animal cloning. *Perspectives in Biology and Medicine, 48*(2), 328–330.

20. Shuster, E. (2003). Human cloning: Category, dignity, and the role of bioethics. *Bioethics, 17*(5–6), 521–525.

21. Shelley, M. W. (1932). *Frankenstein: the modern Prometheus.* New York: Illustrated Editions, 38.

22. Artificial life forms: Genesis redux. (2010, May 20). *The Economist.* Retrieved March 20, 2011, from http://www.economist.com/node/16163006.

23. Centers for Disease Control and Prevention. (2009). Federal and state cigarette excise taxes—United States, 1995–2009. *Morbidity and Mortality Weekly Report, 58*(19). Retrieved from http://www.cdc.gov/mmwr/preview/mmwrhtml/mm5819a2.htm.

24. Ahmad, S. A., & Franz, G. A. (2008). Raising taxes to reduce smoking prevalence in the U.S.: A simulation of the anticipated health and economic impacts. *Public Health, 122*(1), 3–10.

CHAPTER 8: 80 PERCENT ACCEPTED, 20 PERCENT TO GO

1. Lee, P. (2011). *Deloitte technology, media, and telecommunications predictions 2011.* London: The Creative Studio. Retrieved from http://www.deloitte.com/assets/Dcom-Croatia/Local%20Assets/Documents/2011/TMT_Predictions_2011.pdf.

2. comScore. (2011). comScore releases January 2011 U.S. search engine rankings. Retrieved from http://www.comscore.com/Press_Events/Press_Releases/2011/2/comScore_Releases_January_2011_U.S._Search_Engine_Rankings.

3. RISI Wood Biomass Markets. (2010). North American paper trends at home vs. the office—less paper but far from paperless. Retrieved from http://www.woodbiomass.com/news/pulpandpaper/news/RISI-ECONOMISTS-North-American-copy-paper-trends-at-home-vs-the-office-less-paper-but-far-from-paperless.html.

4. Gerdes, G. R., Donahue, N., Eiermann, A. F., & Iwata, J. M. (2010). *The 2010 Federal Reserve payment study: Non-cash payment trends in the United States: 2006–2009.* Atlanta, GA: Federal Reserve System. Retrieved from http://www.frbservices.org/files/communications/pdf/press/2010_payments_study.pdf .

5. Gerdes, G. R., Donahue, N., Eiermann, A. F., & Iwata, J. M. (2010). *The 2010 Federal Reserve payment study: Non-cash payment trends in the United States: 2006–2009.* Atlanta, GA: Federal Reserve System. Retrieved from http://www.frbservices.org/files/communications/pdf/press/2010_payments_study.pdf .

6. IBM Center for the Business of Government. (2010). Telework enhancement act of 2010. Retrieved from http://www.businessofgovernment.org/blog/strategies-font-color-redcut-costsfont-and-improve-performance/telework-enhancement-act-2010.

7. U.S. Department of Health and Human Services, Centers for Medicare and Medicaid Services. (2011). National health expenditures 2009 highlights. Retrieved from https://www.cms.gov/NationalHealthExpendData/02_National-HealthAccountsHistorical.asp#TopOfPage.

8. Hsiao, C., Hing, E., Socey, T. C. & Cai, B. (2010). *Electronic medical record/electronic health record systems of office-based physicians: United States, 2009 and preliminary 2010 state estimates.* Washington, DC: National Center for Health Statistics Health E-stat.

9. Jha, A., DesRoches P. D., & Joshi, M. S. (2010). A progress report on electronic health records in U.S. hospitals. *Health Affairs, 29*(10), 1951–1957.

10. comScore. (2011). comScore reports November 2010 U.S. mobile subscriber market share. Retrieved from http://comscore.com/Press_Events/Press_Releases/2011/1/comScore_Reports_November_2010_U.S._Mobile_Subscriber_Market_Share.

11. SureScripts. (2010). National progress report of e-prescribing. Retrieved from http://www.surescripts.com/media/515306/2009_national-progress-report.pdf.

12. Fesenmaier, D. R., & Cook, S. D. (2009). Travelers' use of the Internet. Washington, DC: U.S. Travel Association. Retrieved from http://travel.utah.gov/publications/newsletters/files/2010_01_21/Travelers%20Use%20of%20the%20Internet%20-%202009.pdf.

13. Cohen, R. A., & Stussman, B. (2005). *Health information technology use among men and women aged 18–64: Early release of estimates from the National Health Interview Survey, January–June 2009.* Washington DC, National Center for Health Statistics. Retrieved from http://www.cdc.gov/nchs/data/hestat/healthinfo2009/healthinfo2009.pdf.

14. SureScripts. (2010). National progress report of e-prescribing. Retrieved from http://www.surescripts.com/media/515306/2009_national-progress-report.pdf.

15. SureScripts. (2010). National progress report of e-prescribing. Retrieved from http://www.surescripts.com/media/515306/2009_national-progress-report.pdf.

16. Ferguson, S. (2010, May 18). IT spending could hit $2 trillion in 2010, says Gartner. eWeek.com. Retrieved from http://www.eweek.com/c/a/IT-Infrastructure/IT-Spending-Could-Hit-2-Trillion-in-2010-Says-Gartner-193999/.

17. Brodkin, J. (2010, May 18). IT spending to rise 4.1% in 2010, Gartner says. Retrieved from http://www.cio.com/article/594199/IT_Spending_to_Rise_4.1_in_2010_Gartner_Says?source=rss_news.

18. Ferguson, S. (2010, May 18). IT spending could hit $2 trillion in 2010, says Gartner. eWeek.com. Retrieved from http://www.eweek.com/c/a/IT-Infrastructure/IT-Spending-Could-Hit-2-Trillion-in-2010-Says-Gartner-193999/.

19. Guevara, J., Stegman, E., & Hall, L. (2011). *IT key metrics data: Summary report.* New York: Gartner, 5.

20. Guevara, J., Stegman, E., & Hall, L. (2011). *IT key metrics data: Summary report.* New York: Gartner, 5.

21. Horrigan, J. B. (2008). Online shopping. Washington, DC: Pew Internet and American Life Project. Retrieved from http://www.pewinternet.org/~/media//Files/Reports/2008/PIP_Online%20Shopping.pdf.pdf.

22. Horrigan, J. B. (2008). Online shopping. Washington, DC: Pew Internet and American Life Project. Retrieved from http://www.pewinternet.org/~/media//Files/Reports/2008/PIP_Online%20Shopping.pdf.pdf.

23. Jha, A. K. (2009). Use of electronic health records in U.S. hospitals. *New England Journal of Medicine, 360,* 1628–1638.

24. Jha, A. K. (2009). Use of electronic health records in U.S. hospitals. *New England Journal of Medicine, 360,* 1628–1638.

CHAPTER 10: THE DYNAMIC FLOWS IN HOW WE THINK ABOUT HEALTH CARE

1. Halverson, G. (2007). *Health care reform now! A prescription for change.* San Franciso, CA: Jossey-Bass.

2. Halverson, G. (2007). *Health care reform now! A prescription for change.* San Franciso, CA: Jossey-Bass.

3. Gerace, J. E. (2009, June 21). Asthma attack signs and symptoms, prevention, and more. Retrieved from http://www.webmd.com/asthma/guide/asthma-attack-symptoms.

4. Yusuf, S., Hawken, S., Ounpuu, S., Dans, T., Avezum, A., Lanas, F., ... Lisheng, L. (2004). Effect of potentially modifiable risk factors associated with myocardial infarction in 52 countries (the interheart study): Case-control study. *Lancet, 364*(9438), 937–952.

5. Chakraburtty, A. (2010, March 1). Exercise and depression: Physical activity benefits for mood and stress relief. Retrieved from http://www.webmd.com/depression/guide/exercise-depression.

6. Institute of Medicine. (1996). *Primary care: America's health in a new era.* Washington, DC: National Academies Press.

7. U.S. Department of Health and Human Services, Centers for Medicare and Medicaid Services. (2011). National health expenditures 2009 highlights. Retrieved from https://www.cms.gov/NationalHealthExpendData/02_NationalHealthAccountsHistorical.asp#TopOfPage.

8. Delamater, A.M. (2006). Improving patient adherence. *Clinical Diabetes, 24*(2), 71–77.

9. Barovick, H., Romero, F., Sanburn, J., Silver, A., Tharoor, I., Webley, K., & Suddath, C. (2011, January 17). The world. *Time, 177*(2), 14–15.

10. Younge, G. (2005, March 23). McDonald's grabs a piece of the apple pie. Retrieved from http://www.guardian.co.uk/world/2005/mar/23/usa.foodanddrink.

11. Shore, R. (2010, November 30). B.C. firm develops apples that won't turn brown when sliced. *Vancouver Sun*. Retrieved from http://canada.com/vancouversun/news/westcoastnews/story.html?id=ae481b3e-54a8-4360-9ff4-faded4a6504a.

12. Plumridge, H. (2011, January 22). Pharmaceutical sector remains genetically challenged. *Wall Street Journal*. Retrieved from http://online.wsj.com/article/SB10001424052748704754304576096290166001426.html.

13. Medical education and simulation. (2010). Retrieved from http://www.meti.com.

14. Smith, G. G. (n.d.) Imaging reimbursement cuts may harm rural practices, patients. Retrieved from http://www.rsna.org/Publications/rsnanews/may06/cuts_may06.cfm.

CHAPTER 11: THE DYNAMIC FLOWS IN HOW WE DELIVER HEALTH CARE

1. Centers for Disease Control and Prevention. (1994). Surveillance for selected tobacco-use behaviors—United States, 1900–1994. *Morbidity and Mortality Weekly Report, 43*(SS-3). Washington, DC: Government Printing Office. Retrieved from http://www.cdc.gov/mmwr/preview/mmwrhtml/00033881.htm.

2. Centers for Disease Control and Prevention. (n.d.) History of the surgeon general's reports on smoking and health. Retrieved from http://www.cdc.gov/tobacco/data_statistics/sgr/history/index.htm.

3. Centers for Disease Control and Prevention. (2010). Vital signs: Current cigarette smoking adults aged > 18 years—United States, 2009. *Morbidity and Mortality Weekly Report, 59*(2010). Retrieved from http://www.cdc.gov/mmwr/preview/mmwrhtml/mm5935a3.htm?s_cid=mm5935a3_w.

4. Halvorson, G. C. (2009). *Health care will not reform itself: A users guide to refocusing and reforming American health care*. New York: CRC Press, 128.

5. Finkelstein, E. L., Trogdon, J. G., Cohen, J. W., & Dietz, W. (2009). Annual medical spending attributable to obesity: Payer-and service-specific estimates. *Health Affairs, 28*(5), 822–831.

6. Centers for Disease Control and Prevention, National Center for Chronic Disease Prevention and Health Promotion, Division of Diabetes Translation. (n.d.). Number (in millions) of civilian, non-institutionalized persons with diagnosed diabetes. Retrieved from http://www.cdc.gov/diabetes/statistics/prev/national/figpersons.htm.

7. Centers for Disease Control and Prevention, National Center for Chronic Disease Prevention and Health Promotion, Division of Diabetes Translation. (n.d.). Number (in millions) of civilian, non-institutionalized persons with diagnosed diabetes. Retrieved from http://www.cdc.gov/diabetes/statistics/prev/national/figpersons.htm.

8. Halvorson, G. C. (2009). *Health care will not reform itself: A users guide to refocusing and reforming American health care*. New York, NY: CRC Press, 113.

9. Halvorson, G. C. (2009). *Health care will not reform itself: A users guide to re-focusing and reforming American health care*. New York: CRC Press, 113.

10. Halvorson, G. C. (2009). *Health care will not reform itself: A users guide to re-focusing and reforming American health care*. New York: CRC Press, 113.

11. Centers for Disease Control and Prevention. (2011). National diabetes fact sheet: National estimates and general information on diabetes and prediabetes in the United States, 2011. Atlanta, GA: Author. Retrieved from http://www.cdc.gov/diabetes/pubs/pdf/ndfs_2011.pdf.

12. Halvorson, G. C. (2009). *Health care will not reform itself: A users guide to re-focusing and reforming American health care*. New York, NY: CRC Press, 113.

13. American Diabetes Association. (n.d.). How to prevent prediabetes. Retrieved from http://www.diabetes.org/diabetes-basics/prevention/pre-diabetes/how-to-prevent-pre-diabetes.html.

14. Brink, S. (2009). The diabetes prevention program: How the participants did it. *Health Affairs, 28*(1), 57–62.

15. American Lung Association. (2010). *Trends in asthma morbidity and mortality*. Washington, DC: Author. Retrieved from http://www.lungusa.org/finding-cures/our-research/trend-reports/asthma-trend-report.pdf.

16. Care Management Institute. (2005). *Asthma: The right thing*. Oakland, CA: Kaiser Permanente.

17. Halvorson, G. C. (2009). *Health care will not reform itself: A users guide to re-focusing and reforming American health care*. New York, NY: CRC Press, 109.

18. Halvorson, G. C. (2009). *Health care will not reform itself: A users guide to re-focusing and reforming American health care*. New York: CRC Press, 109.

19. Halvorson, G. C. (2009). *Health care will not reform itself: A users guide to re-focusing and reforming American health care*. New York: CRC Press, 109.

20. Centers for Disease Control, National Center for Health Statistics. NCHS Health. Asthma prevalence, health care use, and mortality: United States, 2003–05. Retrieved from http://www.cdc.gov/nchs/data/hestat/asthma03-05/asthma03-05.htm.

21. American Heart Association. (2010). *Heart disease and stroke statistics—2010 update*. Dallas, TX: American Heart Association, 18.

22. American Heart Association. (2010). *Heart disease and stroke statistics—2010 update*. Dallas, TX: American Heart Association, 15.

23. United States Department of Health and Human Services. (2011, April 12). Partnership for patients to improve care and lower costs for Americans. Retrieved from http://www.hhs.gov/news/press/2011pres/04/20110412a.html.

24. American Academy of Family Physicians, American Academy of Pediatrics, American College of Physicians, and American Osteopathic Association. (2007, February). *Joint principles of the patient-centered medical home*. Retrieved from http://www.aafp.org/online/etc/medialib/aafp_org/documents/policy/fed/jointprinciplespcmh0207.Par.0001.File.dat/022107medicalhome.pdf.

25. Kaiser Family Foundation and Health Research and Educational Trust. (2010). *Employer health benefits 2010 annual survey*. Menlo Park, CA: American Hospital Association, 75.

26. Emergency care coordination center, Notices. (2009, April 29). *Federal Register* 74(81), 19561.

27. American Heart Association. (2011). Cardiac arrest. Retrieved from http://www.americanheart.org/presenter.jhtml?identifier=4481.

28. Society of Hospital Medicine. (2011). History. Retrieved from http://www.hospitalmedicine.org/AM/Template.cfm?Section=General_Information&Template=/CM/HTMLDisplay.cfm&ContentID=14046.

29. Lindenauer, P. K., et al. (2007). Outcomes of care by hospitalists, general internists, and family physicians. *New England Journal of Medicine, 357,* 2589–2600.

30. Sack, K. (2011, April 14). V.A. shows hospitals can make large cuts in deadly infections. *New York Times,* A3.

31. Sack, K. (2011, April 14). V.A. shows hospitals can make large cuts in deadly infections. *New York Times,* A3.

32. Sack, K. (2011, April 14). V.A. shows hospitals can make large cuts in deadly infections. *New York Times,* A3.

33. Sack, K. (2011, April 14). V.A. shows hospitals can make large cuts in deadly infections. *New York Times,* A3.

34. Vogel, M. (2011). Carving up the budget. *Florida Trend,* 116, 118.

35. Vogel, M. (2011). Carving up the budget. *Florida Trend,* 116, 118.

36. Planetree. (n.d.). Home page. Retrieved from http://www.planetree.org./

37. Planetree. (n.d.). About Planetree. Retrieved from http://www.planetree.org/about.html.

38. University of Miami School of Business Administration. (2011, January). The hospital as town center. Retrieved from http://www.bus.miami.edu/faculty-and-research/conferences-and-seminars/gbf-2011/session-papers/hospital-sprawl.html.

39. University of Miami School of Business Administration (2011, January). The hospital as town center. Retrieved from http://www.bus.miami.edu/faculty-and-research/conferences-and-seminars/gbf-2011/session-papers/hospital-sprawl.html.

40. Thirteen, WNET New York Public Media. (2011). How much do we spend on end-of-life care? Retrieved from http://www.thirteen.org/bid/sb-howmuch.html.

41. Thirteen, WNET New York Public Media. (2011). How much do we spend on end-of-life care? Retrieved from http://www.thirteen.org/bid/sb-howmuch.html.

42. Schorn, D. (2010, August 8). The cost of dying: End of life care. CBS News. Retrieved from http://www.cbsnews.com/stories/2010/08/05/60minutes/main6747002.shtml.

43. Schorn, D. (2010, August 8). The cost of dying: End of life care. CBS News. Retrieved from http://www.cbsnews.com/stories/2010/08/05/60minutes/main6747002.shtml.

44. Schorn, D. (2010, August 8). The cost of dying: End of life care. CBS News. Retrieved from http://www.cbsnews.com/stories/2010/08/05/60minutes/main6747002.shtml.

45. Schorn, D. (2010, August 8). The cost of dying: End of life care. CBS News. Retrieved from http://www.cbsnews.com/stories/2010/08/05/60minutes/main6747002.shtml.

46. Schorn, D. (2010, August 8). The cost of dying: End of life care. CBS News. Retrieved from http://www.cbsnews.com/stories/2010/08/05/60minutes/main6747002.shtml.
47. Bipartisan process proposals for long-term fiscal stability before the Senate Budget Committee, 111th Congress (testimony of David M. Walker). (2009), Retrieved from http://budget.senate.gov/democratic/index.cfm/files/serve?File_id=19555b5a-690e-448b-8516-58577f978ebe.
48. Kelley, A. S., & Meier, D. E. (2010). Palliative care—A shifting paradigm. *New England Journal of Medicine, 363*, 781–782.
49. Chamberlain, C. (2010). *Clinical analysis of adverse drug reactions.* Washington, DC: National Institute of Health.
50. Lazarou, J., Pomeranz, B., & Corey, P. (1998). Incidence of adverse drug reactions in hospitalized patients: A meta-analysis of prospective studies. *Journal of the American Medical Association, 279*(15), 1200–1205. Retrieved from http://jama.ama-assn.org/cgi/content/full/279/15/1200.
51. Editorial Code and Data, Inc., (2011, July 6). High-deductible health insurance plans. Retrieved from http://www.marketsize.com/blog/index.php/2011/07/06/high-deductible-health-insurance-plans/.

CHAPTER 12: THE DYNAMIC FLOWS IN THE ECONOMICS OF HEALTH CARE

1. Centers for Medicare and Medicaid Services. (2010, October 1). Diagnosis and procedure codes and their abbreviated titles. Retrieved from http://www.cms.gov/ICD9ProviderDiagnosticCodes/06_codes.asp#TopofPage.
2. Scarborough, N. (2008). *Medical misdiagnosis in America 2008: A persistent problem with a promising solution.* Franklin, TN: Premerus. Retrieved from http://www.healthleadersmedia.com/content/206010.pdf.
3. Scarborough, N. (2008). *Medical misdiagnosis in America 2008: A persistent problem with a promising solution.* Franklin, TN: Premerus. Retrieved from http://www.healthleadersmedia.com/content/206010.pdf.
4. Mayes, Rick (January 2007). The origins, development, and passage of Medicare's revolutionary prospective payment system. *Journal of the History of Medicine and Allied Sciences, 62* (1): 21–55.
5. Hillestad, R., Bigelow, J., Bower, A., Girosi, F., Meili, R., Scoville, R., and Taylor, R. (2005). Can electronic medical record systems transform health care? Potential health benefits, savings, and costs. *Health Affairs, 24*(5), 1103–1117.
6. Patient Protection and Affordable Care Act of 2010, Pub. L. No. 111-148, § 2713, 131–132, § 4103, 553, Stat. 173 (2010).
7. Othenin-Girard, L. (Senior Producer), Lazarus, D. (Host), Caplan, A. (Guest), & Tanner, M. (Guest). (2011, April, 5). *Arizona proposes fee for obese or smoking Medicaid recipients* [Radio series episode]. Pasadena, CA: National Public Radio.

8. Bittman, M. (2011, July 23). Bad food? Tax it, and subsidize vegetables. *New York Times*, SR1.
9. Hillestad, R., et al. (2005). Can electronic medical record systems transform health care? Potential health benefits, savings, and costs. *Health Affairs, 24*(5), 1103–1117.
10. Hillestad, R., et al. (2005). Can electronic medical record systems transform health care? Potential health benefits, savings, and costs. *Health Affairs, 24*(5), 1103–1117.
11. Hillestad, R., et al. (2005). Can electronic medical record systems transform health care? Potential health benefits, savings, and costs. *Health Affairs, 24*(5), 1103–1117.
12. Hillestad, R., et al. (2005). Can electronic medical record systems transform health care? Potential health benefits, savings, and costs. *Health Affairs, 24*(5), 1103–1117.
13. Hillestad, R., et al. (2005). Can electronic medical record systems transform health care? Potential health benefits, savings, and costs. *Health Affairs, 24*(5), 1103–1117.
14. Hillestad, R., et al. (2005). Can electronic medical record systems transform health care? Potential health benefits, savings, and costs. *Health Affairs, 24*(5), 1103–1117.
15. Hillestad, R., et al. (2005). Can electronic medical record systems transform health care? Potential health benefits, savings, and costs. *Health Affairs, 24*(5), 1103–1117.
16. Hillestad, R., et al. (2005). Can electronic medical record systems transform health care? Potential health benefits, savings, and costs. *Health Affairs, 24*(5), 1103–1117.
17. Hillestad, R., et al. (2005). Can electronic medical record systems transform health care? Potential health benefits, savings, and costs. *Health Affairs, 24*(5), 1103–1117.
18. American Recovery and Reinvestment Act of 2009: Title IV Medicare and Medicaid Health Information Technology; Miscellaneous Medicare Provisions, Pub. L. No. 111-5, § 4101, 467, Stat. 123 (2009).

CHAPTER 14: THE NEW STRUCTURES OF HEALTH CARE

1. Cleveland Clinic. (2011). About us: Overview. Retrieved from http://my.clevelandclinic.org/about/default.aspx.
2. Patient Protection and Affordable Care Act of 2010, Pub. L. No. 111-148, § 3022, 124, Stat. 395-96 (2010).
3. McClellan, M., et al. (2010, May). A national strategy to put accountable care into practice. *Health Affairs, 29*(5), 982–990.
4. Halvorson, G. C. (2009) *Health care will not reform itself: A user's guide to refocusing and reforming American health care.* New York: CRC Press, 67.
5. *Patient Protection and Affordable Care Act of 2010*, Pub. L. No. 111-148,§ 1311, 124, Stat. 173 (2010).
6. *Patient Protection and Affordable Care Act of 2010*, Pub. L. No. 111-148,§ 3022, 124, Stat. 395 (2010).
7. IPMA. (2002). Sick leave abuse: A chronic workplace ill? *IMPA News*, 703–709.
8. Virgin HealthMiles. (2011). Home. Retrieved from http://us.virginhealthmiles.com/pages/home.aspx.

9. Virgin HealthMiles. (2011). Home: Potential savings. Retrieved from http://us.virginhealthmiles.com/pages/home.aspx.

10. GenerationsHP. (2010). What is GenerationsHP? Retrieved from http://www.generationshp.com/about-us.html?877e4ed3a9a597c45742714a77f5409e=89ca6d534ed84348b1ffa0d164be70a3.

11. GenerationsHP. (2010). What is GenerationsHP? Retrieved from http://www.generationshp.com/about-us.html?877e4ed3a9a597c45742714a77f5409e=89ca6d534ed84348b1ffa0d164be70a3.

12. Meyer, J., & Silow-Carroll, S. (2011, February). *A Collins Center special report: Making the investments work: Important benefits and key challenges in implementing health reform in Florida.* (Health Management Associates). Miami, FL: Collins Center for Public Policy, 15.

13. Manatee County Rural Health Services. (n.d.). About us. Retrieved from http://www.mcrhs.org/about.php.

14. Kingsdale, J., & Bertko, J. (2010, June). Insurance exchanges under health reform: Six design issues for the states. *Health Affairs, 29*(6), 1158–1163.

15. Morrison, K. (2009, January 12). Blue Cross and Blue Shield health insurance stores spreading across Florida. *Jacksonville Business Journal.* Retrieved from http://www.bizjournals.com/jacksonville/stories/2009/ 01/12/story5.html.

16. Halvorson, G. C. (2007). *Health care reform now! A prescription for change.* San Francisco: John Wiley & Sons, 197.

17. U.S. Department of Health and Human Services. Health insurance exchanges: State planning and establishment grants. Retrieved from http://www.hhs.gov/ociio/initiative/grant_award_faq.html.

18. U.S. Department of Health & Human Services. Health insurance exchanges: State planning and establishment grants. Retrieved from http://www.hhs.gov/ociio/initiative/grant_award_faq.html.

19. Neuharth, A. (2006, June 23). Traveling interstates is our sixth freedom. *USA Today.* Retrieved from http://www.usatoday.com/news/opinion/columnist/neuharth/2006-06-22-interstates_x.htm.

20. Halvorson, G. C. (2007). *Health care reform now! A prescription for change.* San Francisco: John Wiley & Sons, 196.

Chapter 15: What Health Care Institutions and Practitioners Need to Know and Do in The New Health Age

1. *The American Recovery and Reinvestment Act of 2009* (ARRA), Public Law 111-5, 111th Cong., 1st sess. (2009).

2. U.S. Department of Health and Human Services, Centers for Medicare and Medicaid Services. (2011, February). EHR incentive programs. Retrieved from https://www.cms.gov/ehrincentiveprograms/.

3. U.S. Department of Health and Human Services, Centers for Medicare and Medicaid Services. (2011, February). EHR incentive programs. Retrieved from https://www.cms.gov/ehrincentiveprograms/.

4. U.S. Department of Health and Human Services, National Institutes of Health. (2010, January). Nanoparticle cocktail targets and kills tumors. Retrieved from http://nano.cancer.gov/action/news/2010/jan/nanotech_news_2010-01-12a.asp.

5. Gardiner, H. (2010, March 26). More doctors giving up private practices. *New York Times*, B1.

6. Gardiner, H. (2010, March 26). More doctors giving up private practices. *New York Times*, B1.

7. Gardiner, H. (2010, March 26). More doctors giving up private practices. *New York Times*, B1.

CHAPTER 16: WHAT POLICY MAKERS AND EDUCATORS NEED TO DO

1. He is reported to have first said this in an interview on NPR's Fresh Air (August 31, 1993) (unverified); he repeated it, prefacing it with "As I've said many times…" in "The science in science fiction" on *Talk of the Nation*, NPR (1999, November 30) (timecode 11:55).